# Speaking
## in
# Many Tongues

*To  W.H.F.,*
*D.J.R.,*
*L.B.R.*

*Expanded 2d Edition*

# Speaking
# in
# Many Tongues:

## Essays in Foreign-Language
## Teaching

**WILGA M. RIVERS**

Harvard University

NEWBURY HOUSE PUBLISHERS, INC.

Library of Congress Cataloging in Publication Data

Rivers, Wilga M
    Speaking in many tongues

    (Innovations in foreign language education)
    Includes bibliographical references and index.
    1.  Languages, Modern—Study and teaching—Collected
works.  I.  Title.
PB35.R42  1976      418'.007     76-25589
ISBN 0-88377-064-4

*Cover design: Holly Nichols*

NEWBURY HOUSE PUBLISHERS, INC.

    *Language Science*
    *Language Teaching*
    *Language Learning*

*Rowley, Massachusetts 01969*

First edition, October, 1972
Library of Congress Card Number 72-75494
ISBN: 912066-64-4

Expanded 2d Edition, October, 1976
    5  4  3  2

Printed in the U.S.A.

Newbury House Series

# INNOVATIONS IN FOREIGN LANGUAGE EDUCATION
## Howard B. Altman, Series Editor

*Individualizing Foreign Language Instruction:*
*Proceedings of the Stanford Conference*
Howard B. Altman and Robert L. Politzer, Editors

*Individualizing the Foreign Language Classroom:*
*Perspectives for Teachers*
Howard B. Altman, Editor

*Speaking in Many Tongues:*
*Essays in Foreign-Language Teaching*
Expanded 2d Edition
Wilga M. Rivers

*Changing Patterns in Foreign Language Programs:*
*Report of the Illinois Conference on Foreign Languages*
*in Junior and Community Colleges, 1972*
Wilga M. Rivers, Louise H. Allen, Sandra J. Savignon,
Richard T. Scanlan, Editors

*Individualized Foreign Language Learning:*
*An Organic Process*
Gerald E. Logan

*Performing with Objectives*
Florence Steiner

*Designs for Foreign Language Teacher Education* (forthcoming)
Alan Garfinkel and Stanley Hamilton, Editors,
Bonnie Busse, Lee E. Hawkins, Genelle Morain, Renée S. Disick,
Robert Morrey, Jean-Pierre Berwald and Manuel Pacheco

*Creativity in the Language Classroom*
Irene E. Stanislawczyk and Symond Yavener

*Learner-Centered Language Teaching* (forthcoming)
Anthony Papalia

# CONTENTS

# INTRODUCTION

## A PERSONAL COMMUNICATION:
## FROM THE AUTHOR TO HER READER

We often speak of language as a vehicle of expression—a metaphor which can illumine many aspects of our foreign-language teaching situation. In "Rules, Patterns, and Creativity" I speak of "a vehicle of meaning which (people) do not even realize they are using,"[1] in other words a vehicle which is transporting a person's message somewhere, but which itself is not the object of the trip. Before students can use such a vehicle for their purposes it must be constructed, and this construction demands a blueprint and various stages of production, with tryouts as the various sections and combinations are assembled—tryouts during which what has been assembled to date is used, if only momentarily, for its ultimate purpose. With our language vehicle this ultimate purpose is expression: a person revealing himself to, or disguising himself or hiding himself from, another or other persons. Expression involves all the problems of interpersonal relations. For this reason it is frequently less painful for teachers and students to continue working at the construction of the vehicle than to attempt to try it out for level of performance.

Here I would refer you to the model of foreign-language teaching set out in "Talking Off the Tops of Their Heads,"[2] where I distinguish skill-getting, represented by both *cognition* and *production* (or pseudocommunication), from

---

[1] See p. 13 of this book.

[2] See Chapter 2 in this book. The reader should familiarize himself with the full description of this model before proceeding.

skill-using in *interaction*, which involves both reception and expression and is dependent on motivation to communicate.

The construction of our vehicle presupposes a design. Some particularly talented individuals can put the design into effect without the help of the blueprint; they appear to move directly from model to production which means that they develop their own internal representation from acquaintance with the model. These are the exceptions, however. Most need help in developing a series of blueprints of increasing complexity as a basis for production. Some prefer lessons in drafting blueprints, others can draw them up from experience with a prototype of the vehicle. These blueprints are indicated in my model by the term *cognition* and they represent the system underlying both reception and expression. Our students depend on their blueprints as they put the parts together in *production* so that the vehicle will function. Sometimes students try merely to copy someone else's assembly. This may work for a time but leaves the student bewildered as the assembly becomes more complicated. At this stage only those with comprehensive blueprints, or internal representations, are able to make the mechanism operate as they would like. Construction is not, however, the use of the vehicle—this is represented by the trying-out that continually takes place as the assembly takes form. It is only through such tryouts that the operation of the vehicle can be smoothly integrated and faults corrected and the user gain confidence in handling it.

No analogy should be pushed too far. I have given attention to the differences between the blueprint, the assembly of the vehicle, and its trying out in use in "Rules, Patterns, and Creativity." In "Contrastive Linguistics in Textbook and Classroom" I have shown how knowledge of other blueprints (notably that of one's native language) can be a help only if the systematic nature of blueprints is fully understood and apparent similarities are viewed in relation to whole sections of the design. In "From Skill Acquisition to Language Control" I have reemphasized the fact that mere production of itself is not sufficient. In every lesson it must be regarded as preliminary to actual trying out of what is being learned so that from the earliest stages all learning activities lead to some form of real communication rather than remaining at the level of pseudocommunication through imposed utterances. Techniques for developing a smooth and natural transition from skill-getting to skill-using are described in "From Linguistic Competence to Communicative Competence."

*Interaction* has always been the most neglected part of the essential language activities in our model. With the increasing trend toward individualization of instruction this situation will not be improved unless definite steps are taken to include substantial interaction activities in each program. A student alone with a book or tape, or both, is limited to cognition and production. Working with a few fellow students no more confident than he on the usual type of program, he still lacks the stimulus to use the foreign language for natural purposes. Interaction does not take place in a void. It is not enough to put several people together; there must also be some situational stimulus which naturally elicits an interchange. Interaction is a purposeful person-to-person affair in speech and in most kinds of writing. This interpersonal character of interaction explains why so much teaching and learning of foreign language remain at the production or pseudocommunication level.

In most classrooms there is very little reason or opportunity for students or teachers to reveal themselves to each other: the relationship is a formal and formalized one for which conventionalities suffice. The teacher is there to teach; the student is there to learn what the teacher or the administration thinks he should learn. The usual greetings are exchanged, conventional questions are asked about material presented aurally or graphically, conventional answers arising from the material are expected. Common remarks which may be heard are: "Come to the point, Johnny. We're not interested in your personal history"; "Don't ask silly questions"; "That's nothing to do with it. Didn't you hear the question?" John Holt describes for us the mechanisms students employ to defend themselves in class and protect their real selves from the humiliation and embarrassment which could result if they ventured to express themselves in an uncertain, often hostile environment[3] (and this in their native language). The deeply emotional needs of the individual which must be understood by the teacher if the students are to realize their full potential are discussed in "Motivation in Bilingual Programs." In "Motivating through Classroom Techniques," I take up the psychological aspects of motivation to speak the language and make suggestions for meaningful classroom activities.

G. I. Brown points out that "attempts at communication solely on a rational level are bound to fail when the issues involved have personal relevance for the participants. Personal relevance connotes an affective dimension, people feel and value as well as think about the position they hold. Denying or ignoring the existence of feelings in communication is like building a house without a foundation or framework."[4] No wonder it is more comfortable for student and teacher in the foreign-language class to remain at the level of pseudocommunication. Those who advocate that foreign-language instruction should begin with spontaneous communication and free interaction without any preparation with structured materials are ignoring this affective element.

Spontaneous communication and free interaction are possible in any language only when teachers and their students have built up a warm, uninhibited, confident, sympathetic relationship and when such a relationship also exists among the students themselves. In the first lessons no such state of affairs exists as yet. The teacher's efforts from the beginning should be devoted to building up such relationships through enjoyable, successful experiences in using interesting and amusing segments of language in a multiplicity of ways so that the student begins to feel that he can express real concerns through this new medium and that it is exhilarating to do so. This confident attitude, so essential to development of future speaking skill, is very fragile and

---

[3]John Holt, *How Children Fail* (New York: Dell, 1970). Originally published by Pitman, 1964.

[4]George Isaac Brown, *Human Teaching for Human Learning: an Introduction to Confluent Education* (New York: Viking Press, 1971), p. 6.

can be stifled quite early by a situation where the teacher has the advantage of fluency and is inevitably right while the student is uncertain, groping, and for the most part wrong. Early interaction practice calls for self-restraint and tact on the part of the teacher. Once the students understand the rules of the game—that you do the most you can with the little you have in some meaningful activity shared with others in the group, and that the teacher is there not to condemn but to give a helping hand, a gentle reminder, and much encouragement—confident self-expression is possible even at a very early stage. The types of activities which can be used to give purpose to interaction practice are set out in "Talking Off the Tops of Their Heads." In "Testing and Student Learning" I consider how this approach affects our testing procedures, particularly for effective evaluation of macro-language use as opposed to micro-language learning.

It is because of this fundamental interpersonal factor that methods and techniques imposed on the teacher, efficient as they might have seemed in the abstract in terms of language-learning theory, have always proved successful for some people working with some classes but not for all. The interaction of teacher personality, multiple student personalities, and what each brings into the classroom from the outside can be observed only in unique situations. Take away one student from the group or add one student and you immediately have a new mix. Change the teacher and the situation is no longer the same. All teachers are conscious of this fact which has been the bane of large-scale investigations and experimentation in teaching method.

Is methodology then futile? Not at all. Methodology should be based on what we know about language (what it is and how it operates—still a matter of controversy); what we know about human beings (how they learn and how they learn language and whether these are different processes or merely different manifestations of the same process—another question which is still under investigation); and what we know about people in interaction (a prolific area of psychological study). It is inevitable, then, that methodological recommendations will change as our knowledge of these three factors evolves, with earlier postulates being rejected and new premises accepted. Teachers should keep in touch with findings in these areas and share the excitement of a developing and progressing discipline. "The Foreign-Language Teacher and Cognitive Psychology or Where Do We Go from Here?" and "Linguistic and Psychological Factors in Speech Perception and Their Implications for Teaching Materials" will supply teachers with much new information, particularly in the psychology of perception.

At this point the teacher takes over as a professional person and as an individual with his or her own gifts, insights, and preferences. First, he must know himself and his strengths and weaknesses in interpersonal relations. Then he must know his students: who they are, what their aspirations are, and how they learn as individuals. He will find that their general attitudes fluctuate, not only from generation to generation or from decade to decade but, in this period of rapid change, almost from year to year. (The attitudes of the present generation are discussed in relation to foreign-language programs in "Foreign Languages in a Time of Change.") Senior high school students may still accept what their younger brothers and sisters are already rejecting. In the early sixties, for instance, with a more docile student population, it seemed possible to subordinate the individual to the efficient system for his own good, as seen by his teachers; now the efficient system must be subordinated to individual learning preferences if there is to be a high quality of learning. Undergraduate students speak for themselves in a survey reported in "The Non-Major: Tailoring the Course to Fit the Person—Not the Image," where they express not only their general attitudes toward the learning of languages but their preferences for content of courses. This is a period of plurality of objectives and diversity of learning approaches, a subject I discuss in "From the Pyramid to the Commune: the Evolution of the Foreign-Language Department."

Teachers in this volatile period must understand how teaching and learning relate to each other and interact fruitfully, realizing that either can exist without the other. They must learn to teach in such a way that they do not interpose themselves between the learner and what is to be learned. They must accept and encourage a variety of learning styles allowing for differences in individuals. Some people learn more by the ear than the eye, others learn from printed texts; some learn from abstract reflection, some from concrete manipulation; some learn more slowly than others; some prefer to learn by themselves, while others prefer help, even direction, and need the stimulation of a group if they are to realize their potentialities. Foreign-language teachers for this generation must expect and respect a new clientele and study how they can devise a learning program for students of a type to which they were not accustomed before. These and related matters are examined in "Teacher-Student Relations: Coercion or Cooperation?"

By this time the teacher's head is spinning, maybe. He has listened, he has studied, he has read. None of this is sufficient. The truly successful teacher is highly idiosyncratic. From this plethora of information and recommendations, he selects. He takes from the new what suits his own personality and his teaching style and what is appropriate for the personalities and aspirations of his own students, thus forming his own approach. He is not afraid to innovate, to rearrange, to redesign his courses, because continual reflection and appropriate adjustment and readjustment keep him professionally alive, making him a more interesting person to his students. Above all, he does not remain caught up in his own discipline but sees it in relation to the total educational experience. He sees himself contributing, along with his colleagues in mathematics, in social studies, in guidance, to the maturation process of young minds and personalities. He remains in step with changing approaches to the whole curriculum and views his subject in that perspective. In step? Why should he not be in the vanguard in meeting new challenges and seeking new opportunities? How he can lead while still being true to the essence of his own discipline is discussed in "Individualization of Instruction and Cooperative Learning: Some Theoretical Considerations." Such an approach requires flexibility of mind and sensitivity to professional winds of change. The directions of change which seem to be shaping up at present and the important matter of preparing future teachers who can fit into these new patterns is developed in "Students, Teachers, and the Future."

So we move, let us hope, as a profession into an era of tolerance and acceptance of difference—the era of the commune, where divisive and acrimonious competition to draw teachers in one direction and then in another will appear irrelevant, and the word "best" will be recognized for the subjective and relative term that it is. Let us look forward to a period of "many flowers blooming, daylilies perhaps, but each in its day and hour bringing fragrance to the experience of some."[5] Invite me to visit your garden at that stage so that I can see what your skill and care have brought into being.

Wilga M. Rivers

Cambridge, Mass.
August 1975

---

[5]See p. 162 of this book.

# 1

# Rules, patterns, and creativity*

In 1966, Chomsky shocked many participants at the Northeast Conference by casting doubt on the validity of the direct and uncritical application of linguistic theory to teaching practice. "I am, frankly," he said, "rather skeptical about the significance, for the teaching of languages, of such insights and understanding as have been attained in linguistics and psychology."[1] "It is possible—even likely—" he continued, "that principles of psychology and linguistics, and research in these disciplines, may supply insights useful to the language teacher. But this must be demonstrated and cannot be presumed. It is the language teacher himself who must validate or refute any specific proposal."[2]

With an obvious, though unstated, reference to methods of foreign-language teaching of recent years which it had been believed were consistent with what was known of the nature of language and of the learning process, Chomsky declared: "Linguists have had their share in perpetuating the myth that linguistic behavior is 'habitual' and that a fixed stock of 'patterns' is acquired through practice and used as the basis for 'analogy'."[3] To Chomsky, "Language is not a 'habit-structure.' Ordinary linguistic behavior characteristically involves innovation, formation of new sentences and new patterns in accordance with rules of great abstractness and intricacy."[4] For this reason, he speaks continually of the " 'creative' aspect of language use."[5]

---

* This is a revised version of an article, "Grammar in Foreign Language Teaching," which appeared in the *Modern Language Journal* 52 (1968), 206-11.

Linguistic science has made teachers very conscious of the fact that grammar is the core of language. Without an internalized set of rules, or syntax, they are told, no one can understand or use a language: language is "rule-governed behavior."[6] In the past, many teachers have uncritically adopted habit-formation techniques because language, it appeared, was "a set of habits."[7] Now many are ready to seize upon a new slogan and begin to inculcate rules in the hope of establishing "rule-governed behavior," even though they have only a vague concept of what this phrase can mean as it has been used by linguists or psychologists.[8] In this way they hope to take their students beyond the arid fields of mechanical repetition, where pure habit-formation techniques seem so often to have left them, into the greener pastures of creative production of foreign-language utterances.

Before we decide on any particular approach, we need to clarify our ideas about the essence of language use (which in Chomsky's terms is a question of performance based on competence). We will then select methods appropriate to the type of learning involved in its effective acquisition. It is at this point that there is most confusion.

### Linguistic vs. Pedagogic Grammar

First, it is important to distinguish, as Chomsky has done in *Topics in the Theory of Generative Grammar*, between a linguistic and a pedagogic grammar. A linguistic grammar, as Chomsky sees it, aims to discover and exhibit the mechanisms that make it possible for a "speaker to understand an arbitrary sentence on a given occasion," whereas a pedagogic grammar attempts to provide the student with the ability to understand and produce such sentences.[9]

This leaves the question wide open for the foreign-language teacher. A linguistic grammar is an account of competence (the knowledge of the language system that a native speaker has acquired) expressed in terms of an abstract model that does not necessarily represent, and may not even attempt to parallel, the psychological processes of language use. It can give the informed teacher insights into language structure and clarify for him various aspects of his subject matter, but methods of linguistic description do not *per se* provide any guidance as to how a student may learn to communicate in a foreign language. This is the preoccupation of the writer of a pedagogic grammar who, in the light of what the linguistic grammar has established about the subject matter, decides what are psychologically (and therefore pedagogically) the most appropriate ways of arranging and presenting the material to the students. The form a particular pedagogic grammar will assume will depend on such factors as the objectives of the language course (which devolve from the felt needs of the students), the age and intellectual maturity of the students, the length and intensity of the study, and the degree of contrast between the foreign and native languages.

How, then, can the foreign-language teacher establish "rule-governed behavior" that will enable his students to produce novel utterances at will? In conformity with Chomsky's position, we need to make it possible for the foreign-language learner to internalize a system of rules that can generate an infinite number of grammatical sentences that will be comprehensible and acceptable when uttered with the semantic and phonological components appropriate to specific communication situations.[10] With the word *internalize* we are at the heart of the problem: *"rule-governed behavior" in the sense in which it is used by linguists or psychologists does not mean behavior that results from the conscious application of rules.*

According to Chomsky, "A person is not generally aware of the rules that govern sentence-interpretation in the language that he knows; nor, in fact, is there any reason to suppose that the rules can be brought to consciousness." Neither can we "expect him to be fully aware even of the empirical consequences of these internalized rules"[11]—that is, of the way in which abstract rules acquire semantic interpretations. The behavior is "rule-governed" in the sense that it conforms to the internalized system of rules. These rules are not the pedagogic "grammar rules" (often of doubtful linguistic validity) of the traditional deductive, expository type of language teaching, according to which students docilely constructed language sequences. They are rules, as Chomsky puts it, of "great abstractness and intricacy" inherent in the structure of a language, which through the operation of various processes find expression in the overt forms that people produce.

*Generate*, in the mathematical sense in which Chomsky uses the term, does not refer to some unexpected production of language sequences that reflects originality of thought on the part of the speaker, but to a mechanical process: the outworking of the internalized rules will automatically result in what are recognizably grammatical utterances. When Chomsky talks, therefore, about the " 'creative' aspect of language use," he is not referring to that type of free play with language elements where students, with glib abandon, "create language," grammatical or ungrammatical, to suit their immediate purposes. He is referring to the fact that once the system of rules of the language has become an integral part of the student's store of knowledge he will be able to produce, in order to express his meaning, an infinite variety of language sequences, whether he has previously heard such sequences or not—sequences which are grammatically acceptable, and therefore comprehensible, to the person to whom he is speaking. The mere supplying of rules and training of the students in their use for the construction of language sequences is not in itself sufficient to ensure the "internalizing" of the system of rules so that it will operate in the production of sentences without the students being conscious of its role. Unless foreign-language teachers are aware of the technical meaning of the terms Chomsky was using in his speech on language teaching, they may be left with erroneous impressions of his viewpoint.

### Creative Use of Language

Exercising the language teacher's prerogative that Chomsky has so clearly assigned us, we may well question his statement that it is a myth that linguistic behavior is "habitual" and that a fixed stock of patterns is acquired through practice and used as the basis for "analogy."[12] "Repetition of fixed phrases," he says, "is a rarity," and "it is only under exceptional and quite uninteresting circumstances that one can seriously consider how 'situational context' determines what is said."[13] Despite these assertions, Chomsky himself would be the first to admit that a theory of language performance has yet to be developed. With his continual emphasis on creative and innovative use of language,[14] Chomsky is likely to lead us astray in the teaching of foreign languages by fixing our attention on a distant rather than an immediate goal. It is certainly true that our final aim is to produce students who can communicate about anything and everything in the foreign language, creating at will novel utterances that conform to the grammatical system of the language, but, as in every other area of teaching, we must map out our program step by step.

Creative and innovative use of language still takes place within a restricted framework, a finite set of formal arrangements to which the speaker's utterances must conform if he is to be comprehended and thus to communicate effectively.[15] The speaker cannot "create" the grammar of the language as he innovates: he is making "infinite use of finite means."[16] His innovative ability will exist only to the degree that underlying competence exists—that the set of rules has been internalized. Foreign-language students must acquire the grammar of the foreign language so that it functions for them as does the grammar of their native language: as a vehicle of meaning that they do not even realize they are using.

Basically, the question of how to inculcate the grammar of a language will depend on the type of activity we believe communication in a foreign language to be: is it a skill or an intellectual process, or is it a blend of the two? If foreign-language learning is the acquiring of a skill or a group of interrelated skills, then our students need intensive practice until they are able to associate without hesitation or reflection the many linguistic elements that are interrelated in a linear sequence. If, on the other hand, foreign-language use is an intellectual process, then training is necessary to ensure that students can make correct choices of rules and modification of rules in order to construct utterances that express their intentions.

## Two Levels of Language Behavior

If we can identify two levels of foreign-language behavior for which our students must be trained, then it is clear that one type of teaching will not be sufficient for the task. These two levels may be designated: (1) the level of *manipulation* of language elements that occur in fixed relationships in clearly defined closed systems (that is, relationships that will vary within very narrow limits), and (2) a level of *expression of personal meaning* at which possible variations are infinite, depending on such factors as the type of message to be communicated, the situation in which the utterance takes place, the relationship between speaker and hearer or hearers, and the degree of intensity with which the message is conveyed. If we recognize two such levels a place must be found for the firm establishment of certain basic linguistic habits and the understanding of a complex system with its infinite possibilities of expression. The problem is to define the role of each of these types of learning and their interrelationships in the acquiring of a foreign language.[17]

It is essential to recognize first that certain elements of language remain in fixed relationships in small, closed systems, so that once the system is invoked in a particular way a succession of interrelated formal features appears. Fluent speakers are able to make these interrelated adjustments irrespective of the particular message they wish to produce. The elements that interact in restricted systems may be practiced intensively in order to forge strong habitual associations from which the speaker never deviates (this applies to such elements as inflection of person and number, agreements of gender, fixed forms for interrogation or negation, formal features of tenses). These elements do not require intellectual analysis: they exist, and they must be used in a certain way in certain environments and in no other way.[18] For these features, intensive practice exercises of various kinds can be very effective learning procedures, with the teacher supplying a brief word of explanation where necessary to forestall hesitation or bewilderment. (Lengthy explanations can be a hindrance rather than a help for this type of activity because it is *how* these systems operate that matters, not *why*.)

Practice of this type should not be given in solid, tedious blocks in a determined attempt to stamp in these formal features once and for all. Shorter exercises reintroduced at intervals over a period of time, with interspersed opportunities to use these features in association with other language elements in a communicative interchange, no matter how simple, will be more effective in establishing the necessary control. In this way, the attention of the students will be more directly focussed in subsequent practice on areas which they have found to be of persistent difficulty. Structural practice of this type can be considered effective only if these formal features become readily available to the student when his attention is concentrated on constructing a message—an act which involves the second level of language behavior. They will not become readily available unless the student has early and constant practice in expressing his personal meaning.

At the second level, decisions more intimately connected with contextual meaning may bring into play any of a variety of syntactic structures, so that students will be continually reusing what they have learned. A decision at this higher level has structural implications beyond the word or the phrase, often beyond the sentence. A slight variation in the decision will often mean the construction of quite a different form of utterance. Naturally, then, decisions at the second level involve a more complicated initial choice, which entails further choices of a more limited character. In order to express exactly what one wishes to say, one must view it in relation to the potential of the structural system of the language as a whole and select accordingly. This is the higher-level decision that sets in motion operations at lower levels that are interdependent. The decision to make a particular type of statement about something that has taken place recently involves a choice of register, a choice of degree of intensity, the use of lexical items in certain syntactical relationships that will involve the production of certain morphological elements, certain phonemic distinctions, and certain stress and intonation patterns. The interrelationships within the language system that are involved in these higher-level decisions often need to be clarified in deductive fashion by the teacher or textbook. For effective practice at this level the student must understand the implications and ramifications of changes he is making. This he will best do if the practice involves making decisions in real communication situations devised in the classroom, rather than in artificial drills and exercises. In such interchanges the feedback from the other participants in communication brings a realization of the effect of the decisions the speaker has made.

There must be in the classroom, then, a constant interplay of learning by analogy and by analysis, of inductive and deductive processes—according to the nature of the operation the student is learning. It is evident that he cannot put higher-level choices into operation with ease if he has not developed facility in the production of the interdependent lower-level elements, and so learning by intensive practice and analogy have their place. Genuine freedom in language use, however, will develop only as the student gains control of the system as a whole, beyond the mastery of patterns in isolation. This control will become established only through much experience in attempting to counterbalance and interrelate various syntactic possibilities in order to convey a comprehensible meaning in a situation where its expression has some real significance.

It becomes clear that the second level of language use, which we have just considered, is of a more sophisticated type than the first level. It demands of the student understanding of the interrelationships and options the language system allows. This understanding guides his higher-level choices, yet full comprehensibility depends on his skill in manipulation of the numerous lower-level elements which are set in operation by the higher-level decisions. Too often in the past, foreign-language teaching concentrated on an understanding of the language system as a whole without providing sufficient practice in rapid production of the lower-level elements. This led to hesitancy in language use. On the other hand, more recent methods have worked out techniques for developing the lower-level manipulative skill while leaving the student unpracticed in the making of decisions at the higher level. The language course must provide for training at both levels.

It would be a mistake, however, to believe that practice at the second level should be delayed until the student has learned all the common features of the manipulative type—that is, that the student should first learn to manipulate elements in fixed relationships and not begin until a year or two later to learn the selection process of the higher level. If he is eventually to understand a complex system with its infinite possibilities of expression, he must develop this understanding little by little. The student will learn to make higher-level selective decisions by being made aware at every step of the meaningful use in communication of operations he is learning at the manipulative level. No matter how simple the pattern he is practicing, he will become aware of its possibilities for communication[19] when he attempts to use it for his own purposes and not just to complete an exercise or to perform well in a drill.

As each structure becomes a medium of communication, it takes its place in the evolving system of meaningful expression that the student is internalizing; by using it in relationship with what he has already learned, he sees this isolated operation as part of a whole, with a definite function within the language. As he acquires more knowledge of the language, he will need further explanation of how the various elements he has become accustomed to using interact within sentences and discourse. Such explanations will be brief and to the point. Since their sole purpose is to prevent mislearning through mistaken assumptions about relationships, they will be fruitful only if followed immediately by meaningful practice in the expression of these relationships. Such practice is essential until it is evident that the student has internalized the underlying rules so effectively that they govern his production without conscious and deliberate application on his part.

Whether at the first or second level, practice does not have to be boring and meaningless. It can take the form of games and competitions which call for the production of the types of structures being learned or conversational interchanges within a directional framework.[20] With a little thought, the classroom teacher can find interesting, even exciting ways to practice all kinds of structural combinations and inter-relationships until the student acquires confidence and assurance in their potentialities of expression.

As a further step, and this will be sooner or later according to the age and maturity of the class, the student will need to see the parts and the interacting sections he has learned in relation to the whole functioning system of the language. (Having learned, for instance, different ways of expressing past action, he will need to see how the past fits into the general expression of temporal relationships in this particular language.) In most cases, he will have had more practice in those areas where the danger of native-language interference is the greatest (that is, where the native and foreign languages are most divergent in their usage). At this advanced stage, the student will need to grasp, to understand, without referring to an external and therefore irrelevant criterion,[21] how apparent similarities and differences interact within the complete system of the language he is learning.

But let me emphasize again that the student cannot realize this understanding of the whole before he has experienced, through practice and active use, the functioning of the parts. If he attempts to possess the whole too soon, he will achieve only rote learning of grammar rules and the ability to describe rather than to use the grammatical system. On the other hand, where the teacher can present the system as a whole to students who already have a practical knowledge of the functioning of the parts, he can freely use all kinds of authentic language material, aural and graphic, to demonstrate what he wishes to convey. And by showing how the grammatical system works for real purposes the teacher can convey far more to the students than he can by making numerous abstract explanations supported by isolated, out-of-context examples.

Textbooks and courses of study—and teachers—must make ample provision at appropriate stages for both types of learning discussed here. Neglect of the practice needed to acquire such things as interrelated inflectional systems will force students to make decisions for each element as they proceed, and their use of the language will remain hesitant. On the other hand, it is only by going beyond the practice stage and trying out what they know in communication that students can learn to make the higher-level choices that will bring the lower-level adjustments they have learned into operation at the appropriate moment.

There has been much experimentation in recent years with techniques for the lower-level manipulative operations. We need now to give more thought to effective ways of inducing language behavior at the second level. The learner will understandably take his cue from his teacher. He will see that the use of what he is learning in spontaneous production is his most important task only when his teacher is convinced and convinces him that this is so, and when every exercise and classroom activity leads frankly and naturally to a further opportunity for personal expression in the language. It is often easier for teacher and students to keep on working at a manipulative level, finding immediate satisfaction in the mastery of small elements. The necessary and eagerly anticipated liberation in foreign-language use, however, will not occur unless concentrated effort is directed at all stages toward this very end.

## FOOTNOTES

[1] Noam Chomsky, "Linguistic Theory," *Language Teaching: Broader Contexts*, ed. R. G. Mead, Jr., Report of Northeast Conference on the Teaching of Foreign Languages (New York: MLA Materials Center, 1966), p. 43.

[2] Ibid., p. 45.

[3] Ibid., p. 44.

[4] Ibid., p. 44.

[5] Ibid., p. 44.

[6]S. Saporta uses this term in "Applied Linguistics and Generative Grammar" in *Trends in Language Teaching*, ed. A. Valdman (New York: McGraw-Hill, 1966), p. 86.

[7]William G. Moulton, "Linguistics and Language Teaching in the United States 1940-1960," in *Trends in European and American Linguistics*, eds. C. Mohrmann, A. Sommerfelt, and J. Whatmough (Utrecht: Spectrum, 1961), p. 87.

[8]George A. Miller, "Some Preliminaries to Psycholinguistics," *American Psychologist*, 20 (1965):15-20. Reprinted in L. A. Jakobovits and M. S. Miron, eds., *Readings in the Psychology of Language* (Englewood Cliffs, New Jersey: Prentice-Hall, 1967), pp. 172-79; see especially p. 175.

[9]Noam Chomsky, *Topics in the Theory of Generative Grammar* (The Hague: Mouton, 1966), p. 10.

[10]Ibid., p. 16

[11]Ibid., p. 10.

[12]N. Chomsky, "Linguistic Theory," p. 44.

[13]Ibid., p. 46.

[14]Ibid., p. 44.

[15]J. B. Carroll in "Current Issues in Psycholinguistics and Second Language Teaching," *TESOL Quarterly* 5(1971):103, comments on Chomsky's position as follows: "I do not find any basic opposition between conceiving of language behavior as resulting from the operation of 'habits' and conceiving of it as 'rule-governed' . . . I would define a habit as any learned disposition to perceive, behave, or perform in a certain manner under specified circumstances. To the extent that an individual's language behavior conforms to the habits of the speech community of which he is a member, we can say that his behavior is 'rule-governed'."

[16]Chomsky, quoting Humboldt, in *Aspects of the Theory of Syntax* (Cambridge: MIT Press, 1965), p. 8.

[17]This subject is discussed in relation to all four fundamental language skills in Wilga M. Rivers, *Teaching Foreign-Language Skills* (Chicago: University of Chicago Press, 1968).

[18]It is interesting to note that many of these features, particularly the morphological ones, are excluded by Chomsky from his system of rewrite rules and included in the lexicon as parts of complex symbols. See *Aspects*, pp. 82-88.

[19]Ways of providing such practice are described in "Talking Off the Tops of Their Heads," Chapter 2 in this book.

[20]A directional framework is provided unobtrusively when a discussion is set in motion which requires, for instance, conditional statements: "If you were (the Mayor), what would you (do?)" or past tense situations such as: "When I (came in), were you (talking)?" or "When you were (a baby), did you (cry) often?"

[21]The importance of understanding the operation of the target language as a system is discussed at greater length in "Contrastive Linguistics in Textbook and Classroom," Chapter 5 in this book.

# 2

# TALKING OFF THE TOPS OF THEIR HEADS*

In a description of the Defense Language Institute program I read: "After basic patterns and structures are mastered, the student can proceed to more and more controlled substitution and eventually to free conversation." How delightfully simple it sounds! We breathe the fresh air of the uncomplicated. The student "masters the basic patterns and structures," we provide him with carefully controlled practice, and hey presto! he speaks freely in unstructured situations.

There were times, in days which seem now to belong to another age, when faith in the efficacy of structured courses and controlled drills to produce fluent speakers of another language went unchallenged. We knew where we wanted to go; we knew how to get there; we were happy with our products—or were we? And were they? Are such cries of frustration as: "I can't say anything off the top of my head, it all comes out as phrases from the book" new to our ears?[1] This student complaint of the seventies sounds almost like a paraphrase of the more academic remark of 1948 that "while many students could participate in memorized conversations speedily and effortlessly, hardly any could produce at length fluent variations from the basic material, and none could talk

---

*Paper delivered at the Defense Language Institute English Language Branch, Lackland Air Force Base, Texas, on June 30, 1971, (TESOL Project). Originally published in *TESOL Quarterly,* 6 (1972), 71-81.

on unrehearsed topics without constant and painful hesitation."[2] In almost a quarter of a century we have still not come to grips with our basic problem: "How do we develop communicative ability in a foreign language?"[3] We may intensify practice in the classroom (practice of patterns, practice of variations of patterns, practice in selection of patterns), but how do we engineer the great leap? A child learns all kinds of swimming movements while his loving parent holds him, lets him go a little but is there to support him as he loses confidence; then at some moment he swims. One moment he is a nonswimmer, then he is a swimmer. The movements are the same, the activity is of a new kind—the difference is psychological. How does the nonswimmer become a swimmer? He becomes autonomous in his movements and in his directions: he draws on his own resources; he ceases to rely on somebody else's support; he takes off and he is swimming. How do we get our students to this autonomous stage of language use? This is the crucial point of our teaching. Until we have solved this problem we will continue to mark time: developing more and more efficient techniques for producing foreign language cripples, with all the necessary muscles and sinews but unable to walk alone. "Spontaneous expression," "liberated expression," "creative language use"—the terms may vary with changing emphases in our profession: the goal still eludes us. Let's see what we can do here and now to attack this problem in a direct and practical fashion.

We must examine the problem at the point at which we are stalled. How can we help the student pass from the storing of linguistic knowledge and information about how this knowledge operates in communication to actual using of this knowledge for the multitudinous, unpredictable purposes of an individual in contact with other individuals? We do not need new ways to help the student acquire linguistic knowledge—we know of many from our "twenty-five centuries of language teaching"[4] and each in its heyday has seemed to be effective for this purpose. Here we can pick and choose according to our theoretical persuasion, our temperamental preferences, and our assessment of the learning styles of the particular groups of students with whom we are dealing. In any case, these students will learn according to their personal strategies in the ultimate secret of their individual personalities, even when they appear to be doing as we direct.

We need a new model of our language teaching activity which allocates a full role to the student's individual learning in communication. I propose the following division of essential processes.

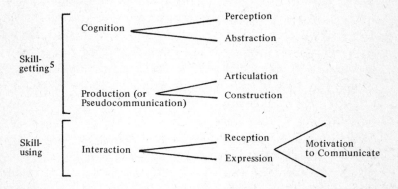

Ability to communicate, to interact verbally, presumes some knowledge (*cognition*) both in the perception of units, categories, and functions, and in the internalizing of the rules relating these categories and functions. I am not concerned here with how this knowledge is acquired and am willing to concede the validity (and probably the necessity) of a variety of approaches to such acquisitions. This knowledge must, however, be acquired. In the process of acquisition the student learns the *production* of language sequences: he learns through doing. Whether we use the terms "exercises" or "drills" or "activities" is immaterial; some kind of practice in putting together smoothly and confidently what he is learning is also essential. The student must learn to articulate acceptably and to construct comprehensible foreign-language sequences by rapid associations of learned elements. No matter how much we relate these activities to real-life situations this practice rarely passes beyond *pseudo-communication*. It is externally directed, not self-originating;

it is a dependent, not an independent, activity. The utterances may even be original in their combinations of segments but the student is not communicating anything that is of real import to him nor receiving any genuine message. This is practice in formulating communications and as such it is valuable practice. It is near-communication with all the outward appearances of communication, but the student does not have to demonstrate in these activities that he has taken the great leap into autonomy: the leap that is crucial. Our failure in the past has been in our satisfaction with students who perform well in pseudocommunication. We have tended to assume that there will then be automatic transfer to performance in *interaction*. We may have encouraged some sketchy attempts at autonomous inter- action, but always with the supporting hand: the instructor or the native speaker leading the group, drawing the student out, directing the interchange.

David Wolfe suggests that progress toward autonomy is hindered by the artificiality of language learning through "drills and exercises which force the student to lie. . . . From the point of view of true linguistic communication," he says, such "seemingly harmless sentences" as *Yesterday I went to the movies, Last night I went to the game, Last week I went to the game* "border on the nonsensical."[6] I do not think that this is the problem. We may maintain that lying is a form of real communication, but, this aspect aside, sentences in drills of this type are pseudocommunication in any case, and it may be clearer to students that this is so if they are sometimes also absurd. In a recent foreign-language text coauthored by the playwright Ionesco, the nonsensical and even whimsical approach to adult learning is purposefully exploited with students playing manipulatively with such sentences as "The teacher is in the pocket of the vest of the watch," "The crocodile is more beautiful than Mary-Jane," and "He says his parents are as big as the Eiffel Tower."[7] Such manipulations are intended to force students to think of the meaning of what they are saying which is one step toward autonomy, and pure nonsense may on occasions be more effective in this regard than the colorless, socially correct actions of Dick and Jane, of Maria and Pedro.

In recent writings on foreign-language teaching there has been increasing emphasis on communication, and on what are being called communication drills. I myself have spoken elsewhere of the necessity for relating the content of drills to the student's own interests: "Participation in the drill can be innovative: providing for practice in the repetition and variation of language segments, but with simultaneous practice in selection, as the student expresses his own meaning and not that of the textbook writer. . . . Practice in selection should not be considered a separate activity for advanced classes: it can and should be included in class work from the very first lessons."[8] "Many drills may be given the appearance of a game, or of elementary communication, by provoking the students into asking the teacher a series of questions in response to cues, or into making a series of comments about the teacher's activities and interests, or those of other students. The more the student is interested in an activity in the foreign language, the more he feels the desire to communicate in the language, and this is the first and most vital step in learning to use language forms spontaneously."[9]

Christina Paulston has developed the communication drill concept in more detail.[10] She groups drills into mechanical drills, meaningful drills, and communicative drills. In mechanical drills, there is complete control of the response so that the student does not even need to understand the drill to produce the correct response (as in simple substitution drills). Paulston suggests that if a nonsense word can be inserted as effectively by the student as a meaningful word, then the drill is of the mechanical type. This is pure production: sometimes merely practice in articulation, at other times practice in constructing an orderly sequence. As such it has its place in the initial phase of introducing a new structure or for practicing some problem of pronunciation or intonation. An example of such a drill would be:

| | |
|---|---|
| Pattern: | I'm reading a book. |
| Cue: | Magazine. |
| Response: | I'm reading a magazine. |
| Cue: | Newspaper. |
| Response: | I'm reading a newspaper. |

In meaningful drills "there is still control of the response (although it may be correctly expressed in more than one way . . .) but the student cannot complete the drill without fully understanding structurally and semantically what he is saying." The following would be a meaningful drill:

| | |
|---|---|
| Question: | When did you arrive this morning? |
| Answer: | I arrived at nine o'clock. |
| Question: | When will you leave this evening? |
| Answer: | I'll leave at six o'clock. |

In a communicative drill, however, "there is no control of the response. The student has free choice of answer, and the criterion of selection here is his own opinion of the real world—whatever he wants to say." This sounds like autonomous interaction, but Paulston continues: "Whatever control there is lies in the stimulus. . . .It still remains a drill rather than free communication because we are still within the realm of the cue-response pattern." She gives the example: "What did you have for breakfast?" with its possibility of an orthodox response such as "I had toast and coffee for breakfast," or the unorthodox "I overslept and skipped breakfast so I wouldn't miss the bus." It is clear that the unconventional student may well turn this into real interaction, but my guess is that the majority of students, feeling insecure in their knowledge of the language, would remain in the area of pseudocommunication.

Adrian Palmer suggests what he calls "communication practice drills."[11] "In communication practice (CP) drills, the student finds pleasure in a response that is not only linguistically acceptable, but also conveys information personally relevant to himself and other people." As outlined, this is an interesting technique. Palmer maintains that "the most powerful technique at the teacher's disposal is his ability to verbally create situations which could be relevant to the student's own life and then to force the student to think about the meaning and consequences of what he would say in such situations." His CP drills are drills in that they center around practice of particular structures such as:

| I would tell | him | to | shut the door |
| --- | --- | --- | --- |
| | her | | turn on the light |
| | them | | bring some food |

He develops them, however, by a somewhat Socratic method:

"Teacher:   'Karen, if you and Susan came to class
at 8 a.m. and it was winter and the room
was dark at 8 a.m., what would you tell
Susan?'

Karen:      (with any luck at all) 'I would tell
her to turn on the light.'

Teacher:    'And how about you, Paul, if you were
with Mary and you wanted to read, what
would you do?'

Paul:       'I would tell her to turn on the light.'

Teacher:    (in student's native language) 'You
as a boy would tell a girl to do that for you?'

Teacher:    (continuing in the target language)
'Paul, if you came alone, and if I was in
the room, what would you do?'

Paul:       'I would tell you to turn on the light.'

Teacher:    'Then I would throw you out of class.' "

In this type of drill Palmer is moving toward interaction in that a student who gives mechanically what appears to be a correct response may well be pulled up short because he has not thought about the implications of his response in the imposed setting. With training in such drills average students would possibly produce more original responses than in Paulston's communicative drills because of the goad of the teacher's teasing and their natural desire to show him they have recognized his stratagem. This type of drill teeters on the brink of interaction but is still in the area of pseudocommunication and production practice because the whole interchange is teacher-directed with the specific intention of eliciting certain structures.

Where do we go from here? We must work out situations, from an early stage, where the student is on his own, trying to use the language for the normal purposes of language: establishing social relations, seeking and giving information, expressing his reactions, learning to do something, hiding his intentions or talking his way out of trouble, persuading, discouraging, entertaining others, or displaying his achievements. When I say the student is "on his own," I mean he is not supported or directed by the teacher: he may well be working with another or other students. In this type of practice the student should be allowed to use anything he knows of the language and any aids (gestures, drawings, pantomime) to fill out his meaning, when he is "at a loss for words."[12] In this way he will learn to draw on everything he knows at a particular moment in his acquisition of the language, and to fight to put his meaning over, as he would if he suddenly found himself on his own surrounded by monolingual speakers of the language. *This experience is not intended to replace the careful teaching of the language we already supply (the skill-getting activities we organize) but to expand it with regular and frequent opportunities for autonomous interaction, thus making full provision for a dimension of language learning which at present is, if not completely neglected, at least given insufficient place in our programs.* As I have said elsewhere: "Perfection at the pattern-drill level, no matter how impressive to the observer, cannot be an end in itself. It is a fruitless activity unless care is taken to see that the skill gained by such training is further extended until the student is capable of autonomous expression."[13] In 1964, I spoke of the need for developing "that adventurous spirit which will enable [the student] to try to meet any situation by putting what he knows to maximum use."[14] In 1968, I wrote "students should be encouraged, at the advanced level, to try out new combinations of elements to create novel utterances. This is what the advanced student would do were he to find himself in a foreign country. He would make every effort to express his meaning by all kinds of recombinations of the language elements at his disposal. *The more daring he is in such linguistic innovation, the more rapidly he progresses.*"[15] On looking back I feel it was a mistake to tag this recommendation specifically to "the advanced student" (a vague entity at best). Where we have been failing may well be in not encouraging this "adventurous spirit" from an early stage with the result that the student finds it difficult to move from structured security to the insecurity of reliance on his own resources, just as the young would-be swimmer clings to his mother's hand or "the foot on the bottom of the pool."

In Savignon's very interesting study "students in the communicative skills program" (which consisted of one hour per week supplementing the regular audio-lingual type course) "were given the opportunity to speak French in a variety of communicative settings ranging from short (1-2 minute) exchanges between a student and a fluent speaker of French in a simulated situation to whole group discussions on topics of current interest. Emphasis was put on getting meaning across; students were urged to use every means at their disposal to understand and in turn to make themselves understood. Grammar and pronunciation errors were expected and were always ignored when they did not interfere with meaning. In other words, the experimenter and the other fluent speaker who participated in these sessions reacted to what was said, not to how it was said."[16] One student commented: "These sessions taught me to say what I wanted to say instead of book conversations."[17] If we compare this remark with that of the student quoted at the beginning of this paper it seems these students did begin to "talk off the tops of their heads."

Just how practice in autonomous interaction can be incorporated into the program will depend on the type of program, but incorporate it we must, giving it a substantial role in the students' learning. We must not feel that interaction practice is somehow "wasting time" when there is "so much to learn." Unless this "adventurous spirit" is given time to establish itself as a constant attitude most of what is learned will be stored unused, and we will produce learned individuals who are inhibited and fearful in situations requiring language use. With careful selection of the activity, such practice can be a part of every lesson, early in the learning process, with expansion of the complexity of the task as the student advances.

Practice in autonomous interaction should be individualized in the sense that it should allow for the different ways students learn, the different paces at which they learn, the different things which interest them, and the different situations in which they prefer to learn. Students should be offered a choice of tasks (things to do, things to find out, problems to solve, situations to which to react) and then be allowed to choose their own way, their own place, time, and company, for handling them. Some may prefer to work regularly with one other person, others may choose a small group, while other may prefer working with the teacher. Some who are loners will prefer working through certain situations by themselves demonstrating their capacity as individuals (and many of these in a quiet way may outpace their fellows through sheer singlemindedness of purpose).

Students cannot be set down in groups, or sent off in pairs, and told to interact in the foreign language. *Motivation to communicate* must be aroused. Occasionally some fortuitous incident or combination of personalities will cause a desire to communicate something in the foreign language to emerge spontaneously, but mostly it will need to be fostered by the intrinsic interest of the task proposed for the students concerned. Such interest will make the interaction which follows autonomous; a genuine communication from one person to another, not just another imposed act of pseudocommunication. Because of the personal nature of the activity we are promoting, the type of reaction to be displayed must always remain consistent with the personality of the particular student. Some people are temperamentally incapable of interacting with a babble of words; to force them to do so is to force them back into pseudocommunication and into mouthing learned phrases. The quality of the interaction will be judged by other criteria: ability to receive and express meaning, to understand and convey intentions, to perform acceptably in situations and in relations with others.

Earlier I suggested various natural uses of language in interaction which can be used for this type of activity. Here I will expand on these and set down a few elaborations of each; any imaginative teacher will think of many others.

(1) *Establishing and maintaining social relations*: greetings between persons of the same and different age and status, introductions, wishes for special occasions, polite enquiries (with attention to the permissible and the expected questions in the culture), making arrangements, giving directions to strangers, apologies, excuses, refusals, mild rebukes, hedging (the gentle art of noncommunication), encouraging, discouraging, and persuading others. Students might be sent to find out from a monolingual native speaker (or one who pretends to be monolingual) how these are enacted in the cultural context of the language being learned.

(2) *Seeking information* on subjects for which students have some basic vocabulary. (At some point finding out specific technical vocabulary can be part of this type of interaction). Once again the native speaker or informant acts as though he were monolingual, or alternatively the students seek the information from other speakers of the language outside of the course or the school. The information may be useful for (1), for (3), for (4), for (8), or even for (11).

(3) *Giving information* about oneself, one's background, one's country, or about some subject in which one is proficient. The student may be giving information to other students learning to do or make something (4), or passing on information gained in (2). Simulated settings like bank or airline counters, customs desks, workshops, or restaurants may be used where the students are confined to the school setting.

(4) *Learning to do or make something*. Possibilities here are limitless. The pressure of intensive courses can be relieved by organizing actual sessions in the foreign language where students work with real-life materials and activities (sports, hobbies, crafts, physical exercise).

(5) *Expressing one's reactions*. The student can be put in real situations or simulated situations where he has to react verbally throughout a television show, at an exhibition of pictures or photographs, or during a friendly sharing of slides.

(6) *Hiding one's intentions.* Each student may be given a mission which he must not reveal under any provocation, but which he tries to carry out within a given period of time. This type of activity carries purposeful use of the language beyond course hours as students try to discover each other's missions.

(7) *Talking one's way out of trouble.* Simulated or real situations should be set up of increasing verbal difficulty where the student must use his wits to extract himself from his dilemma.

(8) *Problem solving.* A problem may involve (2) or (4), or even (6) and (7). The problem presented should be an active one whose solution requires verbal activity or enquiry. As early as 1953 Carroll posed the question whether aural-oral methods might not be more successful "if, instead of presenting the student with a fixed, predetermined lesson to be learned, the teacher created a 'problem-solving' situation in which the student must find . . . appropriate verbal responses for solving the problem" thus being early forced "to learn, by a kind of trial-and-error process, to *communicate* rather than merely to utter the speech patterns in the lesson plans."[18]

(9) *Sharing leisure activities.* Students should have the opportunity to learn and become proficient in the games and diversions of the foreign culture. They should be able to participate in verbal competitions. Where there are special activities associated with festivals or national holidays these should be engaged in.

(10) *Conversing over the telephone.* This is always difficult in a foreign language and should be practiced early. The student should use a phone book in the foreign language and where this is possible make actual calls enquiring about goods, services, or timetables for transport. The help of monolingual contacts outside the course should be enlisted. (Some incapacitated persons and older people living alone would enjoy participating in this type of activity.) This activity can be linked with (2) or (8), and will often involve (3).

(11) *Entertaining.* The student should be given the opportunity to use his natural talents or encouraged through

role-playing sessions to act out in front of a group. He may conduct a radio call-in program or a TV talk show, or groups of students may prepare and present radio or TV commercials (these may involve more or less talking interspersed with mime and are therefore very suitable for the early stages of a course).

(12) *Displaying one's achievements*. Students may tell the group about what they did in (4), (5), (6), (7), or (8), or present and explain special projects. This can be a regular culminating activity to draw together more individualized efforts at interaction.

All of these activities will obviously not be possible for all students from the earliest stage of learning. The teacher will select and graduate activities from these categories so that the attitude of seeking to communicate is developed early in an activity which is within the student's growing capacity. An impossible task which bewilders and discourages the student too early in his language learning is just as inhibiting of ultimate fluency as lack of opportunity to try what he can do with what he knows.

Some people will have deep-seated doubts about accepting such an approach because they foresee that the student will make many errors which may well become ingrained and ineradicable. It was because of such problems that many turned away from the direct method, seeking something more systematic which would seem to ensure more accurate production. Unfortunately, the emphasis on correct production at all times and the firm determination to create a learning situation where students would not make mistakes seems to have led to an impasse for many students. If we wish to facilitate the "great leap" I have described, then a change of attitude toward mistakes during interaction practice is imperative. It is during production (or pseudocommunication) practice that immediate corrections should be made. It is then that we should make the student conscious of possible errors and so familiarize him with acceptable sequences that he is able to monitor his own production and work toward its improvement in spontaneous interaction. In interaction practice we are trying to develop an attitude of innovation and experimentation with the new language. Nothing is more dampening of enthusiasm and effort than constant correction when the student is trying to express his own ideas within the limitations of his newly-acquired knowledge of the language. What is required is for the instructor to note silently consistent and systematic errors made by the student in his presence (not slips of the tongue and occasional lapses in areas where the student usually acquits himself well); these errors will then be discussed with the student at a time when the instructor is helping him evaluate his success in interaction, with particular attention being paid to those types of errors which hinder communication. Such an analytic session may be conducted from time to time with a tape of an actual communication sequence, the student or group of students being asked to detect errors in their own spontaneous production and suggest corrections and improvements. This technique makes the students more alert to their own mistakes and to other possibilities for expressing their meaning which they have not been exploiting.

Many of the types of activities listed may have already found their place in our courses. The originality of the approach lies not so much in the novelty of the activities as in the way in which they are approached. To develop autonomous control of language for communication we must at some time allow the student autonomy, and conversely discourage him from maintaining dependence. We must give the student practice in relying on his own resources and using his ingenuity so that very early in his language learning he realizes that only by interacting freely and independently with others can he learn the control and ready retrieval essential for fluent language use.

## FOOTNOTES

[1]*The Advisor* (Teacher-Course Evaluation, University of Illinois, 1970-71), p. 122.

[2]F. Agard and H. Dunkel, *An Investigation of Second-Language Teaching* (Boston: Ginn, 1948), p. 288.

[3]Throughout this paper I have used the terms "foreign language" and "foreign culture" rather than "English" and "American culture" to remind us that for our

students English is indeed a foreign language and the American culture a foreign culture.

[4]L. Kelly, *25 Centuries of Language Teaching* (Rowley, Mass.: Newbury House, 1969).

[5]I have borrowed the division into skill-getting and skill-using from Don H. Parker, "When Should I Individualize Instruction? in *Individualization of Instruction: A Teaching Strategy*, ed. Virgil M. Howes (New York: Macmillan, 1970), p. 176. More detailed explanation of this model can be found in the Report of the Stanford Conference on the Individualization of Foreign Language Instruction (United States Office of Education, 1971), Position Paper on "Techniques for Developing Proficiency in the Spoken Language in an Individualized Foreign Language Program," prepared by Wilga M. Rivers.

[6]"Some Theoretical Aspects of Language Learning and Language Teaching," *Language Learning*, 17(1967), 175.

[7]Michel Benamou and Eugene Ionesco, *Mise en Train* (New York: Macmillan, 1969), "Le professeur est dans la poche du gilet de la montre," p. 44; "Le crocodile est plus beau que Marie-Jeanne," p. 114; "Il dit que ses parents sont aussi grands que la Tour Eiffel," p. 141.

[8]See Chapter 6 of this book, "From Skill Acquisition to Language Control."

[9]*Teaching Foreign-Language Skills* (Chicago: University of Chicago Press, 1968), p. 109.

[10]"Structural Pattern Drills: A Classification," *Foreign Language Annals*, 4(1970), 187-193.

[11]"Teaching Communication," *Language Learning*, 20(1970), 55-68.

[12]S. Savignon used this technique in her "Study of the Effect of Training in Communicative Skills as Part of a Beginning College French Course on Student Attitude and Achievement in Linguistic and Communicative Competence," Ph.D. diss., University of Illinois at Urbana-Champaign, 1971, since published as *Communicative Competence: an Experiment in Foreign-Language Teaching* (Center for Curriculum Development, 1972).

[13]*Teaching Foreign-Language Skills*, p. 109.

[14]*The Psychologist and the Foreign-Language Teacher* (Chicago: University of Chicago Press, 1964,) p. 78.

[15]*Teaching Foreign-Language Skills*, p. 201. (Italics not in the original.)

[16]Savignon, (1972), p. 25. On pp. 28-9 are listed a variety of communicative tasks used during the practice sessions. Savignon acknowledges her indebtedness to L. Jakobovits, *Foreign Language Learning* (Rowley, Mass.: Newbury House, 1970), Chapter 3, for guidelines in defining these tasks. Professor Jakobovits was the director of her study.

[17]Savignon (1972), p. 30.

[18]J. B. Carroll, *The Study of Language* (Cambridge: Harvard University Press, 1953), p. 188.

# 3

# FROM LINGUISTIC COMPETENCE
# TO COMMUNICATIVE COMPETENCE*

In "Talking Off the Tops of Their Heads" I emphasized the need for providing students from the earliest stages with a great deal of practice in using language for the natural uses of language, that is, practice in interaction (skill-using), and I proposed a number of activities that involved spontaneous and genuine uses of language. Here, I wish to consider the gap in my model between skill-getting and skill-using, and make proposals for a smooth and natural transition from production practice to interaction.

If free, spontaneous interaction practice is an attractive extra in a program which is rigid and mechanical, we should not be surprised to see our students develop a kind of schizophrenia: Personality A, which is submissive and malleable, produces correctly constructed sequences as directed in intensive practice, while Personality B asserts its own individuality, completely ignoring, when engaging in autonomous interaction, what Personality A has been so laboriously practicing. How then can we develop our program so that such a schizophrenic situation will not develop?

The important questions to be considered in movement *toward* spontaneous expression or communicative competence are: *Where do we come from?* and *By what route?* All kinds of routes may be followed to reach a destination. Some instructors unfortunately are not quite sure where the goal is

---

*Paper delivered at the Defense Language Institute English Language Branch, Lackland Air Force Base, Texas, on May 31, 1972 (TESOL Project). Originally published in *TESOL Quarterly* 7 (1973), 25-34.

or how best to get there. They take their students by routes which are circuitous, lead to dead-ends, backtrack, and make the going rough and difficult so that attention is on the going instead of the destination and students begin to feel that the journey itself is the most important thing, completely losing sight of the goal. This is the way it is when students are completely preoccupied with good performance in pseudo-communication. Production practice is necessary for developing linguistic competence, without which there can be no solidly based communicative competence, but it is less demanding for instructor and students than trying to develop communicative competence itself. Consequently, many find it an unexciting but comfortable haven in which to take refuge on the way, and never reach the goal at all. At least they can recognize here something tangible for their efforts.

Other routes, through similar country, lead to the destination directly but they demand effort and persistence. The students to whom these routes are indicated know where they are going and what they will be able to do when they get there. They are prepared psychologically and practically for the goal of communicative competence and all their activities are directed toward it and toward it alone. These students never allow themselves to become absorbed in any activity on the way as an end in itself, but always as a means to a clearly recognized end and as an activity of the same generic nature as the one they have in view.

We see examples of the route-as-goal when instructors are chiefly interested in eliciting near-native pronunciation in imitation and choir-like perfection in construction exercises. We see instructor and students settling down in cozy comfort on the way when smooth and effortless production of correctly constructed sentences, even complicated and intricate ones, satisfies and students rarely engage in authentic interaction.

Merely adding a supplement of interaction activities of the kind elaborated in Chapter 2 will not provide the answer. *Such activities should not be supplemental, but should spring naturally and inevitably from the types of activities engaged in for skill-getting.* The only way to avoid the schizophrenia of Personality A and Personality B is to develop the whole program with Personality B in mind, so that Personality B is free to operate imaginatively at all times. This will not be possible with a patched-up program—something added here and something added there while the bulk of the program is based on wrong assumptions. We must rethink the program so that all efforts are directed toward the perceived goal.[1]

In many programs much effort is put into the production of what are sometimes called "controlled drills" and reliance is placed on a carefully organized step-by-step progression toward the goal. Yet, despite careful planning and fastidious practice, students still stumble and falter when trying to express their own ideas in the foreign language.

I would like to suggest that we look here for the source of our schizophrenia. Our conventional controlled drills are based on assumptions which make them incompatible with our ultimate goal of communicative competence. They are usually based entirely on manipulation of language elements as though that is all language learning consists of. Nor is the answer, as some would suggest, merely a matter of switching over to the learning of explicit grammar rules that we then attempt to put into operation in language material, important as the comprehension of the syntactic rules of a language may be. We must recognize that linguistic competence, "knowing" a language, involves not one but several types of cognitive processes.

Bruner posits three parallel systems in human cognition for processing information and storing it for use, all capable of partial transformation one into the other.[2] They reflect the three ways people can "know" something.[3] If we understand these three ways (enactive, iconic or perceptual, and symbolic) we can analyze in practical fashion what the student has to learn in learning a second language.[4] We can then categorize the various aspects of linguistic competence as belonging largely to one or another of these systems, and devise the types of practice which are most appropriate for the kind of learning involved in each case. (Here we must not be discouraged by people who tell us that nobody knows just what "knowing" a language involves. If we had to wait until complete and irrefutable theoretical knowledge were attained in such a complex area as language acquisition, we would be forced to give up all activity in language teaching. Theoretical advances are sparked and verified through practical observations. We must act on what is known at a particular stage and continually adapt and readapt our procedures as new knowledge becomes available.)

The first representational system in human cognition which Bruner describes is the *enactive.* This system is acquired through manipulation and action by a process of stimulus-response conditioning. In this case we "know" by an habitual pattern of responsive action. Mediating responses transform the stimulus prior to the response and these are processes of understanding which make the response a personal one. Because of this internal transformation of the stimulus different people require different time intervals for making the response. In a foreign language what we can "know" through active response are such things as the arbitrary structural associations which can be set out in paradigms. In actual meaningful language use, however, the other two cognitive systems are immediately involved: knowing the form of a verb ending after a particular pronoun may be an habitual reaction, but knowing when to use that particular ending in the expression of a message is much more complex. There is, therefore, a role, but a limited one, for stimulus-response conditioning in making automatic the production of certain arbitrary elements of surface structure. (Bruner suggests it is also appropriate for learning the production of strange sounds, although, once again, learning when to use the sound as it has been learned and when to adapt and modify it involves other types of representation.)

Bruner's second system of representation is the *iconic,*[5] acquired through perceptual organization and imagery (that is, auditory and visual pattern recognition). Here we build on the inductive recognition of the gestalt: the whole consisting of systematically distributed interrelated parts. The identification of patterns in what we hear and see aids memory. Here we must devise methods for recognition and assimilation of recurring systematic arrangements of formal features and their acceptable rearrangements. Such features as fixed word order in sentence types or in syntactic relationships and structural patterns which continually recur in association with each other are appropriately listed here. Bruner warns us that "affective and motivational factors affect imagery and perceptual organization strikingly." For this reason we must look for individual differences in perception of auditory (and visual) patterning and realize that the disconcerted or embarrassed student will often fail to recognize auditory patterns and may develop, as a result, an emotional block against all auditory activity. The bored student will simply not retain them.

Thirdly, we have the *symbolic* representational system which operates through internalized language and logical processes in the formation of concepts. This symbolic system enables us to categorize and to establish hierarchies of categories, principles, and rules, to bring order into the complexity of what is being learned, permitting "a transition from merely orderly behavior to logical behavior."[6] This systematization of the language may be established inductively by the student himself, but in many cases it can be acquired more rapidly through the deductive medium of the explanations of the teacher or the textbook (using language, "the second signal system," as Pavlov called it). Nevertheless, the student, whether guided or not, must abstract features and synthesize them into rules of operation which will create new meanings. It is the symbolic representational system which processes the many complexities of syntax through which formal features and arrangements of features attain vigorous life in the expression of the infinite nuances of meaning.[7] The student goes beyond the specific instances in which he has seen the forms of language in operation into the creative use of language in novel situations.

These three types of representation coexist in an adult student's cognitive system—they are not stages of learning. Any or all may be appropriately activated at any point in a learning process: it is for us to analyze for what aspects of language learning they are appropriate, and continually interweave them in learning activities as they are interwoven in actual language use, if we wish our students to do more than perform well in exercises of a specific kind.

Types of intensive practice exercises must, then, be varied. Mere repetition and manipulation will help with only a minor portion of what must be known. The associations in a paradigm are arbitrary (I get, he gets), but the notion of paradigmatic variations (the fact that the new language has more or less paradigmatic associations than the student's native language) is conceptual and must be understood before knowledge of the details of the paradigm can be effective in use. Similarly, formal features of tenses are paradigmatic and may be learned by rote, but of themselves they are so much useless baggage. Using them appropriately involves conceptual understanding of the way in which the new language expresses time relationships.

We must develop more and better ways of dealing with the more purely conceptual aspects of language: the patterns of arrangements and the intricate complexities of interacting systems and subsystems of rules.[8] These cannot be assimilated absent-mindedly. In each of these cases "knowing" depends on awareness of abstractions such as similarities, differences, functions, and interactive relationships. Without such awareness the student cannot operate confidently within the new system. This awareness can only develop when the student focuses on abstract operations. Such focus depends on how personally he is involved in correct selection from among the possible variations of the system. We must concentrate on the types of activities which elicit this personal involvement.

In my model I have referred to production exercises as pseudo-communication, and in "Talking Off the Tops of Their Heads" I emphasized the first segment of this term—*pseudo*-communication—in order to contrast it with real interaction activities. Here I wish to emphasize the second segment—pseudo-*communication*—because this, I believe, is the way we can bridge the gap between skill-getting and skill-using. Unless production practice is always regarded as pseudo-*communication,* our schizophrenic situation will continue and our students will not apply what they have practiced in articulation and construction when involved in interaction. Let us elucidate, then, the ways in which production exercises can take the form of pseudo-*communication*.

Passive exercises do not prepare students for active use of language: completely controlled and directed activity does not prepare students for autonomous expression.

Each exercise in which he is involved must demand of the student close *attention, abstraction* (recognition of the requirements of the particular situation), and *active construction* (requiring recall of stored cognitive information and judicious selection). Exercises which can be performed mechanically are useful only for demonstration of associations of forms, of systematic patternings, or of relationships. They allow the student time to see the picture: to observe the interplay of surface elements or grasp the principle. They serve an introductory function, after which they are no longer of use unless it appears later that the student is confused, when they may be reintroduced for clarification or confirmation. They must lead directly to intensive practice in the type of construction which requires the student to produce utterances he himself has selected, until he shows he has control of that particular aspect of the language. Opportunity must then be given without delay for the student to use what he has been learning within the wider syntactic system he has been building up. Thus *every extension of linguistic competence is tested out immediately in natural communicative use.*

Luria has pointed out that grammatical speech will not arise if there is no objective necessity for speech communication.[9] We must create that necessity by the design of our activities.

How then can intensive practice exercises become pseudo-*communication* and gradually lead to real communication? Here I shall set out some guidelines.

1. As each exercise is designed, it should be given a *situational context and a lexical content which are readily transferable to interchanges* between instructor and student or student and student.

*Are we practicing question forms*? Then what is the transferability of items which produce questions with zero probability of occurrence?

> —We are sitting in the hall.
>   Are we sitting in the hall?
> —Janet and I are at the movies.
>   Are Janet and I at the movies?

How often in conversation do we move from statement to question anyway, unless there is a change of reference as in:

> "I've been waiting a quarter of an hour. Have you been waiting too?"

2. After a brief presentation of forms, that is, *teacher-directed practice* to develop familiarity with a particular aspect of the language, the activity should move to interchange between student and student. *Student-directed practice* may take the form of a chaining activity in a large group (e.g., question-answer, question-answer from student to student), or of a small group activity with a student leader. In a small group activity students teach and learn from each other while the instructor listens to see what further directed practice may be required. Small groups which are self-selected also provide for those variations in ability and pace which are so necessary for individual learning.

Student-directed activity moves smoothly into some inter-team competition or game which enables groups to test each other out. For any aspect of language structure a game or simulated activity can be invented which forces the students into *autonomous activity* in which they produce the same types of responses as in an artificial teacher-directed exercise, but this time of their own volition. It is this conscious and intentional progress at all times from teacher-directed demonstration to student-directed application to autonomous student production which makes the further step to *spontaneous interaction* natural and effortless. In this way Personality B is involved early in the practice sequence and is not suddenly called into play in an artificial "extra" activity.

3. With a little imagination even the simplest of structures can be practiced in autonomous production.

*Are we practicing affirmative and negative statements?*
Students can compete in producing the most improbable
statements or set themselves up as a Liars' Club:

> "I borrowed a thousand dollars but I didn't pay it
> back."
> "Last night I flew to the moon and I didn't come back."

*Are we practicing question forms?* A simulated telephone
link may be set up and each student required to ask questions
until he has been able to identify the person calling, until he
has found out what a presumably diffident caller wanted to
ask him, or until he has extracted from the caller what he
wanted him to do. Although this is a simulated situation, it
parallels a possible communication situation.

Another realistic way of eliciting question forms is for the
teacher to give Student A vague instructions to transmit to
Student B. Student B must continue to ask questions of
Student A, and Student A of the teacher, until Student B is
quite clear about what he has to do. When Student B has
completed the required task he reports back to the teacher
on what he has done so that the teacher can verify that the
original message was accurately transmitted.

*Are we practicing indirect speech?* The teacher transmits
information very softly to one student who is expected to
pass on to the class what the teacher has said:

> "He said he saw an accident on the way to class."
> "He said one person was injured."

This can be a three-way transmission:

> Instructor says to Student A: "I don't like rock music."
> Student A says quietly to Student B: "He says he
> doesn't like rock music."
> Student B says to the class: "He said he didn't like rock
> music."

Although this is a structured exercise, it simulates a possible
situation where, for instance, people at one end of a table
cannot hear what their fellow guests are saying.

Another variation of the same activity is the familiar parlor
game of "Confidences" where one person whispers to the

next along the line what his neighbor tells him has been said by the originator of the message. The last person in the line repeats aloud what he thinks he was told and this is compared with the original message. This can be a very amusing activity because of the distortions which creep in as the message is inaccurately perceived and reconstructed by different persons in the group.

4. Whether we are using expansion, completion, or translation exercises we have the possibility of two types: *Type A* which provides only for Personality A, and *Type B* which encourages the emergence of the innovative Personality B.[10]

A Type A *expansion exercise* is purely manipulative. Students are supplied with elements they must insert at the correct places in a basic sentence frame. A Type B expansion exercise provides students with the opportunity to create new sentences from the basic frame by expanding it as they wish as often as they wish. (This activity can become a competition to see which students can expand the meaning of the utterance still further through the addition of another word or phrase.)

> *Type A expansion exercise.*
>
> Basic frame:    He goes to town.
> Instructor:     Often.
> Student(s):     He often goes to town.
> Instructor:     On Saturdays.
> Student(s):     He often goes to town on Saturdays.
>
> *Type B expansion exercise.*

This may be a competition or a chaining activity.

> Student A:  He goes to town.
> Student B:  He often goes to town.
> Student C:  He often goes to town on Wednesdays.
> Student D:  He often goes to town by train on Wednesdays.
> Student E:  He often goes to town by train with his sister on Wednesdays.

The competition continues till students run out of inspiration or possibilities of insertion. Note that students not only have the opportunity to develop the meaning as they wish, but in doing so they reproduce the whole expanded sentence each time as part of their own production.

A similar division can be made in types of *completion exercises*. In a Type A completion exercise a fixed segment is retained, varying perhaps in tense or person in concert with the element the instructor supplies. In a Type B completion exercise, the student can make his own semantic contribution within the syntactic framework he is acquiring.

*Type A completion exercise.*

In the following exercise you will hear the model sentence:

"I took his pencil because he took mine."

Throughout the exercise you will retain a concluding segment of similar meaning to "because he took mine" but as the introductory segment varies you will vary the person referred to in the concluding segment.

| | |
|---|---|
| Model: | I took his pencil because he took mine. |
| Instructor: | He took my book. |
| Student(s): | He took my book because I took his. |
| Instructor: | We took their seats. |
| Student(s): | We took their seats because they took ours. |

*Type B completion exercise.*

Students are asked to invent excuses for aberrant behavior on their own part or on the part of other students in the group.

| | |
|---|---|
| Student A: | I sat in his place because he sat in mine. |
| Student B: | I ate her lunch because she ate mine. |
| Student C: | Mary broke John's pencil because he broke hers. |
| Student D: | My father used my mother's car because she used his. |

The Type A activity may be useful to allow the student time to assimilate the operations of the basic structure, but the Type B activity is essential if students are to develop the command and confidence they need for interaction activities.

Sometimes *oral translation exercises* are used, when the class has a homogeneous language background and the instructor is familiar with this language. In this case, we again have the possibility of Type A and Type B exercises.

In a *Type A translation exercise* students translate rapidly a series of unconnected sentences linked only by their central attention to a difficult point of grammar or an idiomatic turn of phrase. In a *Type B translation exercise* the same attention can be paid to a specific problem of grammar (e.g., use of past tenses) but the sentences in the sequence have a semantic relatedness or a situational development such that the students can simulate a simultaneous interpretation situation, or pretend to relay the information sentence by sentence to a presumably monolingual visitor in their midst. Once again the activity is the same but the situation has an authenticity which prepares students to use the language in real situations when the opportunity arises.

So we could continue. To avoid schizophrenia let us keep most of our production practice time for Type B activities which develop quickly and easily into genuine interaction, that is, use of language for the natural purposes of language.[11] In this way, we will wean our students early from dependence on direction from without, thus preparing them psychologically for the uninhibited autonomy of the confident language-user.

## FOOTNOTES

[1]The perceived goal may, of course, be listening comprehension or reading, in which case a different design will be indicated. Here I am concerned with programs for which facility in oral communication is the goal. I have made some methodological suggestions for listening and reading programs in "Linguistic and Psychological Factors in Speech Perception and Their Implications for Teaching Materials," Chapter 10.

[2]These systems are described and discussed by Bruner in considerable detail in J. S. Bruner, *Toward a Theory of Instruction* (Harvard University Press, 1966), pp. 10-14; and in J. S. Bruner, Rose R. Olver, Patricia M. Greenfield, *et al.*, *Studies in Cognitive Growth* (Wiley, 1966), pp. 6-48.

[3]*Studies in Cognitive Growth,* ibid., p. 6.

[4]In Chapter 9, "The Foreign-Language Teacher and Cognitive Psychology, or Where Do We Go from Here?" I have quoted a number of cognitive psychologists and certain linguists of the generative semantics group who consider that

acquisition of language draws on the general cognitive processes basic to other learning.

[5] In *Studies in Cognitive Growth* this is spelled "ikonic."

[6] J. S. Bruner, *Toward a Theory of Instruction,* pp. 5-6.

[7] It is at this point that much of value can be drawn from Fillmore's linguistic theory showing how the new language expresses universal relations within its own system.

[8] For a more detailed discussion of this subject, see my article, "Contrastive Linguistics in Textbook and Classroom," Chapter 5.

[9] A. R. Luria and F. I. Yudovich, *Speech and the Development of Mental Processes in the Child: An Experimental Investigation,* ed. J. Simon (London: Staples Press, 1959), pp. 28-64.

[10] Type A and B exercises are applied to French in W. M. Rivers, *A Practical Guide to the Teaching of French* (New York, London, and Toronto: Oxford University Press, 1975), to German in W. M. Rivers, K. M. and V. J. Dell'Orto, *A Practical Guide to the Teaching of German* (Oxford University Press, 1975), and to Spanish in W. M. Rivers, M. M. Azevedo, W. H. Heflin, Jr., and R. Hyman-Opler, *A Practical Guide to the Teaching of Spanish* (Oxford University Press, 1976), Chapter 4 in each case.

[11] Natural uses of language and normal purposes of language are distinguished and discussed in W. M. Rivers, "The Natural and the Normal in Language Learning" in H. D. Brown, ed., *Papers in Second Language Acquisition*, special issue No. 4 of *Language Learning* (Jan., 1976).

# TESTING AND STUDENT LEARNING*

I remember an international conference some six years ago at which a distinguished European scholar whose English was not strong suddenly burst into the discussion of an experimental project with the words: *"Why these old tests!"* Although he was referring in this case to statistical tests of significance, the words have remained in my mind: Why these old tests! These words are still only too often applicable in practical instructional situations, despite the excellent books and articles of such friends of the profession as John Carroll, Alan Davies, David Harris, Paul Pimsleur, Robert Lado, and Rebecca Valette.

And tests are becoming older. What was new in the sixties does not adequately assess achievement in the educational climate of the seventies. In this period of rapid change in all educational enterprises, we are foolish not to engage in a little futurology: to analyze trends, predict probable future developments, adjust psychologically to what the future may bring, and plan to meet future needs.

Whether we like it or not, in any foreign or second-language teaching we are swept by the winds of change in general education, in attitudes toward learning, and in community needs. But what has this to do with testing? As Pilliner has stated so succinctly:

> It is axiomatic that (the) content [of tests] inevitably influences the teaching and learning which precede them . . . Properly constructed, (the test) can foster and

---

*Paper read at ATESOL First International Conference, Dublin, Ireland, June 29, 1973. Originally published in M. C. O'Brien, ed., *Testing in Second Language Teaching: New Dimensions* (ATESOL and University of Dublin Press, 1973).

reinforce good teaching and sound learning and discourage their opposites. To achieve these ends, the test constructor must start with a clear conception of the aims and purposes of the area of learning to which his test is relevant.[1]

Reversing Pilliner's emphases, we may say that aims and purposes, construction, and content of tests must be congruent with the aspirations and learning approaches of the day and age. As test constructors, whether for large groups of students from a variety of instructional situations or merely for tomorrow's class, we must not allow ourselves to become so bogged down in the peculiar technical problems of test design that we cannot see the wood for the trees, thus exerting, perhaps involuntarily, a retarding influence on the evolution of foreign-language instruction.

Why do we test anyway? It is salutary sometimes to go back and ask ourselves a question of this type. Is it because it has always been done—because it seems to us of the same order of necessity as the rising and setting of the sun? Is testing an essential part of the learning process? Can we class it as a natural activity? Here we may think of the feedback loop which Miller, Galanter, and Pribram proposed as a model of the molecular unit of human behavior. Miller and his colleagues called their model TOTE (*T*est — *O*perate — *T*est — *E*xit).[2] "In its weakest form," they state, the TOTE asserts simply that the operations an organism performs are constantly guided by the outcomes of various tests."[3] The organism's capability is tested against an existing pattern or criterion. "Action is initiated by an 'incongruity' between the state of the organism and the state that is being tested for, and the action persists until the incongruity ... is removed."[4] This criterion having been matched, the organism moves into the next phase of its activity and is challenged to a new effort by the criterion of that phase.

Here we recognize immediately the principle of the thermostat and we can derive an interesting analogy from it for our students' learning. In this model, the test acts as a plan which controls operations. The test phase "involves the specification of whatever knowledge is necessary for the comparison that is to be made, and the operational phase represents what the organism does about it."[5] The test is, as it were, a source of information or a set of instructions which enables the learner to keep up his efforts till he has matched the criterion, testing and retesting to see how close he is coming to the desired performance. Each time he falls short he makes a further effort to reach the criterion; each time he achieves his aim he moves on to the next phase of activity. In this way the test is an integral part of the learning process: a natural step in any advance. How different this is from the old concept of the test as a hurdle to be surmounted—a hurdle which becomes a discouraging barrier to too many language learners. Here, instead, matching against the criterion becomes a challenge and a guide to further effort. What a gain it would be if we could convey this attitude toward the test to our students: if they no longer feared the test as a threat to their ego, but saw it as an indicator—a sign on the way. In this paradigm, tests are no longer a special activity, set apart from all others and loaded with unique significance. If we think about it, we can recognize here the distinction between the norm-referenced test, where one student's performance is compared with that of other students or matched against some artificial, external standard, and the criterion-referenced test, where the student knows exactly what knowledge he must demonstrate, and either demonstrates it and moves on or cannot demonstrate it and goes back to see how he can improve his performance. This is a revolution in the concept of testing. The student is now responsible for his own learning. When he feels ready to match the criterion, he tests. Note that "he tests": it is not we who test him. If necessary, he later retests. When satisfied that he has matched the criterion, he moves on. Idealistic? Perhaps, but it is in keeping with the changing climate in student-teaching relations, in which the student and his needs are central and in which every student has a right to the opportunity to learn as much as he is able, and as much as he is willing to devote effort to learning. Once the test ceases to be a separate activity, but is interwoven with learning, it may well lose the appearance of what we conceive of as a conventional test.

This being the case, what happens to our "standards"? How do we select those with the level of attainment necessary for specific tasks? This is another question and not an educational one. The educational question must be phrased quite differently. How do we provide the opportunity for each student to attain the highest degree of mastery of a foreign language consistent with his language aptitude, his willingness to devote time and energy, his perseverance, and his interest in the various aspects of language skill and the possible uses of language? A test which is a sorting process for some purpose other than the educational one should properly be assigned to some agency outside of the instructional process. It becomes an admissions procedure, related to job specifications or future study demands. It is not, then, an indicator of achievement or even proficiency, but of what some particular agency is looking for. One agency may need only persons who can read instructions accompanying Japanese stereo equipment; another may wish to accept only students able to read with ease French poetry or experiments in nuclear physics published in English. The person wanting this job, or this form of higher study, will prepare himself to cope with the particular situation; others will not be judged on their inability to do so. The form of the test will again be a set of instructions for the candidate; the appointment or admission he seeks will be an incentive; the student will attempt to bring his language performance into congruence with the set of instructions and thus exit into the specialized realm he is seeking to enter. As Rebecca Valette has suggested, this may mean the setting of national standards—levels for which students can be certified as required. (In the U.S.A., Foreign Service Institute levels of proficiency are often used.)

In this case, the source of the set of instructions is clear. At the general level of skill mastery, the source is not so clear by any means. In the past the test was set by the teacher, guided by the syllabus and ultimately by the officials of the system; or it was set by the teacher "alone," guided usually by the textbook he or she had selected (and, therefore, indirectly by certain contemporary "trends," currents, or emphases of the profession, strained through the prejudices and preconceptions of the textbook writer). Indeed, if the test is to be a set of instructions against which the student may test his developing skills and knowledge, then it must have some clear relationship to his aims and purposes. For this, there must be clear input from the student. There are no "aims of foreign-language instruction." There are only aims of particular students learning a specific foreign language at a particular time and place. This is the age in which the course must be tailored to the person, not the image.[6] It is at this point that the expertise of the instructor comes into play—by assessing in consultation with the student his special needs, then writing the sets of instructions or tests in relation to these needs. In practical terms this may mean a recipe from the student which the teacher transforms into a suitable test.

We may, at this point, look closely in two directions to see where emphasis on the student as learner has led us and see the resulting implications on testing. Apart from a few general suggestions I shall have to leave it to our testing experts to decide what we can do about it. (Some of them are working on it already.) These trends are, however, clearly with us, so we must face their implications squarely. First, each student is an individual with his own preferences as to modality and pace of learning and course content. Second, each student is an individual with a personality to express.

## The Student as Individual

One does not need to open more than one professional journal to meet the words "individualization of instruction," yet the more one reads the more confused one becomes as to what this concept means in actual practice. To some it is a new term for an old concept: self-paced instruction through the use of programmed texts—an activity which in practice draws extremely close to independent study. Independent study for all types of students? Is this providing for individual differences in learning styles and modality and content preferences, or merely for speed of assimilation of what is assigned for learning? Many students, as we well know, do not have the self-confidence to be autonomous learners. This independence can be developed for some with sympathetic encouragement, but meanwhile they prefer to work with others or (is this heresy?) with an instructor. Much so-called individualization is as autocratic in concept as the most rigid teacher-directed classroom, allowing no place for the student to choose other than the independent study of a specific learning packet which his teacher has decreed he shall relish.

Individualizing instruction

> means allowing for the different ways in which students learn and giving the students the opportunity to choose what they want to learn, how they want to learn it, and with whom they want to learn it (independently, with other students in a buddy system, in small groups or large groups, or with a teacher, or program) . . . Individualized instruction will vary according to age and situation, as well as personality and learning style.[7]

As Jeannette Veatch has expressed it: "When human interaction takes place on a level where each respects the other's thoughts and ideas, we are getting close to the secret of truly meeting individual differences."[8]

It is to this last concept that we must look for genuine individualization of instruction. As instructors we must give much thought to the ways our individual students learn and the things in foreign-language learning which "turn them on." The day of the monolithic method and monolithic materials is past. Some students prefer to learn audially, others visually—to some the modality is immaterial. Some learn through abstraction, some through practical, concrete use; some from a book, some from other people; some through a logical progression, some heuristically and, as it seems, almost intuitively. Not only are students different, but so are teachers, and what one can do with ease and composure is difficult for another. There is, then, a move in the selection of materials and techniques toward eclecticism and pragmatism: the teacher seeking what works for him and his present group of students, rather than looking for answers from "experts." The "student liberation" movement means "teacher liberation" as well. This trend is to be welcomed in that it restores to the teacher his professional status, requiring of him that he inform himself as fully as he is able so that he can make decisions which are appropriate to the here and now—interpreting students' needs and interests and incorporating them into learning experiences, which in the present context involve interrelated testing. Genuine individualization leads to diversification of approach and content.

Do students really want or need such diversification or is it a current fad? A 1973 study of 1821 undergraduates at the University of Illinois showed that 63 per cent wanted more listening and speaking while 62 per cent wanted more reading.[9] If these are non-parallel distributions representing distinct preferences for many, as seems plausible, then there is a fair overlap of students, about 25 per cent, who would like more of both, that is, courses which permit them to develop simultaneously in both aural-oral and graphic control of the language, while about 37 per cent at the extremes prefer more exclusively oral communication or reading-oriented courses. The percentages may not be typical for students in foreign-language courses everywhere, but some modification of this distribution seems intuitively to reflect the spread of modality preferences in the community. Content preferences were just as clearly indicated, ranging from practice in communication, learning about contemporary life styles and values, reading of literature, reading of contemporary newspapers and magazines, learning to follow foreign films with ease, translating and interpreting, drawing of information from scientific and technical material, art history, music, cultural and political history, philosophy, and even linguistic analysis. There is no dearth of possible subject matter for any foreign-language learning class. With careful thought and organization much more individualization of content is possible through group work or independent research as students prefer. Groups of students vary. Sometimes we encounter a group in which all the members want to do the same thing; sometimes they divide off visibly. Fortunately diversification will rarely mean a different choice for every student in the group.

Surely such diversification implies real difficulties for testing? If we believe that students must demonstrate the level of proficiency they have reached in comparison with others, then certainly diversity in course content is a complication. If we accept my earlier premise that the test should be an individual matching against a criterion, this need not be so. Instead of better comparative tests, we would seek for a better system of establishing criteria consistent with the student's personal aims and purposes, a system in which the student himself would be involved, so that at any point his progress would be clear and continuous. The test as an extra activity then becomes largely superfluous, unless students request it for the pleasure of demonstrating their achievement. When students enjoy tests as a challenge and an opportunity for displaying what they know, we shall have reached the optimal form and timing of the test. If grades are necessary (and we may question whether they are in most cases), then the grade should be based on what the student has achieved as an individual; they should reflect his personal effort and progress toward an individual goal.

Once the one standard test becomes the goal of all students, we are back where we started. Because of the limitations of the job market or of college entrance, or because some other need for an elite has arisen, it becomes depressingly inevitable that some of the most hardworking students will fail. This is built into the system. Is such artificial "failure" necessary or desirable? If not, let us change the system.

## The Student as an Individual
## with a Personality to Express

Thus far, let's admit it, even our discussion of providing for the student as an individual has been teacher-directed, with the teacher making decisions about what is best for the student. Of course, it has involved the teacher taking the student into his confidence: making sure he understands what he is going to do and why, just what he will be expected to demonstrate and how, what criterion he must match before he moves on. This is built into the concept, for instance, of performance objectives. In the words of a recent book:

> The teacher . . . decides in advance which features of the unit he intends to stress in his classes and what degree of proficiency he wants the students to develop with respect to those features . . . It is up to the teacher to set the level of mastery, but his intention should always be that as many students as possible attain a high score.[10]

If the student is a full partner, he must also have the opportunity to tell the teacher what his expectations for the course are, what particular skills and course content interest him, when instruction is moving too fast or too slowly for him, and, at a particular moment, the specific aspects of his study on which he feels the need to test himself.

In theory, performance objectives seem a good idea: they enable teacher and student to come to a clear understanding of the next step to be surmounted. In practice, in foreign-language learning they can be very confining. A foreign language to be learned cannot be reduced to a multitude of small elements which we accumulate like beads on a string (*this* phonological discrimination, *that* use of the past tense in indirect speech, *ten words* for parts of the body), and who is to say that in each case the student must know these to such an extent that he makes only one spelling mistake in ten examples of their use, or fails to make some distinction in only two cases out of twelve?

For some years now, leaders in our field have been pointing out that use of a foreign language is more than the sum of its parts, that there is macro-language use as opposed to micro-language learning. The micro approach can stultify foreign-language learning even in its early stages. Naturally, if the student is to use language he needs a basic knowledge of phonology, grammar, and lexicon, but these must be practiced continually in some form of real production of meaningful messages. In other words, the student as individual learner must have the opportunity to express himself through the language in terms of his own personality, in some use of the language for the natural purposes of language: as part of an interaction of communication, either giving or receiving, in speech or in writing.[11] If this interchange is a natural expression of personality it cannot be predetermined with an established criterion level of mastery of the nine-out-of-ten variety: the criteria in these cases are comprehension and comprehensibility, qualities which are very difficult to quantify. [12]

In all education (shall we say, in all living) we have this continual tension between man's desire to organize, to bring order to phenomena, to quantify, and unfettered natural growth: between the classical and the romantic impulse, between control and self-expression, between Robert Hutchins and Ivan Illich. As educators we have to keep our balance between the two as the pendulum swings. Performance objectives seem to bring order, clarity, direction, rational progression to foreign-language learning, yet, given preeminence, they stunt the fragile plant they are there to nurture, just as too rigorous pruning and training may produce an espalier but not a free-standing tree in a natural garden.

Here I shall return to one of my favorite themes since 1964:[13] in language learning we have to control language at two levels. There is basic core learning of the phonological, morphological, and syntactical operations of the language and of the interrelationships of these systems with the semantic system. This is what I refer to as micro-language learning. Mastering it is essential, time-consuming, sometimes tedious, hard work, and here the performance objective approach and its related modes of testing may be useful. It is the second level, or macro-level, of the natural use of the new language for the expression of personal meaning which we seem continually to neglect, but which is absolutely essential if the learning of the language is not to be time-wasting "busywork." This macro-language use is not a later advanced stage of study which we are sorry that many of our students do not reach: it is our major purpose in foreign-language instruction which must be encouraged and fostered from the first elementary learnings. It is this level of language use which cannot be confined by the conventional performance objectives if it is to retain that spontaneity which is its hallmark. If we wish to encourage creativity and self-expression in the use of the second language, we cannot decide in advance what features our students will use and the degree of proficiency we want them to demonstrate in the use of these features.

How, then, can this spontaneous language use be tested? Valette says: "Until we know precisely what we intend to teach we cannot measure our success."[14] Perhaps with natural use of language we will never know *precisely* what we must teach, but yet it seems clear that the natural use of language by our students is more important than a clear-cut "measure" of our success. We cannot teach for creativeness in language use with functional comprehension and comprehensibility as the ultimate criteria and then test for mere accuracy of detail, as most standard tests seem to do at present.

It is here that we need better tests than the standard interview for speaking and free composition for writing. Various possibilities have been suggested that involve our giving the student a real task to perform which requires him to seek information and convey information in the language (in speech or writing as his needs require) and then evaluating him on the successful completion of the task. In concrete terms, this suggestion has endless possibilities for actualization at various levels of difficulty and can be adapted to specific uses of language which interest a particular student (the conducting of business affairs, the enjoyment of a film or play, the investigation of a scientific problem). At an elementary stage, the test can entail approaching a monolingual or presumed monolingual speaker of the language to find out such information as his name, age, address, telephone number, and occupation for entering on a file card. More testing along these lines would make the test a natural and enjoyable part of the learning, as was proposed in the earlier part of this chapter.[15] It would also provide a climax to a unit of study which the student could anticipate with pleasure as an opportunity to test himself against a criterion of authentic communication. This type of testing requires imagination and ingenuity on the part of the examiner, and our testing experts could perform a service for the profession in drafting and publishing a number of tests along these lines, with suggested adaptations to keep them varied. Security would not be a problem in these cases because each actualization of the test would take a different turn as the situation was followed through by the student being tested. The result of the test would be rated either successful or unsuccessful (either the student was able to carry the task through to a satisfactory conclusion or he was not), so that the "subjective" element in the judgment of the examiner would not be of any great significance. Clearly there would be variability in the amount and complexity of the communication which took place, but the student would have demonstrated his ability to give and receive information or to interact informally in an acceptable manner.

Carroll tells us that

> . . .from a practical point of view it may often suffice to construct tests that measure only integrated performance based on competence. For example, a general test of proficiency in a foreign language is often found to yield just as good validity when its items are complex, each drawing upon a wide sample of linguistic competences, as when each item has been contrived to tap competence in one and only one specific feature of the foreign language . . . apparently the extent to which a language test should attempt to measure specific aspects of competence depends upon its purpose—that is, the extent to which there is need for diagnosis of specific skills as opposed to a generalized, overall assessment of proficiency.[16]

If, as Pilliner says, the form of the test gives direction to learning, then it is essential that it be consonant with the aim of natural language use if it is to be valid in the contemporary context. Validity is a much-prized concept in testing, yet too many tests continue to be based on the aims of a decade or two decades ago, lagging behind materials and classroom instruction. Thus they retard the evolution of a progressive view of language teaching, instead of clarifying goals for the less informed.

With all global testing, the perennial problem arises: how much accuracy in detail should we expect or require if effective communication is to be the goal? The answer to this must realistically be relative: the businessman out for a contract cannot afford to misunderstand detail or to give assurances which can be misinterpreted. The scientist writing a research paper must state exactly what he intends to state if the equipment is not to blow up when the experiment is replicated. These people need a degree of accuracy not usually essential for the tourist or the captain's wife on a foreign base. Such students would, by their training, realize the need for accurate expression in professional matters and presumably be motivated to work toward it. The businessman, more than the scientific researcher, would understand the need for accuracy in intonational patterns and pitch levels so that he would not sound angry when he was intending to be persuasive. On the other hand, many an emissary in a foreign country has found that a certain degree of foreignness in his speech patterns, far from being a handicap, elicited a greater tolerance on the part of local people toward his early mistakes in adapting to the cultural patterns of their society. More research is needed in all languages into those elements for which an absolute degree of accuracy is required for communication which will not irritate the native speaker, and those which the native speaker will accept as amusing but pleasant indications that the stranger has really tried to learn his language and meet him on his own ground. What we must remember is that we can so easily kill, or at least considerably dampen, the enthusiasm of a foreign-language learner by preferring accuracy of detail to sincere efforts to create spontaneous utterances or write expressive prose. When it comes to micro-testing, we may also remember that the person capable of macro-performance may well be able to cope with the details of the micro-test, but that each person passing the micro-test is not necessarily able to perform acceptably at the macro-level. The fact that the micro-test is so much easier to administer is a danger to us as a profession. If we become addicted to fill-in-the-blank tests and multiple-choice items, we must not be surprised if our students think that this is what performance in a foreign language really is. Let us remember that by our testing they shall know us, far better than we shall know them.

## FOOTNOTES

[1] A. E. Pilliner, "Subjective and Objective Testing" in Alan Davies, ed., *Language Testing Symposium. A Psychololinguistic Approach.* (Oxford University Press, 1968, p. 31).

[2] G. A. Miller, E. Galanter, and K. H. Pribram, *Plans and the Structure of Behavior* (Holt, Rinehart and Winston, 1960). The TOTE unit is described and discussed on pp. 25-38.

[3] Ibid., p. 29.

[4] Ibid., pp. 25-26.

[5] Ibid., p. 31.

[6] This subject is developed in relation to undergraduate level courses in Chapter 13, "The Non-Major: Tailoring the Course to Fit the Person—Not the Image."

[7] Wilga M. Rivers, "Techniques for Developing Proficiency in the Spoken Language in an Individualized Foreign Language Program," in H. B. Altman and R. L. Politzer, eds., *Individualizing Foreign Language Instruction* (Rowley, Mass.: Newbury House, 1971), p. 165.

[8] "Individualizing," in Virgil M. Howes, ed., *Individualization of Instruction. A Teaching Strategy* (New York: Macmillan, 1970), pp. 91-92.

[9] Reported in Chapter 13 of this book.

[10] E. D. Allen and R. M. Valette, *Modern Language Classroom Techniques* (New York: Harcourt Brace Jovanovich, 1972), pp. 21, 37.

[11] I have discussed how we may move in this direction from the earliest stages in "Talking Off the Tops of Their Heads," Chapter 2, and "From Linguistic Competence to Communicative Competence," Chapter 3. See also note 11 to Chapter 3.

[12] In R. M. Valette and R. S. Disick, *Modern Language Performance Objectives and Individualization* (New York: Harcourt Brace Jovanovich, 1972), the distinction is made between "formal performance objectives" and "expressive performance objectives," the latter being "open-ended" with the conditions "less precise" (p. 26), "the actual form such student behavior will assume (being) not as readily predictable" (p. 54).

[13] See Wilga M. Rivers, *The Psychologist and the Foreign-Language Teacher* (Chicago: University of Chicago Press, 1964), Chapter 6: "Two Levels of Language."

[14] R. M. Valette, *Directions in Foreign Language Testing* (New York: MLA/ERIC, 1969), p. 31.

[15]Many of the activities described in "Talking Off the Tops of Their Heads," Chapter 2, could be used as tests of this type.

[16]J. B. Carroll, "The Psychology of Language Testing" in Alan Davies, ed., *Language Testing Symposium* (Oxford University Press, 1968), pp. 56-58. See also J. B. Carroll, "Foreign Language Testing: Will the Persistent Problems Persist?" in M. C. O'Brien, ed., *Testing in Second Language Teaching: New Dimensions* (Dublin: ATESOL and University of Dublin Press, 1973), pp. 6-17.

# 5

# CONTRASTIVE LINGUISTICS
# IN TEXTBOOK AND CLASSROOM*

*Abstract*. The need for a contrastive approach in foreign-language teaching has long been recognized, but in the construction of textbook materials and in classroom practice it has rarely been realized. For pedagogical purposes a useful distinction can be drawn between difference and contrast. Differences can be taught as new items of knowledge, whereas native-language interference must be combatted in areas of contrast. Contrasts should be taught emically not etically, that is, the structural element or the cultural manifestation should be studied as it functions in the foreign language system, not merely at the points where it contrasts with native-language usage. Degree of difficulty may be estimated by the number of elements in contrast, but this criterion does not necessarily apply in the classroom where learning is facilitated if structures can be practiced in an active situation by students who have been prepared for the contrastive nature of language study. Translation may appear to be an excellent exercise in language contrast; it is, however, valuable only at an advanced level of study when students have a wide enough knowledge of the functioning system of both languages to find close-meaning equivalents for stretches of discourse rather than small segments, and to explore the full range of contrast.

*This article reprinted from Monograph No. 21, James E. Alatis, ed., *Contrastive Linguistics and its Pedagogical Implications*, Report of the Nineteenth Round Table Meeting on Languages and Linguistics (Washington, D. C.:Georgetown University Press, 1968), pp. 151-158.

In the past, the empirical judgment of experienced teachers has usually determined the order of presentation and degree of emphasis in textbook materials. Where this judgment has been derived from some systematic observation of student errors it has provided an approximate identification of many areas of language contrast, as evidenced by native-language interference. Gradually the profession has accepted the idea expressed by Fries that 'the most efficient materials are those that are based upon a scientific description of the language to be learned, carefully compared with a parallel description of the native language of the learner'.[1] Yet for some of the languages most commonly taught in our schools and universities, textbooks continue to appear which make little use of the comparative studies which are available while only a small proportion of classroom teachers have the linguistic training to make use of this material without the help of the textbook constructor.

A contrastive analysis of two languages when it is designed with a scientific not a pedagogical intent is not in itself a teaching aid. It must be as exhaustive as its author can make it, in the light of his specific intention, describing with equal care structural contrasts of frequent and of less frequent use or analyzing a limited area in considerable detail. Since the linguist's aim must be to make the description scientifically elegant rather than pedagogically applicable, the analysis will not normally be directly transferable to teaching materials and situations. Chomsky has already emphasized the difference between a linguistic grammar which is an account of competence and a pedagogic grammar which attempts to provide the student with the ability to understand and produce sentences of a particular language.[2] The same distinction may be applied to types of contrastive studies. Fortunately some studies prepared with students' problems in mind are available in the Contrastive Structure Series (University of Chicago Press), although as yet only in a very limited number of pairs of languages.

As Stockwell, Bowen, and Martin have ably demonstrated[3] for pedagogical application a hierarchy of difficulty must be established among the many correspondences. A hierarchy of this type will differ from one established in accordance with purely theoretical premises because 'it is important to distinguish between what may be difficult to explain . . . and what is difficult for the student to internalize—the two may, or may not, be the same'.[4] Once such a hierarchy has been established it must be regarded as 'a set of predictions which must be tested against observation of the problems students do in fact have'.[5] In this article I shall not attempt to duplicate work which has already been done in this area, but shall try to establish certain guidelines for the application of the contrastive approach to classroom work, either by the teacher or textbook constructor.

In the minds of many teachers the notion of contrast is a vague one. It is useful first to distinguish between contrast and difference because each poses a specific pedagogical problem. One language may have a highly developed tone system while another does not. This tone system constitutes a difference of considerable importance, rather than a phonemic contrast. One language may combine elements of various functions in pre-, post-, and medial positions in one unit, whereas the other language may be analytic, arranging elements in linear fashion. In these cases the systems differ to such an extent that comparison of specific elements does not give sufficient information to be pedagogically helpful. For such aspects the new system will need to be taught as an integrated whole without reference to the details of an alien system. For a contrast to be distinguishable at any level, there must be some correspondence at a higher level of structure. Phonemes may contrast in lexical items which are similar in the two languages; there may be contrasting morphemic patterns within syntactic structures of similar applicability (e.g., Language A may require a variety of endings for persons of the verb, as opposed to a simple singular-plural distinction in Language B); within noun phrases there may be a contrasting word order (Language A requiring the order adjective + noun and Language B noun + adjective). If the correspondence is at the level of meaning only, there will be difference rather than contrast: the student will then learn the different way of expressing himself by memorization and practice in appropriate contexts, without reference to the formal characteristics of his native language, and ability to use the new form freely will be a matter of speed of recall. Where there is contrast, native-language interference will be a constant problem: the student's native-language habits will tempt him to follow the pattern of his own language at that point (e.g., using the foreign-language adjective and noun in his native-language pattern of noun + adjective), and intensive practice alone will not be sufficient to free him from this tendency when he is trying to express himself in communication. He will need to be alerted to the specific point at which interference will repeatedly occur, so that he may practice with awareness and concentration and monitor his own production with watchfulness until he finds himself producing the target language forms with ease and accuracy.

Structures will contrast to varying degrees—degree of difficulty for the student being determined theoretically by the number of elements in contrast. In actual language use, however, degree of difficulty will be much more a question of types of choices to be made. Stockwell, Bowen, and Martin[6] have analyzed the possible dilemmas of the student in passing from one language to another in terms of optional choices which the student may make freely in his own or the target language in shaping the meaning he wishes to express, obligatory choices which are the inevitable consequence of his options, and zero choices where the student's problems arise from difference rather than contrast (categories or rules existing in one language but not in the other). In a comprehensive contrastive study emphasis may well fall without distinction on details of the system where there will be greater or less native-language interference or alternatively positive transfer because of structural or functional/semantic correspondence between the native and target languages. When a number of these details operate within a sub-system of the language, where some elements contrast and some are similar in operation, there will be not only the danger of native-language interference at some points but also hesitation and confusion as to the limits of acceptable extrapolation from the native language. At this point, the student must be trained in both that which is similar and that which is contrasting within the sub-system. Many teachers fail at this point and concentrate on teaching only the details which contrast. As a result structures and sub-systems may be taught 'etically' rather than 'emically'. Pike states that 'descriptions or analyses from the etic standpoint are "alien" in view, with criteria external to the system. Emic descriptions provide an internal view, with criteria chosen from within the system. They represent to us the view of one familiar with the system and who knows how to function within it himself.'[7] As soon as a foreign-language structure is taught as though some elements within it function as in the native-language system and some function contrastively, it is not being viewed as a part of the total functioning system of the foreign language, and the student begins to learn the language piecemeal. A student taught in this fashion has great difficulty learning to move freely within the new language system.

The etic approach is frequently employed in teaching the phonological system of a foreign language. Teachers often concentrate on sounds with distinctive features which contrast most obviously with those of otherwise comparable sounds in the native language (i.e., the so-called 'difficult' sounds) while allowing students to produce with native-language articulation sounds with fewer contrasting features. The result is a disruption of the phonological system of the foreign language: sounds produced with incorrect articulatory positions deform neighboring sounds and a 'foreign accent' develops. In concentrating on the sounds which the students find hard to articulate, the teacher often trains them to produce these in such a distinctive and restricted way that the speaker sounds ridiculously pedantic or pretentious to a native speaker, who has learned to produce this sound with variations (within a band of tolerance) dependent on phonological environment or level of discourse. In an emic approach, the student will acquire the phonological system as a functioning whole, learning to discriminate and produce sounds which signal distinctions of meaning within the new language, without being constantly reminded of ways in which it is similar to or different from the phonological system of the native language.

The etic approach may also prevail in the teaching of the grammar of the foreign language. The teacher may concentrate the attention of the students on some feature which functions in a similar fashion in the foreign and native languages at certain points, without making clear the fact that this particular usage is only a restricted part of a wider function which diverges considerably in the two languages. The student may be taught, for instance, that the *futur* in French fulfills the same function as the future tense in English (in *le cortège passera devant l'Hôtel de Ville, passera* fulfills a similar function to *will pass* in *the procession will pass in front of the Town Hall*). This etic type of teaching separates out the forms . . . *era,* . . . *ira,* . . . *ra* from the expression of futurity in the French system of time, and fails to prepare the student for *le facteur va passer dans deux minutes* 'the mailman will be here in two minutes', *je viens dans deux minutes* 'I'll be there in two minutes', and *la direction n'est pas responsable des objets perdus* 'the management will not be responsible for lost property'. The student must learn that what may appear etically to be very different may function emically as one system. What appears to be similar in formation to a structure in the native language may also serve quite a different function in the foreign language, as will soon be clear to a student who, misled by the apparently parallel formation of *I have eaten* and *j'ai mangé,* tries to identify the English present perfect tense with the French *passé composé.*

A similar distinction applies in the teaching of cultural patterns: of values, attitudes, relationships, taboos, and the external manifestations of these. Since language is an integral part of culture, full communication is possible only when the speaker understands the reactions he is arousing in his listener, and the listener is able to identify the intentions of the speaker. In an etic approach, attention is concentrated in the classroom on aspects of external behavior and physically identifiable institutions which appear picturesque and even quaint because they are presented out of the context of interrelationships and functions in the cultural system. As with structural contrasts, that which appears similar may fulfill a contrasting function in the foreign culture while that which appears to contrast by external criteria may have a similar purpose when viewed from within the system. In an emic approach, the teaching of cultural understanding is fully integrated with the process of assimilation of language patterns and lexicon. Through language use, students become conscious of levels of discourse in relation to social expectations, formulas of politeness and what they reveal of social attitudes, and appropriateness of response in specific situations in the foreign culture; through listening and reading they begin to recognize the values which are implicit in much of the foreign behavior. Consequently, instead of being unduly impressed by what is different in the external manifestations of the culture, they come to comprehend contrasts between systems and sub-systems.

From the pedagogical point of view, degree of difficulty must be estimated according to a different set of criteria from those used in a theoretical analysis. A structure which theoretically may be considered more difficult for the student to learn may prove to be less difficult in actual fact because it can be readily transposed into active situations in which the student can practice it frequently. The subjunctive in *il faut que je parte* has usually been relegated by textbook writers to an advanced level in the study of French, yet many students have learned it with ease in the first weeks of study because they have found it useful in communication. Many other structural patterns of wide applicability may be learned similarly at a very early stage despite a high degree of contrast with native-language usage. Stockwell, Bowen, and Martin suggest a criterion of 'functional load' for consideration in establishing a pedagogical sequence of presentation, giving a certain priority to 'patterns which carry a proportionately larger share of the burden of communication'.[8]

From the first lessons students should be prepared by their teacher for the contrastive nature of language formation and function. With this orientation well established, they will be able to absorb many contrasting features of the new language inductively, by a direct method approach, without feeling the need to pause to analyze and describe the differences. A student with such an orientation will more rapidly develop a coordinate language system than a student who is continually seeking to identify in the foreign language equivalents for features in his native language. Mere induction will not suffice, however; to consolidate the use of such contrasting forms, the student will also need systematic drill to develop facility in rapid association of language sequences.

It may appear that the contrastive technique *par excellence* in foreign-language teaching is the translation exercise. Here the student is confronted with native-language forms and structure and required to produce the contrasting forms and structure of the foreign language. It is true that translation in which the exact meaning is transferred from one language to another demands, much more than does speech or original writing, a thorough knowledge of areas of contrast in form and function. It is for this very reason, however, that it is unsuitable as a technique for teaching the details of the language, while being a very profitable and challenging exercise of the student's control of the foreign language at an advanced level. Translation is feasible for the student only when he has a wide enough knowledge of the functioning system of both languages to find close-meaning equivalents for stretches of connected discourse, often longer than one sentence. At the lower levels of instruction students are forced to divide the text into small segments for which they think they can find equivalent segments in the foreign language. Because of the limitations of their knowledge this very segmentation may be an initial source of error as they fail to see the full extent of the contrast in structure.

In the early stages of learning a foreign language, translation of short patterns and simple forms may be a quick way to check whether students have ascribed the appropriate meaning to what they are learning, and whether they have assimilated forms and patterns they have been practicing. In this case the segmentation for purposes of contrast has already been performed for them by the teacher. At an advanced level when students are being taught to translate as a linguistic skill, they should be required to analyze both the source text and their tentative translation for real equivalence. seeking the full extent of the contrasts involved in relation to the context beyond the phrase and the sentence. For such an exercise to provide effective practice in the handling of structural contrast, students should be encouraged to seek a number of alternative solutions in order to explore the full range of contrast, the set of paraphrases they propose in the target language being, to various degrees, meaning-equivalents of the source language sentence or sentences. They should then discuss with each other and with their teacher the contribution of each proposed solution to the elucidation of the basic meaning. They should also be trained to see that effective translation will often involve considerable rearrangement of segments if the full structural possibilities of the foreign language are to be utilized, so that contrasts in forms of discourse will be involved as well as contrasts in structural patterns. When translation is taught at this level of refinement it provides the student with the opportunity to use to the full the knowledge he has accumulated over years of study, and to find by trial and error the acceptable limits of similarity and contrast.

## FOOTNOTES

[1]C. C. Fries, *Teaching and Learning English as a Foreign Language* (Ann Arbor: University of Michigan Press, 1945), p. 9.

[2]Noam Chomsky, *Topics in the Theory of Generative Grammar* (The Hague: Mouton, 1966), p. 10.

[3]Robert P. Stockwell, J. Donald Bowen, and John W. Martin, *The Grammatical Structures of English and Spanish*, Contrastive Structure Series (Chicago: University of Chicago Press, 1965); Robert P. Stockwell and J. Donald Bowen, *The Sounds of English and Spanish*, Contrastive Structure Series (Chicago: University of Chicago Press, 1965).

[4]Stockwell, Bowen, and Martin, p. 282.

[5]Ibid.

[6]Ibid., Chapter 11; Stockwell and Bowen, Chapter 2.

[7]K. L. Pike, *Language in Relation to a Unified Theory of the Structure of Human Behavior*, 2nd rev. ed (The Hague: Mouton, 1967), p. 388.

[8]Stockwell, Bowen, and Martin, p. 292.

# FROM SKILL ACQUISITION
## TO LANGUAGE CONTROL*

Some years ago, in an attempt to be helpful, I undertook to give some lessons in English to a young Italian immigrant to Australia who happened to have wandered into my church and who was making rather futile efforts to make himself understood with the few words he had acquired haphazardly. Very soon, however, he stopped coming for lessons since it was obvious to him that I did not know how to teach a language. I was trying to make him say things like "I went to work yesterday; I'll go to work tomorrow." This, he was sure, was not the way to learn English. What he wanted to know, and as quickly as possible, was the names of all the things he could see around him.

My young immigrant's attitude reflects a very common misconception about language use: that it is essentially a naming process, that the first step in language acquisition must be the learning of labels for all the features of the environment so as to be able to talk about them to others. Many parents have this idea of language and spend time trying to teach their infants the names of all kinds of objects. Recent studies of child language acquisition, however, show that from their earliest efforts at speech children use words not as mere labels but with the operant force of more fully developed utterances.[1]

---

*Originally published in the *TESOL Quarterly* 3 (1969), 3-12.

When a child says "milk," he can mean a number of things. He may be naming a certain familiar liquid; since this desired reaction is rewarded by the obvious pleasure of his parents, he tends to repeat this label to retain their attention. He may repeat the word over and over, engaging merely in word play, enjoying the repetition of sounds and the approving attention he receives as he continues. On the other hand, he may say "milk?" with a look of puzzlement, meaning "Where is my milk? Isn't it time I was fed?" and if he is further ignored he may utter a peremptory "milk!" as a command to his mother to attend to his needs. "Milk. . . ." in a tone of anxiety may mean "Look! I've knocked over my milk. What will happen now?" or it may be a solemn inquiry: "What about my dolly? Isn't she to get a drink too?"

For the child, then, a single word may have all the force of a sentence and carry a number of different meanings, going far beyond its apparent lexical content. Very soon the child expands his utterances to two words, and we see the development of an elementary syntax as he begins to use what Braine has called "pivot" and "open class" words:[2] pivot words forming a small class with few members, frequently repeated, which operate on the larger number of open class words that gradually accumulate as the child's experience broadens. A simple operant like "all gone" ("allgone egg," "allgone milk," "allgone 'nanas") enables the child to extend a basic notion to a number of specific situations. From this stage on, the child's language evolves through a series of syntaxes, identifiable and analyzable at any particular stage of his development; the restricted syntaxes of his early efforts gradually approximate more and more closely to the speech system of those around him until he is finally able to control all its essential syntactic operations. At this stage there is no limit to the number and variety of messages he can convey to fellow speakers of his language. From his earliest attempts at communication, the child needs a grammar; mere labeling will not suffice.

In our second-language classrooms, in recent years we have gone beyond isolated words, mere "vocabulary teaching": we have realized that what the student must learn is to use syntactic patterns. He can acquire new labels later as he requires them, so we teach him a basic vocabulary which he can use over and over again as he practices syntactic operations. We have observed that in the linear sequence of language there are certain strictly formal relationships, within the clearly defined limits of closed sets (e.g., verb systems such as *I'm going, he's going, they're going*). These, we have found, can be learned by steady practice so that no student will be tempted to say* *I's going* or *they's going*. We have found, similarly, that by consistent practice we can teach the restricted word order our language normally requires to convey certain meanings: *I saw him*, not *I him saw* or *Him saw I*. So we have talked of second-language learning as the learning of a skill, the acquiring of a set of habits which must be learned to a point of automatic performance of the sequence. When we are speaking, we do not have time to stop to think about word order, morphological inflections, or invariant syntactical combinations. We need to be so familiar with these details that they fall into place as we speak without distracting our attention from the combinations of meanings we are seeking to express.

This skill-learning approach developed from the common observation that in many classrooms, despite earnest teaching and many exercises on the part of the students, such essential language habits were not being firmly established. Teachers turning to psychological learning theory to see what could be gleaned from it about the effective building in of habits found inspiration in habit formation by reinforcement, or operant conditioning, theory. This approach to learning is drawn from the extensive experimentation of B. F. Skinner and the many experimentalists who have accepted his basic concepts. It has been applied widely in the teaching of many school subjects and is basic to the programming movement.[3]

As applied to teaching techniques and the writing of materials for second-language teaching, Skinner's principles have been interpreted in the following ways.[4] According to Skinner, a response must occur before it can be rewarded, and thus be reinforced. He does not interest himself in what causes the response to occur in the first place. This approach has its obvious application in second-language teaching: naive students cannot invent second-language responses, but these can be elicited by a process of imitation. Imitation is clearly an essential first step in establishing a repertoire of responses in the new language and so we have developed the familiar techniques of mimicking and memorization in elementary second-language classes, as in the memorization of dialogue material repeated after the teacher or tape model. At this stage skill in variation is not sought, but only accurate reproduction.

In conditioning theory, immediate reinforcement or reward increases the probability of a response recurring: the teacher in the second-language classroom supplies this reinforcement by his confirmation of correct responses, as in a pattern drill sequence where the student hears the correct response modeled for him at each step by the teacher or the tape model. With repeated reinforcement, according to the theory, responses become established as habits which are maintained in strength by further reinforcement at intervals as the student uses them to express his meaning in communication. By judicious giving and witholding of reinforcement, responses can be shaped to approximate more and more closely to a desired model. Second-language teachers are familiar with this process which they have long employed for developing finer and finer discriminations in recognition and production of sounds.

Reinforcement after a few occurrences of a response will not, however, ensure that the response will be retained by the student as a permanent feature of his behavior. Unless there is further reinforcement on subsequent appearances, the response-habit will suffer extinction, albeit with some periods of spontaneous recovery before it disappears. For this reason it is essential to reintroduce language material at regular intervals so that the student has the reinforcing, and therefore consolidating, experience of using it correctly on a number of occasions, particularly at the stage when many features of the language are being encountered as novelties in rapid succession. At advanced stages when a great number of features have been integrated into a response framework, the student is forced to draw continually on his previous learning; and his habitual responses, both acceptable and unacceptable, are thus maintained. It is important to remember that incorrect responses will also be reinforced as habitual responses, if the student is not aware of these errors and is satisfied with, and even proud of, his production.

As a repertoire of responses is acquired, Skinner maintains that further responses develop by a process of generalization in which features of novel situations are identified as similar to those already experienced, and established responses find new areas of application. This psychological process is paralleled in second-language learning by the process of analogy as students are encouraged to extend the range of their responses by applying in nearly similar situations the operations they have learned. Analogy is basic to the series of responses in a substitution drill and in other types of exercises which require variation within a limited framework.

A rather naive faith in generalization is perhaps the weakest feature of Skinnerian conditioning as applied to second-language learning. Effective generalization (or production of new utterances by analogy) requires the recognition at an abstract level of a relationship between a new situation and one already familiar, and the combining of new elements in a way which is consistent with this abstract categorization. In a second language where the student's competence (or internalized knowledge of the rules of the language) is partial, this recognition of similarity is guided in really novel situations by his knowledge of parallel structures in his native language. In English we say "I brought it from New York" and "I hid it from John": misled by surface similarities in the native language, the student of French will generalize from "je l'ai rapporté *de* New-York" to "je l'ai caché *de* Jean," instead of the grammatical "je l'ai caché *à* Jean." Valid analogy from one language to another (such as is being investigated in modern studies of language universals) applies at an abstract level of analysis before transformations have produced the distinctive surface features of a particular language.

Even analogizing from one situation in a second language to another in the same language can be misleading. With conditioning techniques the student will have been drilled in transforming utterances either lexically or syntactically to a point of automatic response. Here again he is guided by surface features. In many cases the analogy may be valid; in others the surface features will hide real divergences in usage and the student will fall into error because his knowledge of the language is insufficient for him to recognize the limits within which he may safely analogize.

Despite these limitations, experience has shown that this type of skill practice, systematically developed, does enable students to produce acceptable syntactic patterns on demand in the carefully circumscribed situation of the classroom or laboratory. Properly instructed, the student who is working with the pattern "he's coming" will, on hearing the cue "we," produce the response "we're coming," and continue to produce correct responses even in more complicated sequences. We seem now to have developed techniques for the skill acquisition part of language learning, at least at a formal level. This does not, however, mean that our students on leaving the classroom can participate freely in conversation in the language, producing these acceptable patterns at will. Teachers may well ask: "Where have we been failing? Why are so many of our students after thorough drilling and apparent conditioning still unable to use the language for their own purposes, when spontaneous situations demand more than learned associations?"

Satisfaction with the learning of responses to cues, and even of rapid substitutions, presupposes that language use is the production of language elements in a linear sequence, one item generating the next in succession according to the habit strength of the association. On hearing "Where are you . . .?" most people will complete the utterance with "going." Recent studies of word associations[5] cast considerable doubt on the validity of this approach to the essential processes of language production. Given a cue like "cow," most subjects will produce the response "calf" or "milk," yet sheer strength of linear associations would surely require "cow is . . . ." "Cow, calf" or "cow, milk" rarely appear in succession: word associations are frequently paradigmatic (producing words from the same grammatical class) rather than syntagmatic (or linear) and are drawn from fields of associative structures.[6] To the cue "good," most people will respond "bad" rather than "boy" which would be a common linear or syntagmatic association. (It may be noted that children tend to produce syntagmatic associations more readily than adults. With adults, adverbs produce syntagmatic associations more frequently than other word classes, but even here paradigmatic associations occur.[7])

Perhaps, then, we cite things found together or words frequently occuring in the same utterances. To the stimulus "sword," many will respond with "letter-opener": articles which are conceptually similar but rarely found together or mentioned in close association in speech. Subjects who respond to the cue "fields" with the word "green" are producing neither a paradigmatic nor a syntagmatic association, "green fields" being the association built in by language habits in English. There is clearly an organization among associations which has little to do with linear sequence. Frequency of linear association as the major emphasis in language learning inhibits rather than facilitates real communication. The child learning his native language hears many items in close association, but he does not reproduce these in an automatic fashion. He selects from among them and then uses these selected elements for his own purposes. The child who says "Allgone milk" did not hear the expression in that form. His mother probably said "The milk is all gone" or even "Milk all gone." The child has, at this stage, formed a concept for which he finds the expression "all gone" useful; he then uses "all gone" for his own purposes in a variety of contexts despite his mother's continued repetition of "milk all gone."

In second-language learning, even in a simple structure drill, it is concept formation we should be seeking to bring about, not merely rote learning of items in a sequence. As Miller, Galanter, and Pribram have expressed it: "To memorize the infinite number of grammatical sentences is to by-pass the problem of grammar completely."[8] "The fundamental puzzle . . . is our combinatorial productivity."[9] Even the attempt to memorize a useful selection of sentences for everyday use ignores the real problem that few sentences apart from certain fixed formulas and clichés can be used in an actual situation exactly as learned in the classroom. Just as in perception an association cannot be made with previous percepts before there is recognition of the pattern,[10] so in speech learned associations (sentences, patterns) cannot be useful until the speaker recognizes his requirements for communication as being of a type for which this learned association is appropriate.

Chomsky has attacked the view that language is a "habit structure." He says, "Ordinary linguistic behavior characteristically involves innovation, formation of new sentences and new patterns in accordance with rules of great abstractness and intricacy."[11] He speaks continually of "the creative aspect of normal language use"[12]—the fact that new utterances are similar to those previously heard or produced "only in that they are determined, in their form and interpretation, by the same system of abstract underlying rules."[13] This phrase "creative aspect of normal language use" has led some teachers to think that what is needed is not structural drill but opportunities for the student to "create" new utterances in a free and spontaneous situation, as was formerly the practice in Direct Method classes where students used only the second language from the beginning and tried to communicate in it at all costs. This, as we know, can result in a glib inaccuracy (Frenglish or Spenglish or whatever you will). This carefree indifference to the syntactic demands of the language is certainly not what Chomsky is referring to. According to Chomsky, the speaker-listener must internalize a system of rules that can generate an infinite number of grammatical sentences, and the innovation and creation of which he speaks refer to the production of novel combinations which result from the application of the rules. In this sense our students can only "create" novel utterances when they have internalized the rules, the system of rules then "generating" (in the mathematical sense of this word) new combinations as they require them.

The current vogue for talking about "rules" frightens some teachers. From past experience they know that overt learning of abstract grammatical rules has not been conspicuously successful in producing students capable of using a second language creatively, that is, skilled in speaking (listening, reading, writing) without having to hesitate to consider what is structurally permissible. Chomsky himself uses the term "internalize" for the assimilation of language rules because, as he states quite clearly, the speaker-listener is not generally aware of these rules, "nor in fact is there any reason to suppose that the rules can be brought to consciousness."[14] Here, he is referring to the native speaker, but a second-language learner must also reach the point where he is responding to a rule-system without being aware at each moment of the rules to which his utterances are conforming. It is as well to remind ourselves at this point that Chomsky is not referring to the common "grammar rules" of traditional textbooks, but to rules of "great abstractness and intricacy," the effect of which we observe while being unable to formulate them at the conscious level. The deep structure and the transformational rules of which we read in the literature of generative grammar provide a theoretical model which does not claim to represent the psychological processes of language production.

Miller, Galanter, and Pribram have proposed a model of language production by which we select a higher-level Plan (or strategy) which sets in operation lower-level plans (or tactics, i.e., completely detailed specifications of every operation). [15] In an act of communication, the speaker has a certain freedom of selection initially (for the meaning he wishes to express he selects a certain sentence-type, a time sequence, and certain relationships and modifications within the sentence), but once this initial selection has been made there are choices he is obliged to make at lower levels of structure because of the rule system of the particular language he is using (obligatory inflections, word order, function words, substitutes) all of which devolve directly from his original selection. [16] It is at the level of strategy, or meaning to be expressed, that the speaker exercises choice, that the novel or creative element enters in, this choice necessitating further choices of a more limited character (the tactics) which oblige the student to use certain elements in fixed relationships. Creative, innovative language use still takes place within a restricted framework: a finite set of formal arrangements to which the speaker's utterances must conform if he is to be comprehended and thus to communicate effectively.

We cannot, then, underestimate the importance of practice in the manipulation of language elements which occur in fixed relationships in clearly defined closed sets (systems in which there are a few variable elements but to which new members are not added: e.g., the set "this, that, these, those"). The student must be able to make the necessary adjustments to pass from "I'*m* going" to "he'*s* staying home." At this level the second-language speaker has no freedom of choice. On the other hand, he may wish to say "I'*d* rather go, but he'*ll* stay" in which case he is operating at the higher level of selection, but once having selected his time sequence and his personal references he has no further freedom at the low level of surface manifestations of tense and person. Unless the student is well trained at this surface level of operation he will not be able to communicate freely the many novel messages he has in mind.

It is at the manipulative level that pattern drills (substitutions and transformations) are valuable. Very early in this century, Thorndike had already shown that direct practice leads to transfer of learning where identical elements are involved: you practice A and B, and you are able to use A and B. Chomsky maintains that in normal language, use of "repetition of fixed phrases is a rarity."[17] This is a very misleading statement because the word "phrase" is undefined. At the level of the sentence, or even for substantial segments of sentences, this is undoubtedly a faithful observation of language performance. If the "phrase" is further subdivided, however, into coherent word groups such as *I'm going, before he comes, if I don't see him,* or *to school* as opposed to *to the station* it becomes clear that numbers of segments reappear again and again in identical form, and it is segments like these—the building blocks of the utterance—that are practiced in drills.

On the other hand, Katona discovered that for problem solving an understanding of structural principles led to greater facility in solving new problems and also to longer retention. "We do not learn the examples," he said, "we learn *by* examples. The material of learning is not necessarily the object of learning: it may serve as a clue to a general principle or an integrated knowledge." [18] This is the Gestalt concept of transposition: ". . . the elements are changed, but the whole-qualities, the essence, the principle are preserved in recollection. . . . and we may apply them under changed circumstances."[19] It is at the level of selection, of conscious choice, that the second-language speaker must have a clear conception of the possibilities of variation within the structural system, of the principles which determine the sentence framework and the relationships of the parts within it, so that he is able to set in motion the various elements which will combine in the ways he has learned so thoroughly in order to convey the exact meaning he has in mind. It is this aspect of second-language learning which has been largely neglected in recent years.

The student will acquire this realization of the possibilities of application and combination of what he is learning, not by listening to lengthy abstract explanations (tempting as this activity may be for the teacher), but by using the structural patterns he is learning, in combination with what he has learned, for some purpose of his own. It is not sufficient for him to use a pattern to complete an exercise or to answer as the teacher requires; he must practice selection, from the earliest stages of instruction, in an attempt to combine what he knows and what he is learning in the expression of a message he has personally chosen. (It is in this activity that, under the teacher's guidance, he learns the extent of permissible extrapolation or analogy.) No matter how simple the pattern, it is important in the communication system for its possibilities of occurrence and combination, and it takes its place in the second-language system the student is building up as soon as it becomes a medium of communication, rather than a simple manipulative operation.

All this may seem to be far away from the practical demands of the teaching situation. How, the teacher may ask, can I apply this in the classroom? The following suggestions will, I hope, lead my readers to work out their own applications in conformity with the theoretical position I have been discussing.

Dialogue learning is a common classroom activity for which useful techniques have long been outlined. Nevertheless in using dialogue material many teachers never pass beyond the stage of manipulation: the dialogue is thoroughly memorized; groups, rows, individuals make the appropriate exchanges. The teacher now passes to the next part of the unit. In this type of lesson the essential ingredient of role-identification is missing. As soon as the child acts out the dialogue, as soon as he *is* John or Peter, he is communicating, not merely repeating. Even the inhibited child will speak out if he is being someone else. This acting out of dialogues by various children is not a waste of time. Children will repeat the same material over and over purposefully, and listen attentively to others repeating it if different groups are reliving the roles. When children act out a recombination of the dialogue (one learned from the textbook or one they have themselves created using the well-known segments), they explore further possibilities of combination and application of each pattern to express a variety of meanings. In this way they are preparing for the act of selection when later they wish to express similar meanings. Acting out a dialogue makes even memorization a meaningful activity instead of an artificial classroom technique: even great actors must memorize their roles, and memorization is thus accepted as a normal activity of real life.

Pattern drilling, as teachers well know, may become a parrot-like activity. Even with variations, the student familiar with the technique soon learns to make the necessary adjustments without having to concentrate his attention to the point of personal involvement. When, however, the student asks a question or gives an answer related to someone or something which concerns him personally, even an item in a drill becomes a form of communication. Intensive practice need not, and should not, be divorced from real situations. The lexical content of the drills should be applicable to things the student experiences in and out of the classroom, so that the items are useful even apart from the practice; they should provide meanings with which the student can identify. An alert teacher can easily develop a practice sequence which could feasibly apply to the situation of some or all of the students, with an element of humor or surprise to keep the students' interest. Visual cues for drills not only keep the student alert but force him to think for himself, instead of merely adapting what the teacher is voicing for him. In a carefully structured lesson, the students can be stimulated to provide the elements of the drills themselves: they can be provoked into making a series of statements or questions of the pattern desired through what are apparently only comments on the teacher's appearance or activities, or on their own or other students' intentions or interests. Many a pattern drill can be converted into a repetitive but exciting game which demands concentration. In all of these ways, participation in the drill can be innovative: providing for practice in the repetition and variation of language segments, but with simultaneous practice in selection, as the student expresses his own meaning and not that of the textbook writer. A tape-recording of such a lesson may not sound very different from one made during a stereotyped pattern drill session, the responses of the students following a familiar sequence. The difference, however, is not physical, but psychological: the active participation of the students is personal. Practice in selection should not be considered a separate activity for advanced classes: it can and should be included in class work from the very first lessons.

To sum up then, the student cannot perform effectively at the higher level of selection (putting into operation higher-level choices) unless facility has been developed in the effortless production of interdependent lower-level elements. So learning by intensive practice and analogy variation, under the teacher's guidance, will be features of the early stages of learning a second language, but with immediate practice in selection (within the limits of the known). The student will be continually placing new elements in the context of the functioning system as he understands it at that stage, by interrelating the new with the old. For this he will need to understand what he has been trying to do in his practice exercises. He will be kept continually aware of the relationship of what he is learning to what he knows, so that he can fully realize the systematic function of each new element he has practiced through his endeavors to use it in wider contexts for the expression of his own meaning.

To develop skill in communication in the foreign language the student must have continual practice in communicating, not merely in performing well in exercises, no matter how carefully these may have been designed. The teacher's reward comes on the day when he hears his students using the second language without prompting and without embarrassment for communicating their own concerns. This is language control. When the student has acquired confidence at this level, he will be able to progress on his own, experiencing freedom of expression beyond the confines of learned patterns.

## FOOTNOTES

[1]D. McNeill, "Developmental Psycholinguistics," *Genesis of Language*, eds. F. Smith and G. A. Miller (Cambridge, Mass.: MIT Press, 1966).

[2]M. Braine, "The Ontogeny of English Phrase Structure: the First Phase," *Language*, 39 (1963): 1-13.

[3]See B. F. Skinner, *The Technology of Teaching* (New York: Appleton-Century-Crofts, 1968).

[4]The appropriateness of Skinnerian conditioning in second-language teaching has been discussed fully in Wilga M. Rivers, *The Psychologist and the Foreign-Language Teacher* (Chicago: University of Chicago Press, 1964).

[5]See J. Deese, *The Structure of Associations in Language and Thought* (Baltimore: Johns Hopkins Press, 1965).

[6]"Cow's milk" does appear, but is a different sequence.

[7]Deese, p. 106, gives a table of frequencies of occurrence. For observations of children's associations, see S. Ervin, "Changes with Age in the Verbal Determinants of Word Association," *American Journal of Psychology*, 74 (1961): 361-72.

[8]G. A. Miller, E. Galanter, and K. Pribram, *Plans and the Structure of Behavior* (New York: Holt, 1960), p. 147.

[9]G. A. Miller, *Psychology and Communication* (New York: Basic Books, 1967), p. 79.

[10]The "Hoffding function." See U. Neisser, *Cognitive Psychology* (New York: Appleton-Century-Crofts, 1967), p. 50.

[11]"Linguistic Theory," *Language Teaching: Broader Contexts,* ed. R. Mead, Jr., Report of Northeast Conference on the Teaching of Foreign Languages (New York: MLA Materials Center, 1966), p. 44.

[12]See also *Topics in the Theory of Generative Grammar* (The Hague: Mouton, 1966), p. 11.

[13]"Linguistic Theory," p. 44.

[14]*Topics*, p. 10.

[15]Miller, Galanter, and Pribram, pp. 16, 139-58.

[16]This approach to language production is discussed at length in Wilga M. Rivers, *Teaching Foreign-Language Skills* (Chicago: University of Chicago Press, 1968), pp. 71-80.

[17]"Linguistic Theory," p. 46.

[18]G. Katona, *Organizing and Memorizing* (New York: Columbia University Press, 1940), p. 125.

[19]Katona, p. 136.

# 7

# MOTIVATING
## THROUGH CLASSROOM TECHNIQUES*

How often we hear teachers complaining about their students:

"What can I do? They just *lack motivation*." This, of course, is an impossible statement. Every living organism to survive must have some motivation. Frymier has defined motivation as "*that which* gives direction and intensity to behavior."[1] This type of definition emphasizes the fact that little is known about motivation which, in psychological terms, is a construct inferred from the way an organism behaves. (By the direction and intensity of the behavior we infer something about the inner state of the organism, and in order to be able to discuss and investigate this "something" we call it motivation.)

The complaint: "*They just have no motivation to learn to speak English*" may be a more accurate description of the behavior of some students in school, but even this statement usually reflects a lack of realization on the part of the speaker of the complex and individual nature of motivation. Certain experiments have been performed where teachers had the opportunity to instruct by way of an intercom system

*A paper read at the TESOL Conference in New Orleans, 1971.

fictitious students and then saw their supposed work. These experiments have shown that the teacher's conviction about the degree of intensity of a student's motivation may reflect the picture the teacher has created for himself of this particular student rather than the student's actual psychological state.[2] The students to whom our teacher is referring in the complaint just voiced may not lack motivation to learn to speak English but may have found what seems to the teacher to be substandard, or even incorrect, English quite sufficient for their communicative purposes in the community in which they live. This may also be the only variety of English they hear from those with whom they wish to identify: parents or neighborhood associates. All indispensable communication, as far as they are concerned, may take place in Spanish or Turkish or Navajo. The real problem for the teacher may be: *"My students have no motivation to learn what I teach in my English class."*

So the question, *"How can I motivate my students?"* is not well formulated, nor is the question: *"How can I motivate my students to learn?"* Our students may not appear to be learning what we are earnestly trying to teach them, but every organism, nevertheless, is continually learning. As John Holt tries to show in *How Children Fail*, our students may be learning in our classrooms to protect themselves from embarrassment, from humiliation, and from other emotional concomitants of failure; they may be learning to give us "the right answer and the right chatter."[3] According to Postman and Weingartner "a classroom is an environment and . . . the way it is organized carries the burden of what people will learn from it":[4] consequently, some of our students may be learning from our classrooms that the use of English is a rather meaningless, mechanical activity, or even that it is a vehicle for a teacher's monologues. In either case it would seem to them clearly unrelated to their own concerns or interests.

There are two main strands of psychological thought on the question of motivation:[5] the hedonistic strand which includes the various theories of reinforcement or reward, and the ego-involvement strand in which the individual's self-image and level of aspiration play the determining role.

The hedonistic approach goes back at least as far as Thorndike's Law of Effect. It is discernible in the explanations of many psychologists and notably in those which emphasize reinforcement or reward, and in the pleasure principle of Freud. According to this approach, the individual organism in its relations with the environment is continually seeking to safeguard a state of equilibrium or balance of tension which it finds pleasurable. Excess of motivation disrupts this balance and causes increase in tension which the organism actively seeks to reduce by purposeful goal-directed behavior. Just as excess of motivation is painful to the organism, so is frustration in its goal-seeking efforts which prevents the organism from regaining its state of equilibrium. In this view, motivation can be looked upon as a continual process of individual adjustment to the environment. The individual actively seeks experiences which are pleasurable and avoids those which are painful. This parsimonious view of motivation would seem to provide a straightforward guideline for the classroom teacher. Unfortunately, because of the complexity of the inner state of each organism what is pleasurable for one is not necessarily pleasurable for another, and the teacher must keep these individual differences in mind.

Basically this view would indicate that the teacher should capitalize on the learner's motivated state by keeping the work within the capacity of each student so that he experiences success which is tension-reducing and rewarding. This is the basis of the programmed learning approach. In a well-designed programmed text attainable goals, clearly discernible in carefully elaborated steps, act as incentives and, as each is completed, the student is given immediate confirmation of the correctness or incorrectness of his response. This continual feedback provides reinforcement of what has been learned so that each student is motivated to continue to reproduce responses which have been rewarded and to put forth effort in the hope of experiencing further reinforcing success. Ideally such a stage can be reached by each student only in a completely individualized program where each person proceeds at his own pace. Unfortunately, completely individualized work as presently developed in programmed texts or computer-assisted instruction appears to conflict with the concept of language as primarily a vehicle of communication in which at least two persons by their interaction influence and modify each other's production. We must wait for further technological development of audio components and more imaginative programming before this disability can be overcome. In any case sophisticated materials of this type are still beyond the financial capacities of most schools. In the average classroom the teacher does the best he can in distributing reinforcement within the class group, or within smaller groups for particular activities, hoping in this way to shape behavior progressively in the direction he desires. The result is a classroom largely teacher-dominated as the teacher seeks to manipulate the environment to provide the most favorable conditions for inducing correct language behavior on the part of as many of the students as possible.

The second distinctive view of motivation which is reflected in much modern writing on educational problems maintains that the individual is continually seeking that which enhances his self as he perceives it, that is, that he is striving to achieve what he perceives as his potential. The student is, then, motivated at first in a general, nonspecific way in any situation—in other words, he is ready to take from any situation what there is in it for him. This initial motivation energizes and directs the student's behavior, causing him to attend to and focus on what is new in his environment. This attention is facilitative of learning but must be caught and maintained. It is at this stage that the teacher uses interest-arousing techniques to involve the student. The student is more readily involved if the teacher builds on areas of concern to him at his particular stage of development, thus making the new learning meaningful and increasing its incentive value. Many psychologists believe that the human organism possesses certain autonomous impulses such as curiosity, the desire to know and to understand, the desire to play and explore, and the impulse to manipulate features of the environment. These provide raw material with which the teacher can work to interest the student in the learning process. Through success in language activities and through the satisfaction of recognized and recognizable achievement the student comes to take an interest in the subject for its own sake (that is, an intrinsic interest in learning to know and use English) and what is sometimes called a cognitive drive which is self-sustaining then develops.[5] The development of such an interest in learning English for its own sake is, of course, the final aim of the teacher of English and the best assurance that the student will continue to learn and to seek opportunities to use English after the classroom has ceased to provide his learning environment.

In this latter view, a student's reaction to a stimulus is not predictable from the external conditions as the teacher sees them, but is determined by the student's individual perception of reality. The student may perceive a particular situation as a threat and withdraw from it or react unpredictably to counteract it. This is likely to happen quite frequently in an authoritarian classroom and many English-teaching classrooms are authoritarian: the teacher knows English well, the student does not, and therefore the teacher is always right and always correcting the student. In such situations many a student is forced to adopt strategies to protect his self-image, even, in some cases, to the extent of preferring to be wrong in the first place because at least in this way he knows where he stands and the outcome is less painful. Another student may set himself unrealistic goals which he cannot possibly attain because certain failure which he can blame on someone else is less damaging for him than unexpected failure where he expected to succeed. The teacher who understands this personal character of motivation can help individual students to set themselves attainable goals, no matter what their degree of aptitude, thus building up their self-confidence and increasing their motivation.

Whichever approach to motivation we accept (and as classroom teachers we can learn something of value from each of them),[6] it is clear that motivation is a normal state of the individual. It is for the teacher to identify its individual character and channel it through his design of learning activities. Of itself, motivation is merely raw material.

In the scope of this paper I can consider only a few of the implications of the theoretical positions described, but in each case I shall show how classroom practice in a particular situation will be affected if what is known about motivation is kept in mind.

First of all, *the student is motivated to learn.* We begin, whether we realize it or not, with a motivated organism in front of us. But what, we must ask ourselves, is this student motivated to learn? Perhaps he is motivated to learn enough English to communicate his needs, but not to slog away at uninteresting exercises.

But aren't these exercises necessary? the teacher may ask. What does "learning English" consist of?

—learning to pronounce certain sounds in certain environments;

—learning to use certain lexical items in certain contexts;

—learning to manipulate certain patterns which we can then incorporate into more extensive patterns to express the fullness of our meaning;

—learning to recognize sound-symbol relationships;

—learning to extract meaning from sound or graphic sequences?

As listed, these activities may seem quite irrelevant to Maria or George.

So we narrow down our aims more and more, and we state our behavioral objectives very precisely: we want Maria and George

—to learn to distinguish /I/ from /i/ and to learn to pronounce /tʃ/;

—to learn to ask an information or a yes-no question;

—to learn six parts of the body.

Maria or George may still not be motivated to learn what the teacher has prepared. It is fine for the teacher to "state behavioral objectives" but Maria and George will still not learn unless they see these objectives as relevant to their personal goals. Maria may want to be able to buy some *potato chips* without being asked to repeat what she said over and over again. George may want to be able to ask the price of a comic book or to find out how a battery-powered fire engine works. Carmelita may want to be able to say "That's *my* ball."

How do we achieve our behavioral objectives and those of our students? For some teachers an exercise is an exercise is an exercise (or a drill is a drill is a drill). All exercises (or drills) can be personalized. Only if distinguishing /ʃ/ and /t / are seen as communication problems will Maria be interested, and pronunciation problems can be treated in a communication situation. So can parts of the body, but not in the old format where the teacher asks: "Do I have two heads? Do you have three feet?" This is not even a pretence at authentic communication. A game of *Simon Says* where children have to touch or move parts of the body in the rapid sequence of the competition is a communication situation. Listening to something to which one has to react by drawing something or doing something is communication. Reading something to find out information for one's own interest or in order to tell someone else something is communication. A student who says: "Where are you going tonight?" to another student and expects a reply is learning to communicate. If he says exactly the same words in a mechanical fashion as part of a drill or dialogue because the teacher says this is what he should do, he is learning to do an exercise: he is learning to give "the right answer and the right chatter." This psychological difference is crucial. Remember that the student learns from the classroom, from your structuring of the learning activities, whether English is for communication or not. He learns whether it is part of his reality or just some tedious, artificial chore which someone "up there" has ordained he must perform. Exercises, oral or written, should always be framed as communication exercises: with a credible sequence of ideas and with some relevance to the class group and the class situation (which are the child's reality during his school years). If you lack imagination, learn to involve that of your students. Remember that a student whose interests and concerns are considered respectable and worthwhile in the classroom develops an enhanced perception of himself which increases his motivation to involve himself in purposive behavior within the class group.

What about the child's impulses to play, to explore, to manipulate? These can certainly be harnessed to the language teacher's endeavor. Recently I saw a first grade class in an elementary school bilingual project practicing the full paradigm in Spanish of the verb "to go"—I go, you go, he goes, we all go. . . . A few minutes earlier they had all been lying on mats for their rest period. What an opportunity was being missed! Children of this age love to imitate and mimic. They love make-believe and they identify rapidly with roles which they act out with great enthusiasm. They love movement and they can hardly curb their desire to express themselves vocally. They love stories with much repetition and they insist on each story being repeated exactly as before. Repetitive rhymes and songs are their delight. Instead of look-and-listen activities, or even listen-and-repeat activities, they become absorbed in *listen-do-repeat activities* where they concentrate on the active meaning of what they are saying. And they practice spontaneously at home, showing Mommy and Daddy how it is done, and proudly singing their new song to aunts and uncles. What an opportunity was being missed in that classroom by an elementary school teacher who, suddenly asked to teach Spanish, could think only of how she was taught long ago, instead of exploiting her knowledge of the characteristics and interests of the young child. (In this class too, may I add, many of the children spoke Spanish as a mother tongue.)

It is not only very young children who learn through movement. Many students from lower socio-economic levels where the home environment is not verbal and abstract respond to concrete material for which they see an immediate application. They enjoy learning words and phrases which they can employ immediately in the context of the class or with other children—in the neighborhood or in the school ground. They also learn through activity: through seeing, hearing, touching, manipulating, and through role-playing. The teacher should use visual presentations (flash cards, drawings, projected material); things students can hold, open, shut, pass to each other; music, songs with tapes, guitars, drums; action songs, action poems. The vocabulary taught should be practical; the characters and incidents they hear or read about should never appear to be "prissy" or effeminate. By building on the known characteristics of different types of students we are using their existing motivation for our pedagogical purposes.

We must find out what our students are interested in. This is our subject matter. As language teachers we are the most fortunate of teachers—all subjects are ours. Whatever the children want to communicate about, whatever they want to read about, is our subject matter. The "informal classroom" we hear so much of these days[7] is ours if we are willing to experiment. Do our students watch TV? This we can use by incorporating material they are all watching into our classroom programs. The essence of language teaching is providing conditions for language learning—using the motivation which exists to increase our student's knowledge of the new language: we are limited only by our own caution, by our own hesitancy to do whatever our imagination suggests to us to create situations in which students feel involved— individually, in groups, whichever is appropriate for the age level of our students in the situation in which we meet them. We need not be tied to a curriculum created for another situation or another group. We must adapt, innovate, improvise, in order to meet the student where he is and channel his motivation.

As we design our program it should be possible to involve students in the selection of activities according to their personality preferences. Should all students, even the inarticulate, be expected to want to develop primarily the speaking skill? Some children reared on television may feel more at ease if allowed to look and listen with minimal oral participation until they feel the urge to contribute: these children will learn far more if allowed to develop according to their own personality patterns than if they are forced to chatter when they have nothing to say. Teachers, too, should be aware of psychological research which shows that native language development proceeds at a different rate for girls and boys,[8] with the girls advancing more rapidly, and that the effect of this difference is cumulative. At certain stages, then, one may expect girls to express themselves orally more readily than boys and this again affects differentially their reaction to chattering in a foreign language. Some students may prefer to range beyond the rest of the class in reading and for such children graded reading material for individual selection, covering a wide variety of topics, should be readily available.

Such individualization of choices requires imaginative planning by the classroom teacher who should be willing and ready to go beyond a uniform diet for all comers as soon as children's individual styles of learning make themselves apparent. An experimental study reported by Politzer and Weiss shows that "better results were obtained by the pupils of those teachers who went beyond the procedures strictly prescribed by the curriculum, teachers who were concerned with supplementing the curriculum rather than merely implementing it." It seems, according to this report, that "the efficiency of the individual teacher increase(d) with the amount of his *personal* stake and *personal* contribution to the instructional processes."[9] Can this be less so for the student himself? We know that involvement in personally selected tasks is intrinsically motivating to normal students. This further source of motivation we must not neglect if we wish to channel the student's natural energies.

Ausubel has pointed out that "motivation is as much an effect as a cause of learning."[10] The relationship between the two, he says, is "typically reciprocal rather than unidirectional."[11] By this he means that when we capitalize on the student's initial motivation, focus it, and direct it into satisfying ego-enhancing learning experiences then this satisfaction motivates the student to further learning along these lines. Nothing breeds success like success. As one meaningful learning task after another is mastered, the attractiveness of the tasks increases and the student is motivated to "practice, rehearse, and perform what he has already learned."[12] What more could we seek as language teachers?

In all of this who is the experimenter? It is not the expert nor the consultant but the classroom teacher—the teacher who one day says to himself: "I think I'll reorganize what I have been doing and see if some of these things I have been hearing really work." Progress in improvement of the conditions for learning comes not through funded projects here and there but through the thousands, the millions of classrooms in operation every hour of the week. There has been much enthusiasm in recent years for educational improvement, but from a study of some two hundred and sixty classrooms Goodlad concluded in 1969 that "most of the so-called educational reform movement has been blunted on the classroom door."[13] What of the bilingual program? What of the English as a second language and second dialect programs throughout the country? Their fate too lies behind the classroom door. In other words, they are your personal responsibility. Think of this next time you go into your classroom.

## FOOTNOTES

[1]J. Frymier, "Motivation: The Mainspring and Gyroscope of Learning," *Theory into Practice*, 9(1970): 23.

[2]T. Johnson, R. Feigenbaum, and M. Weiby, "Some Determinants and Consequences of the Teacher's Perception of Causation," unpublished manuscript, University of Wisconsin, 1964, cited by W. B. Waetjen in "The Teacher and Motivation," *Theory into Practice*, 9(1970): 13-14.

[3]New York: Dell, 1970, p. 42. Originally published by Pitman, 1964.

[4]N. Postman and C. Weingartner, *Teaching as a Subversive Activity* (New York: Delacorte, 1969), p. 18.

[5]D. Ausubel, *Educational Psychology: A Cognitive View* (New York: Holt, Rinehart and Winston, 1968), pp. 367-68.

[6]The subject of motivation and implications from theory for classroom practice is dealt with at length in Wilga M. Rivers, *The Psychologist and the Foreign-Language Teacher* (Chicago: University of Chicago Press, 1964), chap. 9.

[7]See, for instance, C. E. Silberman, *Crisis in the Classroom* (New York: Random House, 1970).

[8]Dorothea A. McCarthy, "Sex Differences in Language Development" in *Psychological Studies of Human Development*, eds. R. G. Kuhlen and G. G. Thompson (New York: Appleton-Century Crofts, 1970), pp. 349-53.

[9]R. L. Politzer and L. Weiss, "Characteristics and Behaviors of the Successful Foreign Language Teacher," Stanford Center for Research and Development in Teaching, Technical Report No. 5 (Palo Alto, April 1969) pp. 69-70.

[10]Ausubel, p. 393.

[11]Ausubel, p. 365.

[12]Ausubel, p. 385.

[13]Quoted in Silberman, p. 159.

# 8

# Motivation in Bilingual Programs*

Life today is programmed. We are each fighting our individual battles against the impersonalization of daily transactions and the phony concern for our well-being of those who wish to organize us, sell us a bill of goods, or use us in some way to advance their causes. Strangely enough, some of us do not feel particularly motivated to cooperate with them and are strongly tempted to bend, fold, staple, and mutilate every card they send us. Is it possible that some of our students feel the same way? Perhaps the interest some of us manifest in ways of motivating our students has its counterpart in the concern of business with market research. We have a product, we are sure it is a good product, and we want an increasing number of consumers to like it so that we will have a good program. Where does our consumer, our student, fit into all this?

We will do better to consider the question of motivation from the point of view of the student from the start. We must remember that motivation is the private domain of the learner. As educators, it is not for us to attempt to manipulate it, even for what we see as the good of the consumer. Our role is to seek to understand it and then to try to meet the needs and wants of our students with the best of what we can provide. It is true that our consumers do not

*Paper delivered in Mexico City on November 20, 1974, and originally published in R. C. Troike and N. Modiano, eds., *The Proceedings of the First Inter-American Conference on Bilingual Education* (Arlington, Va.: Center for Applied Linguistics, 1975).

always see clearly what they need and may have only vague glimmerings of what they really want. We can help them clarify these two, so that their natural motivation—that energizing force each living entity possesses—may carry them forward to joyful and satisfying learning under our care and nurture. Note that I said "nurture," not direction. What we seek to stimulate is self-directed learning which results from truly self-realizing motivation.

There are many ways to look at motivation.[1] If we listen to Maslow, we will learn that all human beings have a hierarchy of needs[2] which must be satisfied if they are to reach the stage where the achievement of their potential as individuals becomes an overriding concern, where they seek to develop their aptitude, and increase their knowledge and experience. These needs stimulate motivation, the higher ones coming into play only when lower level needs are gratified.

First, physiological needs must be satisfied. The hungry and the cold cannot be expected to feel the urgent need to acquire another language. Next comes the need for safety, for security and stability, for freedom from the threat of unpleasant and unwelcome change. This level satisfied, students need to feel that they are accepted by teachers and peers and that people care about them as persons. Only when they are respected for what they are and feel that what they can contribute is welcome, that is, when they rise in their own esteem, can their energies be devoted to efforts to realize their potential, to turn their energies to educational purposes which reach out and beyond the immediate and the present.

The implications of this hierarchy of needs are very real for many of our bilingual programs. Are we concerned with our students' basic needs? Are they well-fed and sheltered? Do they feel secure and welcome in the culture of the school? Are they respected as individuals, so that they respect themselves? Are they encouraged to become the types of persons their own culture values, or is the school in a well-meaning but insensitive way trying to turn them into pale imitations of an ideal from a dominant, but alien, culture? If our students are not learning a language as we would like them to, the reasons may well be traceable to unsatisfied lower levels of Maslow's hiearchy of needs. If we are trying to fit them into our pattern, a pattern which will alienate them from those with whom they identify, resistance, not necessarily conscious, but nonetheless real, will prevent them from satisfactorily learning the language we teach.

This is where we need to examine more closely the frequently cited distinction between *instrumental* motivation (a person learns a language as a tool for some pragmatic purpose) and *integrative* motivation (the person is interested in the other language community to the point that he is willing to adopt distinctive characteristics of their behavior, linguistic and non-linguistic).[3] According to Gardner and Lambert, it is integrative motivation which leads to the most effective language learning, yet it is the ultimate demands of just such an integrative impulse[4] that many students in bilingual programs must reject,[5] if they are to retain their place in and usefully serve the communities from which they come. Instrumental motivation they may have, as in many developing countries, and in emerging communities, where the future good of all depends on at least some becoming thoroughly proficient in the use of another tongue. In such situations, what has been called instrumental motivation can provide a strong drive for language mastery. As persons with such motivation experience success in language learning, the sense of achievement and the enhancement of their ego further channel and direct their motivation. We must not violate the private and deeply emotional identification of our students by insisting that they value what we value and share our culturally acquired attitudes.

A compromise may be reached through the valuable activity of role-playing. Situations may be described or set up in which students will act like persons of the other culture, identifying with them completely in characteristic behavior, language, social attitudes, and implicit values, as good actors do. Such acting out will increase their understanding of the other culture and the way the language operates for communication within the culture, while the students themselves are protected psychologically from an identification which threatens their sense of belonging and their deep-seated loyalty to their own community. Puppet plays, similarly, protect the participant and provide an outlet for identifying behavior in the legitimate world of make-believe. Masks have performed a protective function for children at play throughout the world and these also may be used. The inhibited, who cannot bring themselves to act before others and are not adept with puppets, will often speak through the characters in picture stories, as little children do when they are experimenting with social behavior. These various forms of vicarious identification protect the children from much emotional conflict, embarrassment, or possible public failure, because it is not they, but the pictured or modeled characters, who are responsible for what is being expressed or performed.

Apart from the question of conflicting identifications, there are other ways in which our language teaching can threaten students at the levels of security and belonging. Too often, in our classes, we are so busy teaching our syllabus or completing lesson units that we really do not allow our students to learn. Alschuler et al. conclude that, from the point of view of motivation, structure and process may be more important than content.[6] The basic aims of our language programs are to enable our students to communicate freely and without inhibitions, not only in speech, but, in most bilingual situations, in writing as well. Communication is always a two-way process in whichever modality. Genuine communication requires a revealing of the self which leaves one vulnerable to humiliation, ridicule, or searing embarrassment. In an authoritarian situation where there is a "right" answer which must correspond in all particulars to what is in the teacher's mind, the student is even more in jeopardy. Recognized achievement in this case comes through compliance and repression of one's own inspirations and reactions. To encourage authentic language activity, the teacher needs to create a structure and develop a process wherein the individual student feels safe in venturing his own contribution in interaction, where there is a warmth which welcomes what he has to contribute and gives it that serious consideration which builds him up in his own and in his fellow students' esteem.

For these reasons, it is important to break up the second-language class as often as possible, at least into small groups. Full individualization as a structure may not be possible for many reasons and, if it is taken to mean largely independent study, it will not be desirable for more than a small percentage of language-learning activities where communicative activities are to be developed. On the other hand, much more opportunity for interaction is provided by small group structure where groups are self-selected and have purposeful activities in which to engage together. Some will object that much unsupervised production of language will ensue, with the subsequent danger of errors becoming established. Learning activities for the improvement of language control should be separate from opportunities to use the language for communication. Studies of spontaneous speech reveal that native speakers do not produce the perfect structures of an ideal grammar · when talking about things that matter to them. Sentence structure changes direction while one is speaking; mistakes in subject-verb agreement occur; verb endings are omitted; incorrect prepositions slip in; hesitation and fill-in expressions are frequent. Many sentences are not "complete." (What is a complete sentence, we may ask—"Not what she said anyway"—Is this more or less expressive than "The words she spoke do not form a complete sentence"?) If uninhibited speech (or writing) is our final goal, then much practice in speaking (or writing) without the inhibiting, censorious figure of the teacher looming large is essential.

Once lower level needs of safety, belonging, and esteem are satisfied our students' strong drives will be channeled into "self-actualization, self-fulfillment, self-realization."[7] In order to understand this phase, we may draw ideas from the studies of achievement motivation—the inherent desire of all human beings "to achieve something of excellence."[8] If such a desire is natural to our students, why do so many of them seem uninterested in high achievement in their language classes? The answer often lies in the discrepancy between what the teacher perceives as a worthy vehicle for the student's intensive effort and the student's own perceptions. Each child is naturally curious and active, but not necessarily curious or excited about the things which seem to turn the teacher on. Our students may well be striving for excellence in their natural environment among their peers, while the teacher remains completely ignorant of the things which matter to them most.

As language teachers we are fortunate. Language is a vehicle of expression, not an end in itself, and its use is interwoven in life with a multiplicity of activities. If students do not appear to be interested in practicing language use in the ways we have designed, it is the ways we should try to change, not the students.

Here, we may look at the apparent success of total immersion programs, like the St. Lambert experiment,[9] and ask ourselves what elements of these programs could be transferred to a traditional school language-learning situation. The difference is not merely a matter of time spent on the language, but, more importantly, the role the language plays during this time. In an immersion program, the language is integrally interwoven with all the daily activities of the children—their work, their play, the supplying of their wants, the satisfying of their curiosity. This contrasts with many conventional bilingual classes where "language practice" still consists of pattern drills and paradigms. For a second language to be acquired so that it becomes a part of the child's natural repertoire, it must be used in normal activities. Things spoken are intended to be understood, to convey greetings, information, requests, or jests, to which others will react, either verbally or through action or emotion. Things written are intended to be read by someone who might find the information interesting or helpful, not merely so that they may be corrected and graded and returned to the writer.

If we keep this basic principle in mind—language for the normal purposes of language[10]—we may be surprised by a resurgence of energy in its use and curiosity about its operation.

Here, we can learn from innovative teachers of the native language who sometimes find, to their surprise, that all kinds of students can speak and write expressively, when they have something to communicate which they themselves consider significant and someone who cares enough to pay attention to what they have to say. Guidry and Jones report a course in "Cowboy English"[11] at East Texas State University for the "dumb goat-ropers" from small town and rural schools who were noted for their poor record in English courses. A group-produced pictorial essay on the 1973 E.T.S.U. rodeo and a self-initiated theme on "How to Build a Five Strand Barbed Wire Fence in Blackland Soil" told a different story. One student highlighted the basic problem, which exists for many children in bilingual programs as well, when he said: "This is the first time that anybody in a course like this ever asked me to tell them what I know!"[12] These students were engaged, at last, in an act of real communication: in writing about things of deep significance in their daily lives.

What does each of us know about our students' real interests and preoccupations? In a thought-provoking article, "The Meaning of Creativity in Foreign Language Teaching," Birkmaier proposes that we take inventories "of the activities which the student does on his own . . . , of his reading interests and habits, and of the experiences he has had during his short life-span," and that we use these in developing teaching and learning strategies.[13] This is not merely the suggestion of an "expert who has never been in a classroom" but is an approach which has been implemented with gratifying results by practicing teachers. Unfortunately too many teachers are too busy, too well-organized, too successful at eliciting the perfect response, to tolerate the "shavings on the floor" which inevitably accompany a program which evolves from student-initiated and student-centered activity. With language learning, they are thus excluding the very essence of what their program should be seeking—really purposeful and significant language use.

Once we recognize the importance of natural uses of language and a program based on the students' active concerns, we find ourselves involved in the community in which their real lives are lived. Bilingual programs cannot, and must not, be conducted apart from the communities represented by the two languages. Self-actualization and self-fulfillment can be realized in a satisfying way, through service to the community which earns the esteem of the community. Bilingual programs should be so closely linked with their communities that students learning a second language readily go back into their communities to help those who need their newly acquired language skills. If learning English, or Spanish, or Greek involves acting as an interpreter in father's hardware store, pharmacy, or restaurant, or as an amanuensis for filling in medical benefit or income tax claims, students will see indisputable worth in what they are learning. A language can be practiced perfectly well while working with young people in an after-school club or while helping small children adjust to kindergarten life in a strange environment. The language class must go out into the community; it must consider itself part of the community, learning from the community while giving to the community and serving its needs. Bilingual teachers must know the community in its rich diversity, so that they can use the community to develop a program which reflects its preoccupations and concerns.

We talk a great deal about motivation. We worry about motivation. In a program where students are actively learning in a real context and actively engaged in using what they are learning in ways they recognize as worthwhile, the question of motivation becomes an academic one. Both teacher and students are too deeply involved in what they are doing to ask its meaning.

## FOOTNOTES

[1] I have examined the question of motivation in depth, relating various psychological theories to practical teaching situations in Chapter 9 of *The Psychologist and the Foreign-Language Teacher* (Chicago: The University of Chicago Press, 1964) and in "Motivating Through Classroom Techniques," Chapter 7 in the present book.

[2]Maslow's hierarchy of basic needs passes from physiological needs through the needs for safety, belongingness and love, esteem, and self-actualization, the hierarchy being based on relative potency. See A. H. Maslow, *Motivation and Personality,* 2nd ed. (New York: Harper and Row, 1970), Chapter 4.

[3]R. G. Gardner and W. E. Lambert, *Attitudes and Motivation in Second-Language Learning* (Rowley, Mass.: Newbury House, 1972), pp. 11-16.

[4]Ibid., p. 132: Gardner and Lambert state: "Thus the development of skill in the language could lead the language learner ever closer to a point where adjustments in allegiances would be called for."

[5]One overseas student in the U.S.A., on coming into contact for the first time with the notion that cultural values and attitudes are interwoven with language and must be understood and appreciated if the language is to be used as a native speaker would use it, wrote: "We learn these words without their connotations of the culture in English-speaking countries. It is not debated whether or not we need to learn language in relation to its culture. We are trying hard to get ourselves unshackled from the chains of this colonial gift—the language itself. But we have still to learn it—out of desperate need. Shouldn't we rather stop resisting, and start learning it in a more fruitful way? I have no answer to this question: I would be burnt alive, if I said 'yes'."

[6]A. S. Alschuler, D. Tabor, and J. McIntyre, *Teaching Achievement Motivation* (Middletown, Conn.: Educational Ventures, Inc., 1971), p. 60.

[7]Maslow (1970), p. 73. Maslow defines self-actualization (p. 46) as "the desire to become more and more what one idiosyncratically is, to become everything that one is capable of becoming."

[8]Alschuler et al. (1971), p. xviii.

[9]Described in W. E. Lambert and G. R. Tucker, *Bilingual Education of Children* (Rowley, Mass.: Newbury House, 1972).

[10]Normal purposes of language in oral interaction are listed in "Talking Off the Tops of Their Heads," Chapter 2. These categories are expanded and described in more detail, along with normal uses of listening, reading and writing, in W. M. Rivers, *A Practical Guide to the Teaching of French* (New York and London: Oxford University Press, 1975), and the parallel volumes for German, Spanish and English in this series. See also Chapter 3, note 11.

[11]L. J. Guidry and C. J. Jones, "What Comes Out of the Cowboy's Pen? Tailoring the Course to the Student," *American Vocational Journal,* 49 (1974), 34-35.

[12]Ibid., p. 35.

[13]E. Birkmaier, "The Meaning of Creativity in Foreign Language Teaching," *Modern Language Journal,* 55 (1971), 345-52.

# 9

# THE FOREIGN-LANGUAGE TEACHER
## AND COGNITIVE PSYCHOLOGY
## OR WHERE DO WE GO FROM HERE? *

Martin Braine, the eminent psycholinguist, tells the story about his two-and-a-half-year-old daughter who had the habit of using "other one" as a noun modifier, as in "other one spoon." On a number of occasions he tried to induce her to utter the correct form "the other spoon." A typical interchange went as follows: "Want other one spoon, Daddy"—"You mean, you want THE OTHER SPOON."—"Yes, I want other one spoon, please, Daddy"—"Can you say 'the other spoon'?"—"Other . . . one . . . spoon" —"Say . . . 'other' " —"Other" —"Spoon" —"Spoon" —"Other . . . spoon" —"Other . . . spoon. Now give me other one spoon?"[1] Braine uses this as an example to show that children have difficulty in using negative information (that is, correction) for the development of their syntax, a feature of child learning that has been observed by many researchers.

Any foreign-language teacher must nod understandingly on hearing a story such as this and think of similar experiences he has had: when, for instance, after careful and apparently successful practice of the form of a question a student raises his hand and asks, "What means this word, Miss X?"[2] And so our problems continue perennially. It does not

*Keynote address at the Central States Conference on the Teaching of Foreign Languages, 1972.

surprise us when, in this period of innovations, the student working on his individualized packet on the mysterious workings of the direct object in French looks up as his facilitator of learning[3] comes to his carrel in the learning center and says: "*Je comprends le très bien.*" External arrangements may be different, our attitude to our students' learning may have changed so that the pace of activities, even the type of activity, has been adjusted to individual styles, but the problems of language learning remain: those peculiar problems which make the learning of a foreign language a different proposition from the learning of history or science or home economics.

We certainly do not lack statements on how we should go about our task of helping a student to acquire a second language. In fact we seem at times to be almost deafened by a babble of voices. One rather prevalent (and to my mind oversimplified) view is described by Cooper in the following terms: "There seems to be little evidence that the actual language-learning *processes* differ for the child and the adult. Somehow, both have to abstract the linguistic rules underlying the language as well as the sociolinguistic rules underlying its use. Some second-language learners may do this more quickly than others ... but they must do it nonetheless if they are to learn the language. The question which confronts us as language teachers is how we can best structure the language-learning situation so as to exploit the language-learning abilities of the student."[4] The type of restatement in the last sentence, if taken at its face value, obviously does not throw a great deal of light on the problem. It does, however, highlight the need for us as teachers to know as much as we possibly can about the way the student learns and learns language. The approach in the passage cited is that of a number of writers in recent journals who are trying to reexamine teaching problems in the light of the latest findings of linguistics and psychology.

When we discuss language-learning processes at the level of generality of Cooper's statement we must not be surprised to read that these "processes" do not differ for the child and the adult. It is almost self-evident that the language learner must "abstract" and internalize as a part of his own cognitive structure the system of linguistic and sociolinguistic rules if he is to function autonomously in the language, independently of his teacher. We are not surprised, at this undifferentiated level, when the writer tells us that he must do this "somehow."

Basic to Cooper's statement is a theory expounded in several places by Chomsky[5] that the child has innate language-learning abilities in the form of "a linguistic theory that specifies the form of the grammar of a possible[6] human language" and a "strategy for selecting a grammar of the appropriate form that is compatible with the primary linguistic data,"[7] that is, for matching with the language he hears around him (Chomsky calls it "meagre and degenerate data"[8]) the form of a particular grammar from a "fairly restricted set of potential languages".[9] The "strategy" of which Chomsky is speaking is a language-acquisition device (LAD)[10] which proceeds by hypothesis-testing. The child makes hypotheses about the form of the grammar of the language to which he is attending. He compares this with his innate knowledge of the grammar of a possible language[11] which is congruent with the abstract principles of universal grammar and which is capable of generating through ordered sets of transformations the many surface variations of this specific language. (Note that the hypotheses the child is presumed to be making are about deep structure relationships, not the peculiarities of surface structure.)

It is against this theoretical background that we can now consider Cooper's proposals for an actual language teaching situation. Quoting from an article by Vivian Cook,[12] he suggests that the teacher should "permit, and indeed encourage the learner to produce sentences that are ungrammatical from the point of view of the target language. This would be done on the assumption that . . . the second language learner's deviations are not random but systematic and reflect implicit hypotheses as to the nature of the language being learned . . . When he produces sentences which deviate from those of the target language, the teacher's reactions can help him change the hypotheses. Note that the teacher would be more concerned with correcting the *hypothesis* underlying the deviant sentence than with inducing the student to correct the particular *sentence*."[13] Now I certainly agree that we should give our students abundant opportunity to experiment in spontaneous use of the language, knowing full well that in doing so they will produce some ungrammatical sentences. In Chapter 2, "Talking Off the Tops of Their Heads," I have advocated that such opportunities be provided as early as possible in the student's language-learning experience, in association with the structured teaching sequence. This type of free-wheeling gives the student opportunities to try what he can do with what he knows: making "infinite use of finite means" (to use the oft-quoted phrase of Humboldt). It is during such autonomous interaction that we can see what systematic errors the student is making and correct his erroneous hypotheses about the structure of French, or German, or English.

What I am interested in, then, is not so much what is being proposed here but its theoretical underpinnings. First of all, linguistically speaking, it cannot be considered an application in teaching practice of Chomskyan theory. The child's hypotheses about which Chomsky is speaking are, as we have noted, at the abstract level of deep structure. Since the child's knowledge of the grammars of possible languages is said to be innate, his hypotheses about the nature of the language to which he is attending cannot really be deviant and in need of correction, if our interpretation of the theory is consistent. Chomsky says "various formal and substantive universals are intrinsic properties of the language-acquisition system, these providing a schema that is applied to data and that determines in a highly restricted way the general form and, in part, even the substantive features of the grammar that may emerge upon presentation of appropriate data."[14] It is in this sense that the utterances of children learning their first language are no longer considered "errors" by developmental psychologists who base their interpretations on the innateness theory, but rather exemplars of basic structural relations.[15] Extrapolating directly from linguistic theory to classroom practice is not as simple as the quotation from Cooper would make it appear.

In a laudable enthusiasm to keep language teaching practice congruent with the latest theories in other disciplines there seems to be a recent tendency to brush aside what the older learner brings to the second-language learning experience.[16] In the classroom situation that Cooper is describing, the deviations which are "ungrammatical from the point of view of the target language" are clearly at the surface structure level and do not reflect "implicit hypotheses as to the nature of the language being learned" in the sense in which Chomsky has used these terms. We are clearly talking about a different type of hypothesis. As every experienced teacher knows, one of the principal hypotheses underlying the deviant utterances of an older student learning a second language is that the surface structure of the new language will closely duplicate the surface structure of his first language. The first-language learner who hears only surface realizations of the underlying rules of the particular language he is learning (interspersed with some performance errors) and who is surrounded during all his waking hours by the language he is trying to acquire does not have this conflict in his natural language-learning situation. He detects logical relations and begins in a basic fashion to express these relations. It is these relations, as Lakoff has recently observed,[17] which are a part of universal grammar. This explains why young children learning different languages seem to pass through similar developmental phases, producing similar early grammars which represent the same basic relations before they reach the stage of differentiation of the details of the surface structure of the particular language they are acquiring. When, however, even a young child learns a second language, still in a natural, untutored fashion, we have evidence that he too suffers from the interference of the surface features of one language with the surface features of the other.[18]

When the adult learner discovers that many features of the two surface structures are not comparable in their functioning he frequently overcompensates by overgeneralizing divergent features of the new language to instances where the two systems do in fact coincide. (Having learned that a French adjective frequently follows the noun as in *une pomme rouge*, he will overgeneralize to *un crayon long* where the order paralleling the English order, *un long crayon*, would have been appropriate.) The recent research in error analysis reported by Jack Richards[19] shows over half the errors he cites to be interference errors while among the remaining overgeneralization errors many are overcompensatory. Learning the limits of generalization of specific rules in a new language is a problem which can often be handled better by direct instruction, which highlights differences in the surface structures of the native and target languages, rather than by "encouraging" the student to produce deviant utterances according to his current hypothesis until such time as he has had sufficient experience to correct himself. In free interaction we cannot ensure that sufficient opportunities of miscomprehension will occur at particular points of overgeneralization to provide the student with adequate data for the correction of his hypotheses. Nor can we ignore the factor of attention. The student attending specifically to problems of comprehending and expressing his meaning comprehensibly may well not have sufficient cognitive processing capacity available to note and store at the same time signals of the deviancy of certain surface structure features. Inconvenient facts of this type seem to be easily forgotten as soon as we begin to explore again the attractive hypothesis that processes of learning a second language are identical with those for learning a first language. As Stern has put it so aptly: "Once language development has taken place, it produces a lasting structural change. If a new language is learned in later years, it is filtered through the language acquisition device of the individual, modified by his first language."[20]

Unfortunately for the "natural" language-learning argument, recent research has left it far from clear how the child does acquire his first language and some assumptions reflected in current writings on foreign-language teaching appear now to have very problematic status. Many foreign-language teachers seem not to be aware of the fact that very reputable linguists,[21] philosophers,[22] and psychologists have sharply criticized Chomsky's theory of an innate linguistic faculty which enables the child to identify the form of the grammar of the language by which he is surrounded. Schlesinger comments: "There can be no question, of course, that the organism comes to any learning task with some innate equipment; the question is only how much is innate. The soundest approach seems to be to make as few assumptions as possible, and to try to explain with these as much as possible." Bruner says, "I am prepared to believe that in the linguistic domain the capacities for categorization and hierarchical organization are innate and so, too, are predication, causation, and modification."[23] Braine would accept as innate the mechanisms which permit us to perceive temporal position and cooccurrence relations.[24] Ervin-Tripp observes that "order relations seem very apparent to children . . . Order is almost always accurately reproduced in imitations."[25] Bever maintains that "there is not as much innate structure to language as we had thought, if the 'universal grammar' is stripped of those aspects that draw on other psychological systems" (notably mechanisms of perception, learning, and cognition).[26] The present consensus appears to be that it is the logical structures basic to various intellectual processes which are innate, and which distinguish man as a species, not language-specific structures, and that it is these logical structures which make it possible for man to acquire and use language as well as to perform other cognitive operations. In this sense the concepts of "noun phrase," "verb phrase," or "sentence" would not be innate, as McNeill had earlier suggested,[27] but rather the capacity to categorize, to establish hierarchies of categories and relations between categories, the categories themselves being derived from common experiences of man in a human environment. In this sense, foreign-language teachers have always exploited the innate language-related capacities of the students by taking for granted that they can apprehend basic relationships of temporal order, cooccurrence, category, and hierarchy, and such operative relations as agent-action, action-object, causation, and modification.

Even the Chomskyan concept of the child acquiring a language system by hypothesis-testing is by no means uncontested. Braine argues convincingly that the child cannot be proceeding by the testing of hypotheses because real hypothesis-testing is dependent on the reception of both positive information (acceptance) and negative information.[28] Without negative information, that is, correction or rejection of unacceptable sentences, a child cannot test hypotheses about grammaticality. Yet, strong evidence exists that children do learn language from positive information only, even though some of this information is inaccurate (e.g., in cases where the child's deviant utterance is accepted by the adult). Whether children are corrected or not[29] they acquire the language of the community in which they are growing up, and busy parents notoriously miss many opportunities to correct their children's speech, even adopting the children's own forms on occasions, forms which the child is often hearing also from other children of his own age. We also know that children do not adjust their utterances when negative information is provided (even when this is done in an insistent fashion, as with Braine's child at the beginning of this paper)[30] but they continue to operate within their own structural system until it has evolved to the stage where the particular adjustment indicated by the correction becomes functionally warranted. It is, therefore, far from proven that the child acquires his first language by a process of hypothesis-testing. We may like to use this technique in our classes for motivational reasons or to add variety to our approach but we cannot claim at present that it is more than a heuristic on our part.

We are also told frequently these days that children do not learn language from a limited and structured corpus, that children hear language of all levels of complexity, and that it is because of this constant exposure to a full array of language structure and vocabulary from the beginning that the child is able to discover for himself the complete grammar of the language. Some people have asserted on the basis of this presumably scientific information that second-language students should not be presented in the early stages with a simplified form of the language (that is, with basic patterns and a limited vocabulary)[31] but be exposed from the beginning to the full range of language.[32] More recent child language acquisition studies have shown, however, that it is not the case that the child learns from a wide variety of complicated structures and vocabulary. Actually, the child tunes out much of what he does not understand in language which is not addressed to him. Attention and memory play essential roles in comprehension. What the child is not attending to is processed minimally, if at all, and the child's memory span initially is very short. The sentences to which he is directly exposed tend to be short, repetitive, and quite limited in range of structures and vocabulary. This we know from recent investigations of Ervin-Tripp and her associates at Berkeley. Ervin-Tripp quotes a sample of adult speech to a two-year-old child which runs as follows: "Come play a game wit' me. Come play a game with me. Wanna play a game with me? You wanna play a game with me...? Come look at Mamma's colorin' book. You wanna see my coloring book? Look at my coloring book. Lookit, that's an Indian, huh? Is that an Indian? Can you say Indian?"[33] (The same mother was using with adult friends sentences like the following: "It gives me a certain amount of consolation which allows me to relax my mind and start thinking intelligently an' putting my efforts all in one y'know force goin' in one direction rather than jus' y'know continually feeling sorry for yourself.")[34] As for the child himself, Weir has given examples of the speech of her child, David, at three years of age, talking into the microphone with which he had become familiar: "Here's de place. Bad boy bad boy Dave. Bad boy bad boy Dave. Dave is not a bad boy. Mike is a bad boy. Dave is OK but Mike is not."[35] Here we have the child saying over to himself simple noun phrases with modifiers and affirmative and negative declarative sentences with occasional ellipsis.

We must at the present time be extremely wary of basing what we do in the foreign-language classroom on presumed definitive statements about language learning from either linguistics or psychology. As Schlesinger has put it so aptly: "Psychological theorizing about language learning is in its infancy, and generative grammar is not yet fast frozen."[36] Generative grammar is in fact in such a state of evolution at the moment[37] that we bystanders would do well to wait till the dust settles before attempting to shape our classroom practice in any radical way according to principles and structures which tomorrow may be *passé*. Lamendella has concluded that "theories of linguistic description are relevant to language teaching only to the extent that they form part of the data which psycholinguists may use in constructing a cognitive theory of language. It is this theory which may properly be utilized as the theoretical basis for second-language pedagogy."[38] Such a theory of language stemming from psycholinguistics is not yet in sight. As eminent a cognitive psychologist as Bever observes: "I have said little about the effects of general principles of learning on linguistic structure because I do not know anything about how language (or anything else) is learned, while I do have some initial understanding of the mechanisms of perception."[39] Problems of first-language acquisition aside, there are important discoveries in the area of perception, both auditory and visual, which can help us to help our students learn more efficiently and which can give us firmer bases for the designing of learning materials. A little later we shall see what light they throw on particular learning problems with which we are all familiar.

There are, of course, cognitive psychologists who are interested in both problems of learning in general and in language learning. Carroll has quite a deal to say about both in "Current Issues in Psycholinguistics and Second Language Teaching",[40] where he deplores the misinterpretation of his 1965 article[41] in which he had discussed audiolingual habit theory and what he had called cognitive code-learning theory. In his 1971 article he calls for a "meaningful synthesis," suggesting that "if it does not seem too flip to do so," we should call this approach "cognitive habit-formation theory." This article should be read carefully by all those interested in present controversies. Hebb, Lambert, and Tucker have shown recently how Hebb's cognitive learning theory can be applied to language learning.[42] Piaget has devoted his life's work to the relationship between learning and cognitive growth, and Bruner has made cognitive theory accessible to teachers in *"Toward a Theory of Instruction."*[43]

At this stage, a word of warning. We hear a good deal these days about a "cognitive" approach to foreign-language teaching and its proponents speak as though the techniques they propose in some way exemplify the principles of cognitive psychology. When we examine what they are saying a little more closely we sometimes find that they are merely proposing a return to the deductive presentation of grammar rules before practice to make what is practiced presumably more "meaningful" and that this is considered a more "cognitive" way to proceed. I do not intend to consider here the pros and cons of a deductive versus an inductive approach. Kelly traces this controversy back at least to St. Augustine and quotes Lubinus in 1550 as writing: "Now what and how monstrous an absurdity is it . . . to bid them give an account, why they speake Latine right, before they can in any wise speake properly."[44] In a teaching situation both induction and deduction may be very effective depending on the way they are integrated into the total teaching-learning situation. In fact most teachers use one approach or the other at different times, depending on the age and ability of the learners and the nature of the problem under consideration. I am merely concerned here with the very meagre interpretation of cognition which identifies it with a deductive presentation of grammar rules and an emphasis on analysis of structure, useful as these may be at the right place and time. Psychologically speaking, analysis is a cognitive process but so, most definitely, is analogy, requiring as it does the prior recognition of a pattern—the realization that there is something in common between two otherwise different events, which is a process of abstraction. Learning rules is a cognitive process but so is inferencing. We cannot imitate without activating a cognitive process.[45] It is noteworthy that small children find it difficult to imitate an utterance: they either interpret and rephrase it, or they answer a question or perform an action.[46]

A cognitive psychologist would make no attempt to establish a value hierarchy for these processes. He tries to find out what takes place when we perform any of them. He is interested in different strategies of learning and the stages of maturation at which each becomes dominant, or is, in Piaget's system, at least a possible operation for the child. He is interested in how we recognize phonic or graphic patterns and the interpretations we impose upon them. He is interested in short- and long-term memory. He is interested in

what makes any object of learning or any situation meaningful to a particular student. Essentially he is interested in what
goes on *inside* the organism: how we observe, interpret,
interrelate and comprehend, reorganize and use *any* material
for learning, because all living is learning. From what he
discovers he is able to make suggestions for improving
institutionalized learning (that is, in-school tasks), recognizing that no process or procedure is appropriate for all
types and conditions of learning.

For the cognitive psychologist, then, cognition "refers to
all the processes by which the sensory input is transformed,
reduced, elaborated, stored, recovered, and used . . . Given
such a sweeping definition, it is apparent that cognition is
involved in everything a human being might possibly do; that
every psychological phenomenon is a cognitive phenomenon."[47] This processing of input and preprocessing of output
is what we need to understand if we are to teach a foreign
language. It is here precisely that we have much to learn from
the experimental findings of the psychology of perception
which has made great strides in recent years. Psychology is
not an alien science coming to strange conclusions which
contradict what we ourselves observe. Much of what the
psychologist discovers appears to us to be "common sense"
because he is describing the operations of the human
organism. Thus recent psychological studies in perception
help us to understand experiences enshrined in such familiar
expressions as: *he was only listening with half an ear,*[48] *it
was just on the tip of my tongue,*[49] *you took the words right
out of my mouth,*[50] and *you can tell he's French by his
accent.*[51]

I shall now take two common problems of foreign-
language learning and show how recent theories of perceptual
processing can help us to analyze and deal with them.

A teacher may ask: *If listening is a passive or receptive
skill, why do students sometimes seem to hear what was
never said?*

Studies in perception make it clear that listening is far
from being a passive skill, and the same may be said of
reading (which shares with listening certain processes in a

different sense modality).[52] Listening involves an active cognitive processing. Far from being an act of reception it involves the construction of a message from phonic material, with the result that the message we construct may sometimes be different from the message the speaker intended. There are three stages in the aural reception of a message and changes in the original message can occur at each stage. First, the listener must recognize in phonic substance sound patterns in bounded segments related to phrase structure (here we are helped by the rhythm of speech). At this stage we are dependent on echoic memory which is very fleeting. Unless we interrelate meaningfully the segments we detect we lose them as echoic memory fades. To extract a message, then, we must immediately begin processing, identifying the groupings we have detected according to the content of our central information system, that is, according to knowledge we have already stored. (This store of knowledge is, of course, limited at first in the foreign language, but expands as we continue to learn.) We recirculate this organized material through our immediate memory thus building up an auditory memory of it which helps us retain the segments we are processing. It is valuable, then, for the language learner to recapitulate mentally what he is hearing as he processes its meaning (this is a form of subvocal matching). Much of this processing of incoming information takes place during the pauses in speech, so speech which has been speeded up within segments is still comprehensible if the pauses are slightly lengthened so that the overall presentation rate remains the same. There are implications here for presentation of listening comprehension materials on tape, especially in view of the modern emphasis on normal rate of speech from the early stages.

It should not surprise us that when we are listening to a language with which we are not very familiar we often lose whole segments here and there even though we comprehended them when they were uttered. At this stage we must interrelate incoming segments with those we have retained and hold some in immediate memory to interrelate them with what follows, so that we can construct a sequential meaning for the utterance and for the sequence of utterances. We are then, by our organization, anticipating the full form of the message, and this explains why we often supply a completion when the speaker hesitates. The more we can gather the incoming information into meaningful chunks[53] the more we can retain. It is therefore important to train students in the perceiving of groups of words as units. To achieve this we should encourage our students to repeat what they hear in meaningful segments, and we should ask questions which require meaningful segments, rather than single words, as answers. It is also important to train students to hold longer and longer segments in their memory to improve comprehension.

Having constructed *our* meaning from what we are receiving, we recode this for long-term storage, that is, we reduce it to the "gist," and this is what we recall when asked about it. When we ask students questions about what they have been hearing, we should always encourage them to give the answers in their own words in the foreign language rather then expecting them to repeat exactly what they heard. This encourages real processing rather than superficial "playback," and gives practice in retrieval of the coded material.

It is clear from this analysis that attention plays an important role in comprehension. If attention wavers, we identify the wrong segments, we skip some segments, and we construct a different, idiosyncratic message. We know also that reinforcement plays a role in maintaining attention, so listening should be accompanied by some activity through which the student can demonstrate his comprehension and experience the pleasure of success. If he can do this through some form of personal expression in speaking or writing, the student learns at the same time that comprehension of a message is part of a communicative act. Set is also a significant factor. We hear what we expect to hear. In normal communication the context (the situation, the time of day, the persons interacting) helps us in interpreting a message. If we miss a segment or two, or if some of what we have heard "slips our mind," we fill in the gaps from expectations based on previous experience in such situations. This is why listening comprehension is facilitated when there is a visual or situational element, or even some background noises on the tape to indicate that the speakers are in a railroad station or at the seaside.

Emotion affects our cognitive processing. Personal thoughts and apprehensions take up some of the limited processing capacity, interfering with interpretation and retention of what is being perceived. It is natural, then, that the nervous or embarrassed student cannot "hear" well, or "hears" what was never said. The more disconcerted he becomes the more he grabs at semantic clues here and there and tries to process some kind of message. It is also natural for a student to forget what he heard and understood, and be unable to recount it. Material which is relatively unfamiliar cannot be gathered into large enough chunks, processing capacity is overstrained, and there is not enough cognitive energy left for the listener to rehearse and recode for storage what is being interpreted. In this case the student understands as he hears each segment but cannot store a sequential message.

For our second problem we imagine our teacher complaining:

*My students rattle off drills (or write out paradigms; or whip through packets) all right, but they never seem to remember anything from one day to the next.*

How familiar this sounds! These students are relying on short-term memory for their answers, particularly in drills and exercises where all the elements are supplied. In aural-oral drills particularly, the rhythm of the cues helps the students to produce the answers with a minimum of cognitive processing. Since they are not personally identifying the salient regularities in the material they are "rattling off" they are not forming concepts which they can relate to other information in the long-term store. Each utterance is a relatively unrelated new experience. Once a concept is formed, each utterance in a series becomes a variation on a theme which permits rehearsal and recirculation of the concept for recoding in long-term memory. Sentences in most drills and exercises are semantically empty for the student in the sense that they have no personal reality for him as a reflection of his present experience: they become exercises in manipulation of language segments which is purposeful only as manipulation. Mechanical, nonmeaningful activity does not use up a great deal of processing capacity—just enough to imitate, more or less accurately, and make minor adjustments. As a result a process of *time-sharing* takes place on the following pattern:

> *je mange du fromage . . .*
>> (That boy with the red hair looks interesting.)
> *je mange des pommes . . .*
>> (He's drumming rhythmically with his fingers.)
> *je mange des carottes . . .*
>> (I wonder if he likes dancing.)
> *je mange de la viande . . .*
>> (Ah! he prefers cinnamon gum.
>> I must remember that.)

It is no wonder, then, that the point of the drill never reaches the long-term store from which it could have been retrieved the next day or a week or two later.

Other problems which I would like to have considered, had the time allowed, are the following:

*We've practiced and practiced that structure but they still get it wrong when they try to say something on their own.*

*Mary's the first to recognize when something is wrongly pronounced, yet her own pronunciation is nothing to write home about.*[54]

*They say every sentence we utter is one that's never been heard before. Most conversations don't sound that original to me.*

And finally one remark I heard recently at a discussion on individualized instruction:

*Where do all these paragons come from who go off in a corner by themselves and work like mad? I know mine would just goof off!*—which brings us into the whole area of the psychology of motivation![55]

Carroll observes that "the 'new orthodoxy' in linguistics and psycholinguistics has made certain statements that have made second language teachers almost despair of their profession."[56] Teachers, he says, need to be constantly reminded of practices that "have long been the property of good language teachers, from the days of Gouin, de Sauzé, Palmer, Sweet and other pioneers ... because they tend to develop, under the pressure of new fads and theories, a kind of professional panic and anxiety about their work."[57] The busy teacher, exhilarated or wearied by a long day working with impatient and ebullient students, hardly needs to read: "that people can learn, is an undeniable fact of life; that people can teach, is an interesting hypothesis, but unsubstantiated."[58] As a witticism it is worth recalling for the next faculty meeting, but as teachers we realize it is mere playing with words. It is based on a view of teaching (the teacher as authority figure)[59] which is by no means axiomatic. That teachers are "managers of the learning process"[60] is equally authoritarian. It is time to return to the concept of teaching which Dewey expressed so aptly in 1897 (the tradition is, of course, even older): "the child's own instincts[61] and powers furnish the material and give the starting point for all education. Save as the efforts of the educator connect with some activity which the child is carrying on of his own initiative independent of the educator, education becomes reduced to a pressure from without[62] ... The teacher is not in the school to impose certain ideas or to form certain habits in the child but is there as a member of the community to select the influences which shall affect the child and to assist him in properly responding to these influences."[63] With this concept of teaching, we select, from among practices we know, those which are appropriate to the various aspects of language acquisition, refining them in accordance with theory and experience.

The simple answer to the problem is not merely "individualization." An individualized program, just as much as a classroom situation, presupposes materials with built-in learning approaches. Without guidance students may work in ways which are quite inefficient for language acquisition, just as an uninformed teacher may work inefficiently in class. Analyses of problems like those above show the types of useful indications we as teachers can gain from an understanding of cognitive processes—information that will help us to understand the problems of individual students and to design materials and activities with which they will be successful because we are not demanding of them responses which are beyond their processing capacities at a particular stage. If teachers are to be required more and more to prepare or adapt materials themselves as individualization becomes more widely accepted as an approach to school learning, they will need to think carefully about how students learn and arrange the conditions and "select the influences" accordingly. To quote a famous poet: "Men must be taught as if you taught them not."[64]

## FOOTNOTES

[1]M. Braine, "On Two Types of Models of the Internalization of Grammars," in Dan I. Slobin, ed., *The Ontogenesis of Grammar* (New York: Academic Press, 1971), pp. 160-61.

[2]Example cited in Susan Ervin-Tripp, "Structure and Process in Language Acquisition," in James E. Alatis, ed., *Bilingualism and Language Contact: Anthropological, Linguistic, Psychological, and Sociological Aspects,* Monograph Series on Languages and Linguistics No. 23 (Washington, D. C.: Georgetown University Press, 1970), p. 340.

[3]Gilbert A. Jarvis says, "In the present sense of the term, we shall have to get 'teachers' out of our schools and replace them with facilitators—facilitators of learning." See "Individualized Learning—Where Can We Risk Compromise?" in *Modern Language Journal*, 4 (1971): 376.

[4]R.L. Cooper, "What Do We Learn When We Learn a Language," *TESOL Quarterly*, 4(1970): 312. In this article Cooper has provided us with a number of interesting insights into language learning. I have extracted from it the particular sections quoted because in them Cooper has described in a succinct fashion a particular viewpoint which I wish to analyze and discuss.

[5]Notably in *Aspects of the Theory of Syntax* (Cambridge: MIT Press, 1965); *Cartesian Linguistics* (New York: Harper and Row, 1966); and *Language and Mind* (New York: Harcourt, Brace and World, 1968).

[6]"Possible" in the sense that it is congruent with the particular form of innate equipment with which each human being is endowed and is, therefore, a language of a type which a human being can learn naturally.

[7]Chomsky, *Aspects*, p. 25.

[8]Chomsky, *Language and Mind*, p. 76.

[9]Ibid.

[10]For a full description of LAD see D. McNeill, *The Acquisition of Language: The Study of Developmental Psycholinguistics* (New York: Harper and Row, 1970), pp. 70-71.

[11]Chomsky, *Aspects*, p. 30.

[12]V. J. Cook, "The Analogy between First and Second Language Learning" in *IRAL* 7(1969): 216. After examining the research on first language acquisition of the mid-sixties, Cook sets out four requirements which would need to be met by a method of teaching foreign languages which could claim to be based on these theories. The suggestion taken up by Cooper is one of these requirements. Cook concludes: "No method can at present claim to fulfill these requirements. It remains to be seen whether they can in principle be fulfilled, whether, in fact, the analogy of first and second language learning is sound."

[13]Cooper, pp. 312-313.

[14]Chomsky, *Aspects*, p. 53.

[15]McNeill (1970), p. 36.

[16]Cooper, while claiming that "first and second language learning are analogous" and that a second language is not "learned in any fundamentally different way than a first language," nevertheless lists some of the "cognitive differences" in the two situations. "In spite of these differences," he says, "there seems to be little evidence that the actual language-learning *processes* differ for the child and the adult." In the present state of knowledge I would say that there is very little evidence either for or against such a conclusion because there has not been to date a great deal of experimental research into the specific language learning processes of the adult. The question is, therefore, still an open one.

[17]In "The Arbitrary Basis of Transformational Grammar," *Language*, 48 (1972): 76-87, George Lakoff says: "The theory of generative semantics claims that the linguistic elements used in grammar have an independent natural basis in the human conceptual system . . . In generative semantics, possible grammars are limited by the requirement that the nonphonological elements used have a natural semantic basis, independent of the grammar of any particular natural language" (pp. 77-8).

[18]Roar Ravem, "Language Acquisition in a Second Language Environment," *IRAL*, 6 (1968): 175-85.

[19]Jack C. Richards, "Error Analysis and Second Language Strategies," *Language Sciences*, no. 17 (October, 1971): 12-22.

[20]H. H. Stern, "First and Second Language Acquisition" in *Perspectives on Second Language Teaching*, Modern Language Center Publications No. 1 (Toronto: The Ontario Institute for Studies in Education, 1970), p. 64.

[21]As an example, see Ernst Pulgram, Review Essay on Noam Chomsky, *Language and Mind, Modern Language Journal*, 55(1971): 474-80.

[22]See Nelson Goodman, "The Emperor's New Ideas" in S. Hook, ed., *Language and Philosophy* (New York: New York University Press, 1969), pp. 138-42.

[23] J. Bruner, "On Cognitive Growth" in J. Bruner et al., *Studies in Cognitive Growth* (New York: Wiley, 1966), p. 43.

[24] Braine, p. 171.

[25] Ervin-Tripp, p. 335.

[26] T. G. Bever, "The Cognitive Basis for Linguistic Structures" in J. R. Hayes, *Cognition and the Development of Language* (New York: Wiley, 1970), p. 352.

[27] McNeill, pp. 70-71.

[28] Braine, pp. 155-68.

[29] E. Lenneberg says that even "children suffering from gross and criminal parental neglect" learn to speak the language of their community, in "A Biological Perspective of Language" in E. Lenneberg, ed., *New Directions in the Study of Language* (Cambridge: MIT Press, 1964), p. 67.

[30] For a similar example see D. McNeill, "Developmental Psycholinguistics" in *Genesis of Language*, F. Smith and G. A. Miller, eds., (Cambridge: MIT Press, 1966), p. 69.

[31] See L. A. Jakobovits, "Psychological Perspectives on Individualized Foreign Language Instruction" in H. Altman and R. Politzer, eds., *Individualizing Foreign Language Instruction* (Rowley, Mass.: Newbury House, 1971), p. 94.

[32] See L. A. Jakobovits, *Foreign Language Learning: A Psycholinguistic Analysis of the Issues* (Rowley, Mass.: Newbury House, 1970), p. 25.

[33] Ervin-Tripp, "An Overview of Theories of Grammatical Development" in Slobin, p. 194.

[34] Ibid.

[35] R. Weir, "Some Questions on the Child's Learning of Phonology", in Smith and Miller, p. 162.

[36] I. M. Schlesinger, "Production of Utterances and Language Acquisition" in Slobin, p. 100.

[37] Here I am referring to the active controversy between "classical" transformation-generative grammarians who are further developing Chomsky's system and the generative semanticists like Lakoff and McCawley who have an affinity with case grammarians like Fillmore. Lakoff tends to the view that what is innate and universal is an apprehension of logical categories and meaningful relations rather than abstract syntactic principles of a potential language. The various linguistic schools of thought have provided interesting (and often unexpected) insights into the way language operates. These we should draw on in constructing teaching materials and in helping students learn language, but we should use caution at the moment in making definitive statements about language learning based on one particular theory rather than another.

[38] J. T. Lamendella, "On the Irrelevance of Transformational Grammar to Second Language Pedagogy," *Language Learning*, 19 (1969):270.

[39] Bever, p. 350.

[40]J. B. Carroll, "Current Issues in Psycholinguistics and Second Language Teaching," *TESOL Quarterly*, 5(1971): 101-14.

[41]J. B. Carroll, "The Contributions of Psychological Theory and Educational Research to the Teaching of Foreign Languages," *Modern Language Journal*, 49(1965): 273-81.

[42]D. O. Hebb, W. E. Lambert, and G. R. Tucker, "Language, Thought, and Experience," *Modern Language Journal*, 55(1971): 212-22.

[43]Cambridge:The Belknap Press of Harvard University Press, 1966.

[44]For a full discussion of the induction-deduction controversy down the ages, see L. Kelly, *25 Centuries of Language Teaching* (Rowley, Mass.: Newbury House, 1969), pp. 34-43. Lubinus quotation p. 37.

[45]Ervin-Tripp, p. 316, states that "at a minimum, it can be shown that imitation requires perception, storage, organization of output, and motor output. In addition, before the storage phase there will be interpretation if the material is interpretable." See also Hebb, Lambert, and Tucker, p. 218.

[46]Ervin-Tripp, p. 317.

[47]U. Neisser, *Cognitive Psychology* (New York: Appleton-Century-Crofts, 1967), p. 4.

[48]Discussed in Ervin-Tripp, p. 317.

[49]See "The 'Tip of the Tongue' Phenomenon" in Roger Brown, *Psycholinguistics* (New York: The Free Press/Macmillan, 1970, pp. 274-301. Originally published 1966.

[50]For further information on this phenomenon see Chapter 10, "Linguistic and Psychological Factors in Speech Perception and Their Implications for Teaching Materials."

[51]See Ervin-Tripp, p. 323.

[52]Both listening and reading are discussed at length in Chapter 10 in this book.

[53]This term was used by G. A. Miller in his famous article "The Magical Number Seven, Plus or Minus Two: Some Limits on our Capacity for Processing Information," *Psychological Review* 63 (1956):81-96.

[54]As well as the processes outlined in note 45 for imitation, the student's own production of sounds when speaking is dependent on articulatory skill and kinesthetic feedback which vary from individual to individual so that the student's internal representation of the sound may not be reflected accurately in his production. Students also vary in their inhibitions about making "strange" sounds or in adopting these sounds as a permanent form of expression. Also during production other factors are competing for the limited processing capacity of the individual. For a full discussion, see Ervin-Tripp, pp. 316-26.

[55]I have dealt with this aspect of psychology at length in Chapter 7, "Motivating through Classroom Techniques."

[56]Carroll, pp. 108-9.

[57]Ibid., pp. 112-13. It is interesting to note that Gouin referred to his method as "psychological" or "natural."

[58]Jakobovits, "Psychological Perspectives," p. 91.

[59]Ibid., p. 97.

[60]Report of the Committee on the Process of Contracting in Foreign Language Learning in Altman and Politzer, p. 123.

[61]Views on instincts have changed considerably since 1897, but the sense of the passage is clear and startlingly contemporary.

[62]John Dewey, "My Pedagogic Creed" (1897), reprinted in M. S. Dworkin, ed., *Dewey on Education* (New York: Teachers College Press, 1959), p. 20.

[63]Ibid., p. 24.

[64]Alexander Pope, *Essay on Criticism III.*

# 10

# LINGUISTIC AND PSYCHOLOGICAL FACTORS
## IN SPEECH PERCEPTION AND
## THEIR IMPLICATIONS FOR TEACHING MATERIALS*

Speech perception, it must be admitted, is a subject about which very little is known with any certainty. How is it possible, we may ask, for a person to extract a message from a continuous stream of sound which trained phoneticians find difficult to segment when the acoustic signal is recorded on a spectrogram. Yet, despite linguists and psychologists, understanding utterances is the common experience of every normal human being, and despite our ignorance of its nature we continue to train students who can understand not only their native language but foreign languages as well.

There are many questions about speech perception for which at present we can expect no definitive answers. Some maintain that the reception of a message is determined by the operation in reverse of the same processes as those involved in its emission. For this view there is as yet little experimental evidence and some that would seem to refute it.[1] Others consider that we perceive an oral message by covertly constructing a parallel message with which we compare it for

---

*This article reprinted from *The Psychology of Second Language Learning*, eds. Paul Pimsleur and Terence Quinn, (Cambridge University Press, 1971).

fit—if this is so, speech perception must be considered a special case of speech production. Still others consider speech perception a distinctive process in which the decoding rules draw on different factors from the encoding rules of speech production, with semantic cues playing a predominant role. Most linguists have concentrated on the system of rules which must be internalized if speech production is to be a theoretical possibility and Chomsky at least sees no difference between the knowledge of the language which must be posited for hearing and for speaking. The model of such a system of rules is a description of competence with no pretence at describing performance.[2] Psychologists, on the other hand, must concern themselves with the behavioral reality of the systems of rules elaborated by linguists, attractive as these may be as theoretical models, and they cannot accept without experimental evidence identity of process in performance for the two aspects of the communication act. As applied linguists we are caught in the middle and for our practical purposes we may be led sorely astray if we accept a theoretical model as a representation of psychological reality without looking for experimental validation.

Many writers have classified the comprehension of speech as decoding, and left it at that. This term is deceptively simple for a process which involves first perceiving that there is a systematic message rather than accidental noise in a continuous stream of sound, then apprehending and identifying within this stream bounded elements (segments) which the listener has never heard in exactly this form before, each segment having a distinctive structure and combining with other segments within a more extensive organized system. As the listener seeks to interpret the message he is hearing, this structuring within and among segments requires that he retain elements he has already apprehended until their relationships with succeeding elements have been established, and that he then engage in a continuous readjustment of his interpretation of each developing structure in view of what has preceded and in anticipation of succeeding segments. The listener is thus engaged in a continuous process of analysis and synthesis, in which factors of attention and memory are vitally involved. Comprehending a message is not merely attending to a stream of sound and establishing some construction at the whim of the listener: there is a highly complex structured system involved which has an existence apart from this particular listener and speaker and which is known to varying degrees of complexity by both. Nor is comprehension the passive reception of an already structured message. Since the speaker and the listener in a communicative act are different persons whose competence in the language is never identical, it is quite possible for the message perceived to be structured differently from that intended by the speaker. With a message in a language which is not the native language of one of the two participants the discrepancy in competence may be considerable and the probability that the message perceived will be identical to the message emitted will be correspondingly reduced. The structure apprehended by the listener in the stream of sound will also be influenced by situational context and by such personal factors as set, fatigue, and emotion. As a result, the message one person finally receives will not correspond precisely to the message another person would have perceived in the same communication sequence. Listening comprehension is an area in which linguistic and psychological factors are inextricably interwoven and as a phenomenon it can never be explained purely from the point of view of the psychologist or of the linguist. Insofar as it is a performance phenomenon it can be investigated empirically as behavior (behavior involving two persons), but such investigation will be peripheral unless it takes into account what the linguist has to say about competence and the organization of the language system.

There is reason to believe that the act of perception is not a purely passive one. It is an act of construction rather than of reception.[3] In continually varying sounds we recognize a phonemic system: combinations of sounds with certain complexes of distinctive features which we have come to accept within a certain band of tolerance as sounds of the particular language to which we think we are listening. Should we anticipate that an utterance will be in a specific language, we will not perceive the same combinations of sounds as we would have perceived if we had been expecting another language, although the sound signal itself will not have changed. As we listen for a particular language we will not be disconcerted by variations in sound sequences which represent the same morphemes because we have internalized a system of morphophonemic rules which enable us to adjust our construction appropriately beneath the level of conscious attention and effort—we are, however, 'hearing' the variants even if these are not made distinctly because this is what learning this language has made us expect.

Beyond this, we perceive in a continuous sound signal units and groups of units which as yet no machine has been able to identify consistently except when utterances have been shaped to conform to certain restrictions which suit its program. These segments are perceived by the listener as belonging to groupings which possess a meaning at a deeper level of analysis because of the categories to which we assign the whole, and often parts, of each segment and because of the interrelationships we perceive among these categories, categorization extending to larger and larger internally structured segments until the ultimate category of the discourse itself is reached. The groupings we perceive form a rhythmic pattern which helps us retain what has been apprehended in earlier groupings long enough to interrelate it with later groupings in such a way as to make the utterance meaningful. When we know a language well, these rhythmic groups seem to form a pattern of rise and fall of the voice in harmony with meaningful content which may itself be a construction of the mind, rather than an uncontestable acoustic fact, as certain recent experiments seem to indicate.[4] Lieberman hypothesizes that it is meaningful content which suggests to us an appropriate learned intonation pattern in some cases so that we perceive what we expected even when the speaker has deviated from what we had anticipated.

We can detect in the process of perceptual construction three stages which should be kept in mind in the designing of teaching materials. The first stage, sometimes called 'sensing', is a stage of rapid impressions, only roughly identified and differentiated and is relatively passive and receptive. At this stage we impose some rudimentary segmentation on what we hear. We are dependent on echoic memory which is very fleeting (it has been estimated to last for a few seconds), so actual items heard are not long retained unless they are interrelated in some meaningful way with other items. The rapid synthesis of impressions which we form is a construction resulting from our familiarity with the phonemic system, the morphophonemic rules, and the broad syntactic categories. As a result, much of what we have actually experienced auditorily does not pass on to the second stage because in our first rapid selection we have rejected as 'noise' elements that did not fit in with our initial construction. These sensory items then pass from echoic memory and can have no further effect on our interpretation.

The second stage is one of identification through segmentation and grouping. We segment and group at various levels as we apply the phonotactic, syntactic, and lexical collocational rules of the language to which we are attending. This identification is not the identification of an input identical with that of previous auditory experiences, since what we are identifying we may never have heard in exactly that form before. It consists of an identification of configurations of attributes which distinguish categories, and then of wider categories of which the already identified categories are the attributes. In this way associations are aroused within the centrally stored information system. This identification process is an active, detailed one which processes the signal it is receiving sequentially, interrelating the segments it has already identified and those it is identifying within the phrase structure of the utterance. At this stage memory is still auditory, but because of the initial grouping in a rhythmic form which is tentatively meaningful, insofar as the phrase structure has as yet been apprehended, the auditory segments (or 'chunks' in G. A. Miller's terminology) are more easily retained.[5] It is because of this greater power of retention that we can suspend judgment where there is ambiguity of structure, holding perceived segments in our mind, ready to make the necessary adjustments as the form of the phrase structure becomes clear.

There is considerable discussion as to whether this process is one of analysis-by-synthesis. It seems difficult to explain the conversion of auditory information, received from outside the nervous system, into cognitive meaning. According to the analysis-by-synthesis hypothesis, as we listen we construct a parallel message within our own cognitive system, according to the organized rules we have internalized, and compare it for match, or fit, with what we are perceiving aurally. This hypothesis seems to tally with our common experience of supplying words when others pause, or of believing we are following with comprehension another person's message when suddenly we are disconcerted by the next element and have to revise our projection of the form of the utterance. The hypothesis is in some ways an attractive one, but as yet a satisfactory model of the process which could operate in real time has not been developed. Further, analysis-by-synthesis cannot explain common substitution errors. If the input on which our matching is based is an acoustic signal, then it should be impossible to 'hear' words which have not been uttered, yet this is a common experience springing from our projection of the probable form of the utterance to which we are attending. It seems plausible, therefore, that we are engaged as we listen in some form of anticipatory projection, with adjustive correction should the utterance not conform with our expectations. This projection is based on our familiarity with the phrase structure, morphology, and lexical collocations of the particular language to which we are listening, as well as the extra-linguistic factors of situation and gesture. The less familiar we are with these elements the more difficult we find it to comprehend and retain what we hear because of our inability to anticipate appropriately. The development of an adequate model of comprehension must, however, await more substantial knowledge of the actual processes involved from the psychological point of view.

Whatever may be the precise nature of the identification process, we would not remember what we had perceived were it not for the third stage, that of rehearsal and recoding of the material, which must take place before what we have perceived enters into long-term storage. (Although this is called here a 'third stage' it must be considered as taking place simultaneously with the ongoing interpretative process.) Rehearsal refers to the recirculating of material through our cognitive system as we relate it to what follows and at times readapt what we have already interpreted in what we have already heard. Without rehearsal the auditory material in the memory would fade very rapidly and we would not be able to follow the line of thought in an utterance or series of utterances. It seems, however, probable that we do not store the material exactly as we first perceived it; rather we recode it in a more easily retainable form. A number of experiments seem to support the hypothesis that long-term storage (after thirty seconds) is in deep structure form:[6] that is, that the material perceived is detransformed and the basic semantic information retained, perhaps with transformational markers which enable the listener to re-capture the original form if necessary. This hypothesis is consistent with common experience: when asked about what we have heard, we tend to give the gist of it, usually in simple active affirmative declarative sentences (which are referred to in the literature as SAAD). Such sentences are closest to base strings to which obligatory transformations only have been applied. It is optional transformations (such processes as passivization, nominalization, and self-embedding) which seem to be dispensed with for storage although the semantic markers of such transformations as affect meaning (e.g., question, negation) are retained in the base. A series of simple kernel-like utterances is more redundant than utter-ances with a number of transformations which combine information and this redundancy aids memory. Recoding for retention must be performed immediately and without conscious attention or the listener misses part of the next grouping while he is rehearsing the recoding of the preceding segments. It is through recoding that the listener clarifies interpretatively relationships between what is being attended to and what has already been assimilated, and this establish-ing of meaningful associations is essential to storage and later recall.

At this point it is interesting to consider Fillmore's proposal that grammatical subject and object are surface features.[7] Real meaning is in the deep structure: not only the semantic contribution of the lexicon, but also the semantic aspect of syntactic relations. It is of interest that in psychological experiments on recall, the logical subject as expressed in an agent *by*-phrase has proved to be a more effective prompt than a nonagent *by*-phrase,[8] which seems to indicate the psychological reality of Fillmore's agentive and to give added support to the notion that information is stored in deep structure form.

The three stages in speech perception which have been described form in practice one complex operation. It is reasonable, however, to presume that the efficiency of the whole process will be increased if listening comprehension materials are so constructed that the student has specific practice in the various types of operations he must perform almost automatically in an integrated series if he is to comprehend speech at a normal speed.

It has sometimes been suggested that students should begin the study of a foreign language by being plunged into a 'bath' of foreign-language speech, that for some time they should listen only until they begin to absorb the language through continual exposure. (This has also been termed the 'sunburn' approach.) In the light of our analysis of the processes of speech perception, this method has little to recommend it. If the segmentation we make in the initial stages is vital, and if ready comprehension is to some extent dependent on our ability to project an anticipated message, then all that the 'sunburn' procedure can do is to familiarize the student to some extent with the general sound aura of the language, not the significant sound patterns, and encourage an attempt at segmentation based on native-language habits. It is our competence in the foreign language which enables us to segment and group meaningfully. Where the student does not as yet possess some degree of competence, he may be able to perform some rudimentary semantic decoding where mime and visual images are introduced to supply clues to meaning, but it is then not clear to what degree the student is merely decoding the visual or kinesthetic signal system. With this prop removed he may remember some precise associations of specific phrases but he will have learned little upon which he can later build a system of decoding.

It is hardly a great step forward, however, to suggest that listening comprehension will grow as competence in the language is established. We can do better than that.

The first stage of speech perception is one of rapid, fleeting impressions, crudely segmented before the echo of the stimulus has disappeared from the memory. The initial selection is vital and normally related to syntactic groupings. (Where the structure is complicated the listener may resort momentarily to the less certain ground of purely semantic decoding, which in its simplest form is based on the order of semantic elements and their probable relationships.) We can help the student at this stage by ensuring the prolongation of the auditory image.

In the early stages students should be encouraged to repeat to themselves the segments they have apprehended, first as stretches of sound, then in an attempt at syntactic grouping. The very effort of repetition forces the student to segment the stream of sound in some fashion, the auditory image is longer retained, and the student has time to relate segments and to readjust his developing interpretation. Experiments at Harvard have shown that speech can be speeded up within segments and still be comprehensible so long as the pause between segments which is essential for cognitive processing, is slightly lengthened, so that the actual rate of presentation is not increased.[9] The student should be trained to use the pause for conscious processing, until early segmentation has become automatic. Early listening comprehension materials should, then, be kept within the limits of structural patterns being learned, so that rapid identification of syntactic groupings is possible. Once the student has made an incorrect segmentation, he has lost the sound image and further adjustments must be made by conjecture and inference. Training in listening comprehension by parallel production is more than mere imitation: it forces concentration on segmentation as well as providing guided practice in the production of well-formed segments, thus integrating with listening comprehension an operation which is basic to creative speech production as well.

At the next stage, the student must identify more precisely and interrelate the segments he is holding in his short-term memory. Unless he is able to interrelate these meaningfully into larger groupings he will lose what he has so far retained. This is where the student will gain from systematic training from the beginning in the recognition of structural features. If he is ever to reach an advanced stage of listening comprehension where he can enjoy and later discuss all kinds of materials, he will need to be adept at rapid recognition of many indicators of structure. He must be able to categorize words and word groupings (in the practical sense of recognizing their function). He must be able to recognize rapidly sentence shape by identification of clues to question form, negation, coordination, subordination. He must recognize clues which indicate condition, purpose, temporal relationships. Such features are frequently signalled by initial words which should be apprehended immediately so that the mind can concentrate on less clearly marked syntactic relationships. He must be able to recognize rapidly signals such as prepositions, articles, and auxiliaries which help him discern constituents of phrase structure, and he must identify immediately—in order to discard them—prop words and hesitation words which add nothing to meaning but take up precious storage space (e.g., "vous voyez," "d'ailleurs," "effectivement;" "kind of," "you know," "I think"). Students should have frequent practice in repeating as units in meaningful contexts word groups of high frequency which contrast with those of their own language, and further practice in detecting these in listening materials. Exercises can be designed especially for practice in apprehending and matching orally certain types of structure (e.g., left-branching, right-branching, or nested constructions). Progressively developed these can be amusing exercises for laboratory practice. Once the student has been trained to listen purposefully and can identify readily the various clues to syntactic interrelationships which have been listed, his mind and memory will be free to concentrate on the lexical content of the message, using what he knows of reality to supply meaning when his knowledge of the foreign lexicon fails him.

Next there is recoding for retention. Here we may gain some ideas for teaching materials from the suggestion that information perceived aurally is detransformed for storage and is mostly recalled in simple active affirmative declarative sentences. We can aid the automatization of this process by giving students direct practice in such recoding. It is surface structure in the foreign language which is troublesome to the student because it is here that languages are differentiated and contrast. The student needs practice in detecting the main relationships (in Fillmore's terms the agentive, objective, instrumental, locative, among others); he needs training in abstracting these from the complications of the surface form and reducing the relationship extracted to a more basic form of expression: in other words he needs practice in giving the gist of what he hears in simple form. This he can then store, leaving his mind free to concentrate on incoming information. Exercises should be developed which force recognition of such deep structure relationships by using as prompt words for recall those which correspond to the agent, instrument, or objective. It is the deep structure relationships which constitute language universals and in the recognition of these relationships the student is able to draw on his cognitive abilities beneath the level of surface structure complications. Students should also be given exercises in which they are presented first with the essence of what they are to hear in basic, kernel-like sentences and are then required to listen to the same substance in more complicated form with numerous transformations. Students who are not trained to decode and recode in the foreign language will inevitably develop the habit of automatically converting what they hear into a simplified form in the native language, thus wasting much valuable time and energy in translation and retranslation and never developing speed and ease in direct comprehension.

One of the perennial problems in modern language teaching has been the development of fluent direct reading. Students have been trained to read fluently recombinations of foreign-language speech they have learned, and even carefully graded readers kept within specified limits of known vocabulary and structure, but when they are finally allowed to read less controlled materials it becomes apparent that they have not developed a technique for extracting meaning directly from the foreign-language text. Many fall back into mere translation; others adopt a predominantly semantic strategy, seizing on lexical elements they recognize here and there and constructing some garbled version which shows they have not understood the basic structuring of the meaning. Research into the act of reading for meaning has shown that the processes involved parallel those of listening comprehension: first, there is recognition in a fast impressionistic way of segments which for comprehension must be identified as meaningful segments of phrase structure; there is the necessity to interrelate these according to basic relationships, holding one segment in the mind and suspending judgment until other segments are identified and combined with it in a meaningful way.

There is the same need for rapid recognition of categories, of sentence shapes, of markers, of constituents of phrase structure and for penetrating beneath surface complications to basic relationships. In view of this similarity of processes, the teaching of fluent reading could be considerably facilitated by combining it with a program of training in listening comprehension. The effort at rapid segmentation (the identification of the essential relationships of the underlying phrase structure), the holding of chunks in the memory while awaiting confirmation of anticipations (that is, while waiting to see that the projected sentence is congruent with the actual sentence), the extracting of the gist (that is, the reduction to deep structure): all of these operations must be performed again in relation to the graphic medium. When the student is being trained in these specific operations for listening comprehension he should be made to realize their applicability to the other medium by being encouraged to read rapidly material based on the same content as what he has heard, and at other times to listen to oral presentations based on similar content to what he has read. The reading should not be done aloud, however, since hearing himself read and concentrating on how he is reading hinder the student in his rapid identification of the graphic symbol.[10]

Similar exercises to those outlined for listening comprehension should be developed for reading comprehension:

reading the gist in simple active affirmative declarative sentences before reading a highly transformed version, practice in recounting in detransformed form what has been read, practice in detecting the deep structure relationships beneath the surface forms, rapid identification of cue words to structure and sentence shape. This is another whole area of concern and must be set aside for another time. All good teaching, however, is teaching for transfer (or, as in this case, transposition), and teaching of listening comprehension should be no exception.

# FOOTNOTES

[1] I. M. Schlesinger, *Sentence Structure and the Reading Process* (The Hague: Mouton, 1968), Chapter 6.

[2] Noam Chomsky, *Aspects of the Theory of Syntax* (Cambridge: MIT Press, 1965). "To avoid what has been a continuing misunderstanding, it is perhaps worth while to reiterate that a generative grammar is not a model for a speaker or a hearer. It attempts to characterize in the most neutral possible terms the knowledge of the language that provides the basis for actual use of language by a speaker-hearer. When we speak of a grammar as generating a sentence with a certain structural description, we mean simply that the grammar assigns this structural description to the sentence. When we say that a sentence has a certain derivation with respect to a particular generative grammar, we say nothing about how the speaker or hearer might proceed, in some practical or efficient way, to construct such a derivation" (p. 9).

[3] For a full discussion with supporting experiments, see U. Neisser, *Cognitive Psychology* (New York: Appleton-Century-Crofts, 1967), Chapter 7.

[4] P. Lieberman, "On the Acoustic Basis of the Perception of Intonation by Linguists," *Word*, 21 (1965):40-54.

[5] G. A. Miller, "The Magical Number Seven, Plus or Minus Two," *Psychological Review*, 63 (1956):81-97.

[6] J. Fodor and M. Garrett, "Some Reflections on Competence and Performance" in J. Lyons and R. J. Wales, eds., *Psycholinguistics Papers: Proceedings of the 1966 Edinburgh Conference* (Edinburgh: Edinburgh University Press, 1966) pp. 148-51.

[7] C. J. Fillmore, "Toward a Modern Theory of Case" in David A. Reibel and Sanford A. Schane, eds., *Modern Studies in English—Readings in Transformational Grammar* (Englewood Cliffs, N. J.: Prentice-Hall, 1969), pp. 361-75.

[8]A.L. Blumenthal (1965), as described in R. J. Wales and J. C. Marshall, "Linguistic Performance," in Lyons and Wales, pp. 70-71.

[9]Harvard Center for Cognitive Studies: *Sixth Annual Report 1965-66*, p. 18; *Seventh Annual Report 1966-67*, pp. 30-31.

[10]Ibid., *Seventh Annual Report*, p. 32.

# 11

# FOREIGN LANGUAGES IN A TIME OF CHANGE*

Recently, I have been reading a very interesting booklet—the student evaluation booklet of a very well-known university—and I read some very provocative things in it. As teachers we have been deploring the dropping of the foreign-language requirement in many universities, but what does the student say?

"As a foreign language requirement this course contains all the necessary grammar and vocabulary except for words of frustration, hostility, and anger. A good dictionary will fill in those educational gaps."

"(This course) ruins most students' averages, it ruins their morale, it ruins their social life by staying in and studying so much, and it really ruins any desire that any would have to learn a foreign language."

As teachers we are bewildered by these reactions to our carefully structured, well designed, pedagogically sound programs. One student writes: "I sincerely urge you . . . . to quit treating students as infants with your highly structured, foolproof, unemotional (sequence)." So virtues become vices.

---

*Address given at the School-University Foreign Language Articulation Conference at the University of Illinois at Urbana, October 28, 1971.

Yet we felt we were responding to the spirit of the times. Our students wanted emphasis on speaking rather than reading: didn't we give them that? No more silent classrooms: everyone could participate actively for thirty minutes out of thirty minutes. We provided them with the opportunity to work on their own with a "personal tutor" in the language laboratory. We gave them contemporary reading materials when they reached that stage. *What has happened to our students?* Where have we gone wrong? Does the fault lie with ourselves and our programs?

The title of this article is: "Foreign Languages in a *Time of Change.*" We may well ask: isn't every period a time of change? It has become a truism to say: Yes, but ours is a period of *rapid change*.

We have all heard of *culture shock*: it is the experience a person has in a foreign culture when suddenly all the familiar psychological cues that help him function in his own society are changed. In his new situation he has to ask himself how he should act and react to others, how he should time his actions, what is the correct social behavior. Why, he wonders, do these people seem indifferent to things which seem to him to be so important, even matters of principle. Everything in this new society is so strange and incomprehensible that he is disoriented and disturbed. In a recent book Alvin Toffler speaks of "future shock." "Future shock," he says, "is a time phenomenon, a product of the greatly accelerated rate of change in society. It arises from the superimposition of a new culture on an old one. It is culture shock in one's own society, but its impact is far worse."[1] He sees society at present as suffering from confusional breakdown.[2] *We* are caught in it; *our students* are caught in it: in a revolution in societal patterns, institutions, and values where familiar cues no longer provide a sufficient guide.

For us this is intensely confusing; for our students it is carrying them away from us fast in a developing pattern of new attitudes and values. Attitudinal changes which gradually evolved over a generation may now be effected within a decade. Unless we realize this and seek to understand these new attitudes and values the dislocation of our educational efforts will grow worse despite our well-meaning, even decisive, actions.

Many of us knew depression and war. We had to rebuild. We had to work hard, to delay gratification until we had achieved intermediate goals, to submit ourselves to years of discipline to attain the affluence we have today. *This generation is born with it and bored with it.* This generation is the first in history that has a prolonged and leisured youth (as distinct from adolescence) with opportunities for intellectual, emotional, and moral development without the demands of societal responsibilities.[3] As the sociologists keep telling us, our young people are entering a post-industrial society in which many of the careers for which our generation had to prepare themselves with such assiduity will not exist (or will not exist in the forms in which we know them) when our students emerge from their prolonged youth to take their place in the larger society. To this generation, learning something to pass an examination as a passkey to career opportunities is meaningless. With "open admissions" we cannot even use acceptance into a college as a goad.

As Toffler has put it: "The technology of tomorrow requires not millions of lightly lettered men, ready to work in unison at endlessly repetitious jobs, it requires not men who take orders in unblinking fashion, aware that the price of bread is mechanical submission to authority, but men who can make critical judgments, who can weave their way through moral environments, who are quick to spot new relationships in the rapidly changing reality."[4] If as Postman and Weingartner have pointed out "a classroom is an environment and . . . . the way it is organized carries the burden of what people will learn from it,"[5] many foreign-language classrooms have been preparing students excellently for the demands of industrial as opposed to post-industrial society. Haven't we been teaching students to work in unison at endlessly repetitious tasks, and to take orders in unblinking fashion, with mechanical submission to authority?

The new society requires—

—men who can make critical judgments;

—who can weave their way through moral environments;
—who are quick to spot new relationships in the
  rapidly changing reality.

Where does foreign-language study fit into this new educational picture?

For Toffler it has no place at all. It is the first thing he eliminates. In his chapter, "Education in the Future Tense" we read: "Tens of millions of children today are forced by law to spend precious hours of their lives grinding away at material whose future utility is highly questionable. (Nobody even claims it has much present utility.) Should they spend as much time as they do learning French, or Spanish or German?"[6] Later he says:

> "Anyone who thinks the present curriculum makes sense is invited to explain to an intelligent fourteen-year-old why algebra or French or any other subject is essential for him. Adult answers are almost always evasive. The reason is simple: the present curriculum is a mindless holdover from the past."[7]

The attack is widespread. Toffler is only one voice. As foreign-language teachers we cannot put our heads in the sand. *Do we have an answer?* It cannot be a glib one; it must come from a careful study of the situation we are in.

Let us look, then, for further information. If our youth is passing through a revolution, what are the trends of this revolution? Here I would like to take up four illuminating observations of Professor Kenneth Keniston of the Department of Psychology at Yale. In an article: "You Have to Grow Up in Scarsdale to Know How Bad Things Really Are," he points to four trends in the thinking of our youth.[8] They are as follows:

> 1. A revulsion against the notion of quantity, particularly economic quantity and materialism, and a turn toward concepts of quality. (Keniston reminds us of the slogan of the French student revolt in 1968: "Long live the passionate revolution of creative intelligence.") This brings an emphasis on quality of experience, on the expressive, the aesthetic, the creative, the imaginative, even the fantastic.

2. A revolt against uniformity, equalization, standardization, and homogenization (against the "technologization of man") with the demand that individuals be appreciated not despite their differences but because they are different, diverse, unique, and noninterchangeable.

3. A continuing struggle against psychological or institutional closure or rigidity in any form, even the rigidity of a definite adult role, and the extolling of the virtues of openness, motion, and continuing human development. (Here we may think of the present resistance to requirements—any requirements.)

4. A revolt against centralized power and the complementary demand for participation. It is in this sense that students are demanding "relevance" in their educational program: a chance for the student to participate in his own educational experience in a way that involves all of his faculties, emotional and moral as well as intellectual.

Our highly structured system worked with another generation in another era. How can we meet the demands for quality of experience, for appreciation of difference, for openness and participation, while preparing people who can make critical judgments and face new relationships and new attitudes, even moral ones, without reactions of shocked withdrawal?

I think as foreign-language teachers we can, and I believe, moreover, that we should cease apologizing for our subject and trying to slip it in without people noticing, under the protective cloak of institutional requirements. *We do have something to contribute to the whole education of adolescence and youth*, but not by merely continuing to do as we have always done.

What do we need, then? Newer, more scientific methods that some guru is going to present to us in a neat package? It is certainly not new methods we need, but a new attitude: one that is less harassed and less pressure-bound by an earnest desire to teach more and more material. We need an attitude which allows the student to learn, that waits for the student to learn, that allows the student choices in what he shall learn.

In our earnestness, in our anxiety to do the best academically by our students, in the educational lag in our thinking which has carried over from the days when we had in our classrooms an elite, a chosen few, who pursued the esoteric study of a foreign tongue, we have structured and shaped learning experiences which have become homogenized and inflexible and have gradually eliminated (sometimes not so gradually) all but the fittest—those who seemed to us to fit best into the pattern of our often stereotyped advanced courses.

Now our students reject rigidity and structure, quantity of learning, and imposed experience. No wonder there is tension and often abrasive tension. In our concentration on how students learn a foreign language, we have forgotten *how students learn*. To quote Earl Stevick of the Foreign Service Institute: "We must no longer look at (the learner) only as 'linguistic man'—man regarded only as a potential internalizer and producer of alien sounds, words and patterns. Any language student is an entire social being."9

What have we, as foreign-language teachers, to contribute to our student's quality of life, to his development of critical and moral judgment, to his ability to adapt and readapt to changing attitudes and circumstances?

I think we are ideally suited to share in this function. Isn't ours the only subject which rudely thrusts the student into inevitable contact with other modes of thought and expression and forces him to think more critically about his own, and which also gives him vicarious experience in confronting and adapting to new ideas and attitudes? This is true only if we teach the foreign language with such an end in view, not, of course, if our sole aim is the drilling of irregular verbs and the mastery of the use of accents.

As I have said elsewhere in this regard:10

"The . . . . contribution of foreign-language study that is truly educational, in the sense that it expands the student's personal experience of his environment, and truly humanistic in that it adds a new dimension to his thinking is the opportunity it provides for breaking through monolingual and monocultural bonds. Such an experience reveals to the student that there are other ways of saying things, other values and attitudes than those to which his native language and culture have habituated him. Through this process he may develop new attitudes to ideas and peoples that will reduce his bondage to the familiar and the local while increasing his sympathy for persons of other cultures and languages. The new-generation student in our schools is internationalist and interculturalist in his aspirations; he is also brutally direct in demanding the rationale of what we are doing and what we are asking him to do. This basic contribution which foreign language can make to his development is one which he would welcome, but he must see that what we do in our classrooms really achieves such a purpose or he will drop out as soon as he conveniently may. If, as Harold Taylor has said: "The first task of education . . . . is to raise the level of awareness and response to *all* ideas, events, people, and objects,"[11] then foreign language taught with this end firmly in view can still claim that it has has a rightful place in the overall educational program of the school."

All this is very idealistic. What is the reality? Why do we find it so difficult to demonstrate this type of teaching in actuality?

Here we may listen to another student voice:

"Most people forget what they learned so soon after they've finished that even those who someday make it to Europe or South America can't use it. Besides, in this electronic age, the ideal of a multilingual Renaissance man is pitifully camp. You can travel farther and learn more about 'other cultures' on acid than on a world tour."

and again:

"too many books, too much stress on grammar, too little emphasis on their culture."

Are these complaints rather about the content than about the subject itself?

Perhaps we have been unable to get away in our thinking from the ideal, which comes from the days of selective high schools and privileged undergraduates, that all foreign-language students should be expected to attain near-native mastery of the language in all skills: an ideal which is impossible in the time available to us in most situations (and here I am not thinking of courses for foreign-language majors). We aim at near-native mastery for all and design our courses accordingly, then we leave up to eighty per cent of the students somewhere along the way, sometimes not very far. When they realize how little they know and how little they can use it, they become frustrated and hostile, and they grow into parents and community leaders opposed to such an experience for their children. How familiar this is to all of us! Can we realistically claim that *all* students need to attain this kind of language mastery?

We must decide what it is that we want every student to carry away even from one year's experience of foreign-language study. If it is a change in attitude and in his attitude to his own language and to language and communication as such—then we must design our program so that such an outcome is really achieved and evident. I submit that we have been giving too much thought to the formal structure of our programs while retaining the same old content: individualized instruction, computer-assisted instruction, writing behavioral objectives, systems approaches, or what you will, are still tailored to the present and future tense in Level One, the past and conditional tense in Level Two, the awesome subjunctive in Level Three.

At this point let me insert a warning. We cannot shift gears and move from an emphasis on skill-learning to the changing of attitudes without knowing something about the whole question of the effect of prior attitudes on the learning of controversial material; otherwise we may very well reinforce prejudices. We know that controversial material which fits in with our existing evaluative framework is readily retained whereas we tend to retain implausible material from the other side. In fact in their initial selection for retention from what we give them our students may misunderstand, distort, discount, or even reverse, in accordance with their own biases, the implications of what they are hearing, seeing, or reading.[12] Then if we limit ourselves to facts about a particular culture, these are very perishable, as we well know, and we may unwittingly be increasing the possibility of culture shock for our students when they encounter the realities, rather then helping them to understand what they see or hear. The attitude of the teacher who is dazzled and can see no wrong in the foreign culture can arouse rigidity and hostility. What we are out to develop is an openness to new ideas and new ways of expression and a tolerance of difference. We must learn how to achieve this.

What about the high percentage of our students (seventy or eighty percent in many cases) who will never be with us long enough to achieve mastery? Should we be honest and say we cannot give them anything which is worthwhile in the year or two they are with us? Or can we take a look at our programs and restructure them?

Here I am going to propose that whatever our situation: college, high school, junior high school, elementary school— wherever foreign-language study is begun—we design a two-stage program.

Stage One would be designed as terminal, designed so that whoever passed through it would have gained something of educational and humanistic value, even if he never studied a foreign language again in his lifetime. This would also be the stage for creating interest and enthusiasm in some, who would then wish to go on to Stage Two because they really wanted to master the language. Stage One would then be an end in itself and not merely the elementary stage of Stage Two, and certainly not *pre-* anything.

*What would we aim for in Stage One?* At the moment, I would say four things.

*First: An introduction to language itself through a specific foreign language*, gearing our study to the way language operations express meanings and the many ways meanings can be encoded; the way our language expresses our way of looking at things and the way another language expresses another people's way of looking at things. This study would be frankly contrastive.

For many years we have professed to be teaching our students to understand how language operates and to understand the operation of their own language better through the study of a foreign language. Most of this protestation has been lip-service. Are we really going to work out how to do this interestingly and significantly?

*Second: an introduction to another people through language*: the way another people thinks, feels, values, and acts in contradistinction to our own preoccupations, attitudes, and reactions. (This I have already written about at some length.)

*Third: An experience of being another people*, communicating as they do, acting as they do, relating as they do. Here our students learn the language and live the language. Language knowledge acquired is immediately acted out. Rules internalized become channels of communication. Practice in production is immediately incorporated into some form of authentic interaction.

*Fourth: An experience of communicating with another people*: speaking with them (where possible), writing to them, working and playing with them where a neighboring community makes this possible, sharing with them in joint or exchange projects (Here I would call your attention to a recent article of Dwight Bolinger of Harvard: "Let's Change Our Base of Operations" in the *Modern Language Journal* 25 (1971): 148-156.)

Methodologically we would aim at involvement of all students in planning, in group research and interaction, in interdisciplinary exploration, in human contacts in nearby communities or through correspondence.

Such a course would not be a waste of time for those who wished to master the language. It would foster attitudes which would carry them through the long, and often tedious, stages of disciplined language study. Our Stage Two students would not be a conscripted, but a self-selected, clientele with considerable experience in the area and an autonomous desire to do what they were doing.

I can already hear the old objections: Isn't this lowering standards? How are we going to test these courses across the board so as to satisfy administrators and parents? (For too long we have allowed the latter problem to hamstring our endeavors at realistic change.) There need be no "lowering of standards." Since the objectives will be different, we will expect different outcomes, a different type of achievement, and we will design different tests to conform with our objectives. We will expect to test, for instance, for certain understandings, for certain attitudes, for a new freedom we hope our students will have achieved. Such a test may very well mean no test at all in the conventional sense of the word. The present approach arouses hostility and frustration in many. Isn't it time, then, to consider new structures and a new content more congruent with the thinking and aspirations of the present generation of students?

Obviously such an approach will involve careful planning and preparing of materials, with perhaps pilot projects to work out the best way of proceeding. The present situation requires some intensive original thinking. As a profession, I believe we are capable of carrying such a project through.

I cannot dwell here on Stage Two which will be more akin to the language-learning situation to which we are accustomed. We would, however, now have a better motivated and a better prepared group, both from the point of view of linguistic awareness and cultural comprehension, a group which had chosen to study the language with the acknowledged purpose of seeking a high degree of mastery. What more could we ask for? Here I could say much about our need to shift gears too if we wish to conserve this group through the necessarily laborious period of developing comfortable competence of operation in the foreign tongue.

But let us not just talk or listen. Let us get down to some hard study and planning for the implementation of such a program.

## FOOTNOTES

[1] Alvin Toffler, *Future Shock* (New York: Bantam Books, 1970), p. 11.

[2] Toffler, p. 343.

[3] This view is put forward by Kenneth Keniston, Department of Psychology, Yale University, in "You Have to Grow Up in Scarsdale to Know How Bad Things Really Are," *New York Times Magazine*, April 27, 1969, reprinted in *The University Crisis Reader*, vol. 2; *Confrontation and Counterattack*, eds. I. Wallerstein and P. Starr, (New York: Random House, 1971), pp. 453-68.

[4] Toffler, p. 402.

[5] N. Postman and C. Weingartner, *Teaching as a Subversive Activity* (New York: Delacorte, 1969), p. 18.

[6] Toffler, pp. 409-10.

[7] Toffler, p. 410.

[8]Keniston, pp. 464-65.

[9]E. Stevick, *Adapting and Writing Language Lessons* (Washington, D. C.: Department of State, 1971), p. 14.

[10]"Teacher-Student Relations: Coercion or Cooperation," Chapter 15 in this book.

[11]Quoted by A. E. Lean in *And Merely Teach* (Carbondale: Southern Illinois University Press, 1968), p. 58.

[12]D. Ausubel, *Educational Psychology: A Cognitive View* (New York: Holt, Rinehart and Winston, 1968), p. 390.

# Fʀᴏᴍ ᴛʜᴇ Pʏʀᴀᴍɪᴅ ᴛᴏ ᴛʜᴇ Cᴏᴍᴍᴜɴᴇ:
## THE EVOLUTION
## OF THE FOREIGN-LANGUAGE DEPARTMENT*

The great monolith of the foreign-language department is splitting and cracking. Its foundation is disintegrating and falling away, or so it seems, and the effect is being felt right to the apex. Our beautiful aesthetically proportioned pyramid is threatened. Of course many of us haven't given too much thought to its lower structures for some time. We had our graduate students: our future professors with such fine minds (were there any others?). There were, of course, our majors, whom we regarded as potential graduate students, and then that lesser breed, the future secondary teachers who helped us pay our way. Were there a few minors? They obviously could not be serious or they would be majors. And that vast anonymous mass at the base in the service courses? Like the poor, they were always with us, for after all without the working poor how could an elite cultured class give its full attention to intellectual and aesthetic matters?

Paralleling this hierarchy of students we had our own inner core. At the apex were the senior professors, the scholars, concerned only with the elitist graduate student, preferably in thesis advisement on a one-to-one basis: the

---

*A paper presented at the Annual Meeting of the Association of Departments of Foreign Languages, Chicago, Illinois, December 26, 1971. Originally published in the *ADFL Bulletin* 3(1972): 13-17.

established scholar engaged with the most brilliant of the incipient scholars. Next came the aspiring younger faculty, the scholars of promise, interested only in the majors, and of these preferably the few destined for graduate study. Somewhat lower were our less scholarly, practical colleagues teaching teachers how and what to teach, and at the base the graduate assistants doing their time, poor souls, with the required courses, as we've all had to do in our day. No wonder there is alarm and consternation at the threat to the base: we cherish our antique monument as it is, because it memorializes in concrete form the glories of a past age.

Perhaps we need a new image for ourselves and for others. Instead of our well-proportioned pyramid, orderly and coherent, where each section fits into its place supporting the whole in anonymity and impersonality, we need a real community: a community of scholars, of learners at every level, in keeping with the true meaning of the word "scholar." I suggest that we renounce our historical monument and that we become a commune—an untidy, nonhierarchical, interacting, interdependent, evolving commune. And what shall we have in our commune? Plurality and diversification in unity, innovation and interaction in mutual tolerance and acceptance. In this way, if we are sincere in our conversion, we can provide for all types of students the truly humanistic experience which our discipline offers. We must renounce the idea that foreign-language study has a utilitarian value (although it may have for a few) and concentrate on developing people: interesting people who have read and experienced beyond the limitations of their own language and their own culture, flexible people able to react with equanimity to new ideas and ideals and to see them in perspective because of their wider experience in another culture and in another age. In this way what we have to offer can be of value to all who come to us no matter how short their stay and no matter what their future role.

Idealistic? Maybe. A little whimsicality will help us to take ourselves less seriously, and to worry less intensely, in this period of rapid change which is affecting, whether we will or not, our institutional role and our clientele. The new image I propose is not as fanciful as it may seem but its implications cannot be realized overnight. The establishment of our commune is not merely a question of breaking down caste and challenging authority structures. Of the latter there will always be some. Even in a commune natural leadership patterns evolve as events and necessity sort out the decision makers from the followers. The significant change must be in our attitudes within the community: in the development of a new acceptance of difference and a new appreciation of diversity of gifts and interests.

How, then, does our commune differ from our pyramid? First the monolith disappears—that monolith where each step is preliminary to the next and each leads on inevitably to the apex. Stop at one step and where are you? Nowhere in particular—merely somewhere on the way. Within the commune there is a plurality of tasks and achievements, each one a worthwhile accomplishment in itself. People come and people go; some stay, some leave, some return. Whenever they are within the commune they are fully participating members—they belong, they count, they are respected—for every contribution of effort and interest helps to create and maintain the commune. He who leaves takes away with him a complete experience, perhaps shorter and less intense than if he had stayed, but in any event not a partial experience that is merely anticipatory and unsatisfying in its incompleteness.

So much for our metaphors. Let us express them rather in terms of courses and student-teacher interaction to make them comprehensible and practical. We need courses at every level which provide for a diversity of interests and time-objectives, courses which have satisfying content in themselves and are not merely preliminary to some future experience. In this sense a fair proportion of our courses can be designed as "terminal," so that the student who completes the course but goes no further can take away with him a full and enriching experience, while the student who continues will find his later experiences facilitated and illuminated by what went before. The secret is in the approach we take when planning our courses. As we are forced to compete for student interest in an open market we will need more and more to conceive and plan our courses imaginatively and realistically with the interests of a diversity of students in mind. We can no longer afford to regard our lower level courses, for instance, as "elementary" and "intermediate" (the very words enshrine a preparatory concept). Thinking of them as preliminary courses we try to include in them all the grammar we think our future majors should know until our students gag with revulsion. We often withhold till the fourth semester any material that is intellectually stimulating and then provide snippets from various centuries, surely worthy when seen in their literary context but utterly boring to the naive literary student.

Does a terminal course, in my sense of the term, necessarily have to be a "review of the grammar," ensuring that the short-term student takes away a thorough picture of the workings of the subjunctive and the intricacies of the pronominal system? Is this what he will quote with pleasure when looking back on his undergraduate days? Surely we can provide a choice for our students: a preparatory diet for those who intend to continue and are willing to prolong an arduous apprenticeship for the promise of future mastery, and, paralleling this, a stimulating and provocative offering for those who will leave us at the end of the semester. When are we going to do some serious research into the amount of grammar a person really needs to know actively in order to comprehend, and the amount of concentrated learning required for him to be able to recognize the rest when he needs it in the context of interesting material? Recent psychological research in reading and listening shows that there is a significant heuristic element at work in comprehension. Shouldn't we set some of our best graduate students to finding out which aspects of language structure must be thoroughly assimilated and which can be deduced from our knowledge of setting and semantic associations (particularly in languages with a large commonality of outlook and cultural context)? Once we have substantial research evidence in this area we may find we can reduce considerably the grammar content in terminal courses and use our time, and our students' time, for the type of confrontation with ideas and attitudes which we recognize as one of the major educational contributions we can make to undergraduate education.

A language is a vehicle. What about content? Are all students, or even most, at the lower levels interested in learning the language in order to read the literature? For those who are we bring the literature to them, carefully selected in theme and development to interest and stimulate them intellectually, while still linguistically within their capacity of comprehension. Some, let us face it, are interested rather in current affairs and the preoccupations of their contemporaries in the other culture. For these why not use the newspapers and magazines of the day as the major course content? The interpretation of such contemporary documents will certainly challenge our understanding of present-day life and institutions and their roots in earlier periods. Some students are fascinated by the clash of attitudes, values, and behavior patterns between cultures: if so, we can provide opportunities for them to see the other culture and their own through foreign eyes—often a startling experience. Is it drama and film they seek? These we can provide. Should they wish to learn only to communicate, to comprehend and be comprehended, it should not be such a struggle for us to eliminate from our courses the written exercises they no longer need. If they wish only to read but not to discuss in the foreign language, surely this too is a legitimate interest. For far too long we have allowed a commendable obsession with fairness in grading to preoccupy us so that in order to ensure that all are rewarded alike we serve for all an identical, often insipid and tasteless diet which few enjoy.

For a plurality of student needs we must provide a plurality of content. But why not also a plurality of approaches? Once again with the best of intentions we have insisted that all be taught alike despite the differences in their learning patterns and the equally important differences in the natural instructional styles of their instructors. Here again uniformity has led us to colorlessness and lack of spontaneity. A little less scrupulous identity of treatment may lead to some unevenness in the offering, but it can also liberate the natural talents of young instructors and the potential exuberance of the instructed. At this stage of vigorous rethinking of our programs we do not need a voice *ex cathedra* to tell us what is the new pattern to which we must conform, thus establishing a new orthodoxy of the hetero- dox. We need the excitement of experimentation within our own institutions, a healthy enthusiasm for one's own brainchild, that child who flourishes despite the pessimism of those who do not recognize its hidden vitality. We need many flowers blooming, daylilies perhaps, but each in its day and hour bringing fragrance to the experience of some. Excellent teaching has always been uneven in its distribution, depend- ing as it does on the presence or absence of gifted individuals who stand out in the memory of the instructed.

I have talked at some length about the transients. Let us consider now those who will stay in the commune and draw from it a major part of their undergraduate experience. I cannot deal here with all aspects of the undergraduate program although there is much one could say about each. Let me keep to one or two facets which are particularly close to my own interests and in serious need of development. Here I shall begin with the language program for majors and minors. It is not enough to say, ostrich-like, "Send them abroad for a year," thus saving ourselves the taxing effort of seeking solutions for some of the toughest problems with which we have to deal. The year abroad undoubtedly helps but not all can participate and in our commune the interests of all are our concern. Let us face the fact that the improvement of language skills at the so-called "advanced" level is one of the most difficult of our tasks and yet it is the area toward which the least research and inquiry have been directed.

First we must meet the student where he is. Students complain about the gap between their intermediate course (or their high school experience) and the advanced courses. How do we explain this gap? It is very real to instructors and students alike. Two folk-explanations are prevalent: "nobody has taught them anything in their earlier courses" and "the students are a feckless lot; if they really cared they wouldn't keep on making the same mistakes." If the same situation persists from year to year with successive groups of students and we know the most energetic language teaching is going into the earlier courses, perhaps the time has come to look more critically at ourselves and our courses at this level. Most of the instructors, being trained in literary scholarship, want to teach literature primarily so they proclaim loudly that they are not there to teach the language. The students, they say, should know the language already. In their anxiety to protect themselves from such an unwelcome task they conveniently forget the many years it took them to perfect their own knowledge of the language (and this applies to the native speakers among them too) and the pitifully short language programs still prevalent in this country.

Because extra language work is, however, a clear necessity, we set up some language courses and farm these out as perennial chores for less influential or more accommodating members of the department. Anyone can do it, so sometimes the task is undertaken by a young literary scholar who wants a semester with little preparation so that he can write up that article from his thesis. Few materials are available at this level so the same old book does the job. Since very few are really interested in the design of the courses the language is chopped up into unnatural and unpalatable segments—a unit of diction this semester (such terrible pronunciation!), a unit of syntax next semester, not forgetting a unit or two of composition (no one has taught them to write decently in the language, and they'll need this skill for their literary papers). Finally, we allot four hours, or even eight hours, to intensive conversation (the hardest of all to teach but fobbed off most frequently·on untrained and often completely inexperienced native speakers who proceed to do all the talking for want of familiarity with techniques for eliciting speech).

Have we ever stopped to consider seriously whether language can be learned effectively in this piecemeal fashion? To learn language well one has to enjoy learning it so that one is eager to know how to express oneself more correctly or more elegantly. The many snippets of knowledge the student needs are assimilated into his functioning system only after conscious and alert attention is directed to them. Sometimes in language departments we seem to have a puritanical fear of students enjoying what is good for them.

A typical student comment quoted from the course evaluation booklet of my own institution will arouse acquiescence from many unenthusiastic instructors shanghaied into language teaching: "No matter what the language, grammar reviews are all the same: distasteful but good for you, sort of the cod liver oil of language courses."[1] What we need to consider is: can syntax be learned efficiently apart from conversation, composition, and diction? Syntax taught in isolation is a linguistics rather than a language course, an important course to be sure but requiring a different content from that served up in the usual "syntax course." Sometimes the syntax course takes the form of a rather simplistic course in translation, where students translate short, detached sentences containing specific "points of grammar." This is not conceived, however, as a serious course in translation where the student will study the nonmatching nature of surface structures and of syntactic representations of semantic substance. A genuine translation course would train the student to extract the thought content from stretches of English discourse and reexpress this in the formal structures of another language. Here we would be teaching a specialized craft which can become a passion. Such a course is a long way from our little artificially constructed translation sentences which are doing violation to language as a living, functioning entity. Living language involves at once all of the aspects we are now teaching separately, with the addition of the converse element of perception.

We need, then, apprenticeship classes where living language is taught as a whole, where the seamless garment is despotted, stretched a little here, shrunk a little there, and worn spots are invisibly mended, but where the fabric is preserved in its integrity. In such courses syntax is considered as it is needed, diction as it is needed, semantic structure, communicative competence as they are needed, but all within the context of purposeful activity, because only then does the language come alive. Instead of talking desperately about something or other for four, five, eight hours a week in a

---

[1]*The Advisor* (Teacher-Course Evaluation, University of Illinois, 1970-71), p. 125.

"conversation class," the group undertakes some project together and in carrying it through uses the language, improves its use of the language, corrects its use of the language: an advanced language class, a living language class—call it what you will, it is the integrated activity which counts. A series of language courses of this type can be designed so that each will unobtrusively zero in on specific problem areas. Is it diction which is defective? The course may focus on play and poetry reading for pleasure. Is written French the problem? Activities will be designed that require the writing of a large number of letters or reports that will have some destination: perhaps in the exchange of information with a group outside the university; an activity may be designed in the first part of the course that must be carried out in the second half, such as the writing of a scenario for a radio drama or a film based on an incident which took place in the country where the language is spoken; the class may take over the regular writing and editing of a daily or weekly departmental newspaper. If general language practice is sought, activity or "case packets" can be designed which lead the students into simulating problem-solving situations which require them to search out information in printed sources and from native speakers on campus, to discuss their findings together, and to write some form of report for final presentation. During such activities gaps in the knowledge of syntax will continually reveal themselves, but the students will be taught to seek out the facts themselves from reference material or from the instructor as they need them, or to teach each other, rather than being subjected to the fourth, (fifth, sixth?) formal exposition of the workings of the object pronoun system. Such an activity class may well be linked to literary or cultural subjects and serve as an opportunity for students to familiarize themselves with wider areas of interest as they seek to discover how certain themes have been expressed at certain periods in literature, how certain ideas have been worked out in drama, or how certain aspects of life are experienced in another culture. Interesting content is needed for a language class. Such a class will differ from an introductory literature course, however, in that the purpose of the course will be quite frankly the perfection of language in use.

If we make available a series of courses of this type of varied interest and emphasis we can provide for the discrepancy in student needs. Four courses of this nature would not form a sequence to be taken by all in strict order: some would need all, some none; some would be interested only in the second and the fourth, others in the first or the third. Instructors could concentrate on improving and varying the offering of a course with a particular emphasis on an area in which they were most interested. But here comes the crunch. Our students, we are told, "prefer" literature classes—they are bored with language classes.

There are perhaps readily identifiable reasons why our students seem to prefer literature. Literature courses are at present taught by specialists who love their specialty; interesting, even exciting materials are readily available; professors spend much time preparing, finding supplementary materials, encouraging lively debate; students soon sense which are the "real" subjects which "count" in the department. Let us take the obverse which clearly applies: language classes for the most part are not taught by specialists who love their specialty; interesting and exciting materials are not readily available; professors teaching such courses as an imposed chore resent spending time seeking out, or preparing personally, materials which will not provide that idea for a future article and which will not be regarded as "scholarly production" when they are being considered for promotion or tenure; students soon sense that these courses are held in low esteem by fellow-students, professors, and their own instructor.

The situation will continue as it is at present until as foreign-language departments we are willing to accept the need for highly qualified, respected, imaginative, academically rewarded language specialists. I am not speaking of linguists, philologists, or phoneticians, but language teachers who know how to design materials and write materials, and who can integrate language use with intellectually stimulating, thought-provoking, exciting activity. To do this effectively they will need to have an informed knowledge of many areas, but they will be devoted specialists nevertheless. We need specialists in contemporary language and language learning who are also informed about different approaches to teaching, who can teach in teams, who can use students to teach their peers, who can help students to learn without interposing themselves in the learning process. We need specialists who understand that testing is primarily a device to encourage learning; who do not consider group work a kind of cheating, or take-home examinations, or open-ended or open-book examinations, as "lowering standards;" who can see the virtue in a student's discussing his paper freely in class and then going home to rewrite it in a final version or being permitted to retake tests to improve his grade. There are many well-attested devices for improving the quality and quantity of learning which are suspect to many of the stalwarts of the pyramid, but which will seem merely humane and fruitful in the commune, where change is not feared but welcomed when it promotes the good of the greatest number. I have called for proper recognition of language teaching specialists, but it must now be clear that such a group could be subversive, promoting a quiet revolution in our inner circles.

So that we do not create a group of initiates at odds with the rest of the commune, and so that other areas may profit from the shared spirit of innovation and renewal, we need a seminar for study and discussion where all future professors will have the opportunity to thrash out in common the problems of the total commune, where each can come to understand the preoccupations of the other, where our future professors will be shaken out of the ruts into which their own educational experience has settled them, where they will get to the roots of the educational problems facing them and acquire the flexibility to solve them that comes through knowledge and understanding of their causes. In other words, we need enlightened training for our teaching assistants, not in teaching techniques for tomorrow's class but as preparation for a long career. We need imaginative professors who will accept teaching assistants as co-workers, team members in the teaching of all kinds of courses, showing them innovative and stimulating learning situations in progress and giving them freedom to create others. This we can have in the free and unguarded, unsuspicious atmosphere of the commune as we could never expect it on our separate steps of the pyramid.

Teacher training, graduate preparation? There are many other areas which need a fresh wind blowing into the corners and through the doors of offices and classrooms. Let us establish our commune and these areas too will gradually open themselves up for intensive discussion and cooperative action.

# 13

# THE NON-MAJOR: TAILORING THE COURSE
# TO FIT THE PERSON—NOT THE IMAGE*

Acknowledgment. The author wishes to acknowledge the active cooperation in the gathering and processing of these data of her colleagues at the University of Illinois at Urbana-Champaign: Milton Azevedo (Spanish, Italian, and Portuguese), Vincent Dell'Orto (German), Rasio Dunatov (Slavic Languages and Literatures), Hans Hock (Linguistics), William MacDonald (Center for Asian Studies), Richard Scanlan (Classics), Bruce Mainous (Unit for Foreign Language Study and Research), Lawrence Aleamoni and Eileen Cohen (Measurement and Research Division of the Office of Instructional Resources), Paulette Pelc (research assistant), Harriett Weatherford (secretary to the U.F.L.S.R.), and the many instructors who generously gave class time in the last week of the Fall semester, 1972-73, to allow the completion of the questionnaire.

'Know thyself' said the inscription on the Temple at Delphi. This is a fine piece of philosophical advice. May I amend it to a practical recommendation: 'Know thy students'. We may ask ourselves: what do we really know about our students? What are their backgrounds, their interests, their needs, their prejudices, their attitude toward foreign languages and foreign-language learning? Who do we consider to be 'our' students in any case? Our majors? Do these constitute the largest group in our classes? How well do we know our elective students, our minors, the students in our elementary and intermediate level classes?

For many of us, by far the most numerous group of students is represented by 'the hordes of kids taking the

*This article reprinted from K. Jankowsky, ed., *Language and International Studies*, Georgetown University Round Table on Language and Linguistics (Washington, D.C.: Georgetown University Press, 1973). Copublished in *ADFL Bulletin* 4 (1973), 12-18.

foreign language requirement over our dead bodies' as one of our colleagues recently expressed it.[1] Most of these are studying the foreign language unwillingly and bitterly, so recent articles in the field would have us believe. Is this really so? Have we bothered to find out? Do we know our students?

At the University of Illinois at Urbana we have just administered a 75-item questionnaire to 1821 students of twelve languages at five levels of instruction (elementary: 101 and 102; intermediate: 103 and 104; advanced: 200 level). For the major languages taught on · campus we had the following numbers of subjects: French 733, German 518, Latin 98, Russian 129, Spanish 180. We also received information from students of Arabic, Chinese, Classical and Modern Greek, Modern Hebrew, Hindi, and Persian. Through computer analysis across a number of different intersections we now have a much fuller three-dimensional picture of the population of the language classes at a big Midwest state university than ever before.

Of our sample, 63% were fulfilling a requirement: the graduation requirement of the College of Liberal Arts and Sciences (993 students) or Departmental requirements[2] from areas as diverse as Agriculture, Architecture, Aviation, Biology, Commerce (187 students), Communications, Education, Engineering, Library Science, Music, Physics, and Physical Education. Another 20% were electives, 8% were minors, and 9% were majors.[3] For many of us, it is this last 9% whom we consider to be really 'our' students—or at the most the last 17% (if we add on the minors). These are the 'serious' students who fill our classes at the advanced level (200 and above), so we presume, and are receiving the close attention of our full-time faculty in a large state university.

Actually, our overall survey shows that only 35% of students at the 200 level are majors (57% in Russian, 48% in French, 40% in Spanish, 30% in Latin, and 23% in German). Does that surprise you? It did me. Who are all these students, the 62% in the first two semesters of the advanced level, of whose presence we are only dimly aware? In the following discussion, I shall consider all these non-majors as one group, namely electives, since many electives find that by completing two courses at the advanced level they can count their chosen subject as a teaching minor, while very few students have been required to complete a foreign-language minor by their major department. Since no one has compelled these students to join us, they must like us. Isn't it time we got to know our departmental guests? We shall look more closely at this group in a moment because they represent only 11% of our sample.

First of all, let us consider some general attitudes of students at all five levels of instruction in the College of Liberal Arts and Sciences, a total of 1500 students in the sample. Since many of us have worked with these students at one time or another, we think we know something of their background, their attitudes, their interests, and their aspirations. Let us examine first some assertions about them that we hear frequently in professional discussions.

(1) We all know that most students today see absolutely no use in learning a foreign language.

In our data, only 29% see no use for foreign languages in their life-style, that is, less than one-third.

(2) Students are perhaps not against foreign languages as such, but, we are told, they certainly are against requirements of any kind.

In our data, only 32% (again less than one-third) say that they do not think any form of study should be required.

(3) It is often stated that our young people feel that English is spoken so extensively in other countries that there is no point in learning a foreign language.

Only 21% of the students in our sample, that is, one in five, subscribes to this view.

(4) Even if our preconceptions up to this point do not correspond with our students' expressed attitudes, it is widely accepted among us that, in the Midwest at least, Americans feel very isolated from contact with foreign languages: they rarely hear a foreign language spoken and few of their acquaintances can speak one.

In our data 25%, or one in four of the 1821 students in our survey, have parents who speak a foreign language, while 66% have friends who speak a foreign language. In fact, one student gave as his reason for selecting German as the language to study: "I want to know what my Grandpa says when he gets mad and yells at me!"

(5) If none of the above holds true for the majority of our students, at least we know they do not see any relevance to their career interests in foreign-language study.

At the University of Illinois, 45% (just under one-half) say they are preparing to work in a field where knowledge of a language will be useful. (The 9% of our sample who were foreign-language majors were certainly not sufficiently numerous to determine the overall direction of these responses.)

(6) A common complaint from opponents of a foreign-language requirement has been that grades in the foreign-language courses bring down the student's grade-point average and compromise his future plans.

This proved to be untrue to an almost embarrassing degree when the students' estimates of their foreign-language grades showed an overall level of 82% of A's and B's as compared with 75% for their all-university grade-point average. The students' estimates of their foreign-language grades were consistently above their all-university grade-point average at all levels of instruction except for 104 (fourth semester) when many students exercise their privilege to be graded on a pass/fail basis (pass = D) instead of by letter grade. (Even in 104 the average class still achieved 70% of A's and B's to 76% for their all-university grade-point average.)

(7) Whatever else proves not to be true, it is generally accepted that for the majority of students at the elementary and intermediate levels these four semesters of foreign-language study are an unpleasant and unprofitable experience.

In our elementary and intermediate courses, approximately one-fifth of the students class themselves as electives or future majors and minors. Of the four-fifths who are requirement students one-third say they would have chosen to study a foreign language had there been no requirement and one-third of those who are studying the language only because there is a requirement say they enjoy studying the language anyway.

Calculating from different computer-produced breakdowns of data, we find that the sum of those who chose to study a foreign language on an elective basis (E), plus those who would have chosen a foreign language even if there had been no requirement (ER), plus those who are in the class because of the requirement but enjoy studying the foreign language nevertheless (R) yields the following percentages of students at the four levels of elementary and intermediate study who do not feel they are being forced to spend time on what does not interest them:

| | E | | ER | | R | | |
|---|---|---|---|---|---|---|---|
| 101: | 25% | + | 23% | + | 17% | = | 65% |
| 102: | 23% | + | 20% | + | 13% | = | 56% |
| 103: | 22% | + | 24% | + | 12% | = | 58% |
| 104: | 22% | + | 21% | + | 21% | = | 67% |

Interestingly, as an internal validation, these figures dovetail very neatly (with allowance made for a certain number of students who did not answer particular questions and the addition of rounded percentages) with the affirmative responses at these four levels to the item: "I can see no use for foreign languages in my life-style":

| | |
|---|---|
| 101: | 31% |
| 102: | 37% |
| 103: | 34% |
| 104: | 29% |

Isn't it time that as a profession we stopped being on the defensive and dropped our "nobody likes me" stance? We would do better to begin investigating what we should be providing for this large percentage of students of goodwill who seem to like us despite ourselves. I am wondering what kinds of percentages our colleagues in other departments would achieve on these same questions in their required courses.

(8) How is it then, some may ask, that student groups opposed to foreign-language study feel they are representative of student opinion in general when the students' stated attitudes across such a representative sample do not support their position? An important clue is to be found in a much smaller 1972 survey of student attitudes at the University of Illinois for which 141 randomly selected students in the elementary and intermediate French classes were polled.[4]

There was an enormous discrepancy between the percentage of students at these levels who felt language study was of importance and the percentage of these same students who felt that their friends considered language study important: a discrepancy of 42%! (Fifty-one per cent considered foreign-language study important, 9% thought their friends regarded it as important.) It would seem that the large numbers of students who would like to learn a foreign language or who enjoy foreign-language study feel that they are in a minority because of the intense propaganda against required foreign-language study by a vocal few. In the spring of 1973, after four months of intensive effort to enlist the support of all L.A.S. students, an activist student group at the University of Illinois was able to produce signatures against the L.A.S. foreign-language requirement from about one-third of the students in the college. This percentage was thought by some professors in other departments to show that two-thirds of the students were "apathetic." On the contrary, the percentage of signatures obtained is quite consistent with the data on student attitudes discussed in the last section.

(9) Finally, some say our students would be much happier if we were to give up the attempt to teach them to understand and speak the language. In his article, "Research Findings and FL Requirements in Colleges and Universities," Jakobovits (1969) reported on a 1968 survey at the University of Illinois (a self-selected 500 questionnaires were returned out of 5,000 distributed, as compared with our 1821 questionnaires administered across twelve languages at five levels of instruction). In this article, Jakobovits stated: "Two available surveys of college students' interest in FL study indicate that . . . one-half consider the primary goal to be development of a reading knowledge of the language" (Jakobovits 1969: 452). One of the studies to which Jakobovits alludes is that of Robert Politzer at Harvard University in the early fifties, "Student Motivation and Interest in Elementary Language Courses." In this period of rapid change a study published in 1953 hardly represented the Now generation even in 1968. Actually the Politzer study showed that at that time "87% endorsed greater emphasis on

oral proficiency ... 53% accepted the reading aim, 39% voted for speaking." This study was, of course, pre-Sputnik.[5]

In our data in 1973, 63% in the elementary and intermediate courses wanted more listening and speaking, while 62% wanted more reading. If these are nonparallel distributions, as seems plausible, then there is a fair overlap of students who would like more of both (that is, courses which permit them to develop simultaneously in both areas), while some 36 to 38% at the extremes prefer more exclusively aural-oral courses or more specifically reading-oriented courses. The existence of these segments of the student population with decided preferences for either specifically aural-oral or visual learning experiences has already provided a regular clientele for specialized courses set up by the foreign-language departments at the University of Illinois, as I shall discuss later.

It is interesting to note that two-thirds of these students expressed interest in foreign-language newspapers and magazines as course reading material; this proportion corresponded well with those who expressed interest in learning more about current affairs in the country where the language is spoken. Only 20% wanted more scientific and technical reading, a figure which did not surprise the French department which had been forced for several semesters in succession to cancel a fourth semester option in this area for lack of sufficient registrants. (For the few who did register the problem was solved by admitting them to the reading course for Ph.D. students into which they settled happily with the graduate group.) That 50% of the students expressed an interest in more readings in literature when most departments already supply generous proportions of such readings reflects the continuing interest that great works of literature hold for students of the Liberal Arts and Sciences.

To summarize the expressed preferences of the L.A.S. requirement students:

> They want to listen and speak more.
> They want to read, not only literature, but also newspapers and magazines which will keep them informed about current affairs.

They want to learn more about the people who speak the language and see more films.

Only 20% are interested in more scientific and technical reading (increasing to 30% in German and 32% in Russian, but falling to 12% in Spanish).

They do not want more grammar, or more writing of the language.

Interests vary when we look at the departmental requirement students, represented in our sample by students of Commerce, Communications, Agriculture, Engineering, Music, Education, Fine and Applied Arts, Aviation, Architecture, and Physical Education. To some degree these are elective students, since they have chosen the foreign language instead of other subjects on a Humanities list.

Because of small sample size the following remarks cannot be considered reliable; but, in whimsical vein, we may say that Music students would be happiest with a group of Aviation students: talking and listening to each other, singing and making music, reading literature, but also newspapers and magazines so that they may learn about people and events in other countries. Not even engineers (=5) and agriculturalists (=17) are interested particularly in scientific or technical reading (0%-6%), and Commerce students (=187) are not particularly interested in learning to write the language, read its literature, or enjoy its music. They prefer to listen and speak, read newspapers and magazines to catch up on current affairs, and relax with films.

No one wants more grammar. As one student said: "Less grammar. The grammar kills me!" (French 104). As a profession, we must begin to take much more seriously this constantly voiced complaint of our students. Of course, internalization of the rules of grammar is basic to all active use of a language; but it is equally certain that strong dislike of a particular aspect of study impedes effective learning. It cannot be beyond us to find ways of making the learning of grammar more functional, integrating it more closely with natural language activities. We also need to find out just how much grammar and what areas of grammar in particular are essential for comprehension of the written and spoken word. We need to prepare new types of grammar books to suit the needs of the students in our specialized courses. Surely these matters are important enough to be given priority in our experimentation and research.

What are we doing to meet these expressed interests of our students? Different things are being attempted in many places, but here I would like to describe for you our own attempts to provide for a plurality of student needs and interests in the French Department at the University of Illinois. Our German Department has described its own rather different approach in two articles which appear in *Changing Patterns in Foreign Language Programs.*[6] Their initiative seems to have met with considerable student approval, since by the end of the fourth semester the students were declaring two to one that they enjoyed learning German even though it was a requirement.

## The Non-Major at the Elementary and Intermediate Levels

The French Department program for the elementary and intermediate courses is in a process of development. I can point out here the directions we are taking,[7] but with 1,250 students in some sixty classes, taught by about fifty instructors, all engaged in graduate studies, the guiding principle must be *festina lente.* To hasten the development of a program responsive to all needs, the department devotes considerable time and effort to preparing its graduate assistants for their teaching career. Not only is careful attention given to the improvement of their teaching techniques (through demonstration classes, regular discussion of how material may be presented to maintain student interest and promote effective learning, preparation of quizzes and tests as group projects, and classroom visitation), but the instructors are encouraged to consider and debate the broader implications of language learning and curriculum development through a full-credit graduate course in the College Teaching of Foreign Languages to which representatives of other departments frequently contribute. For those interested in more specialized research and discussion there is an advanced seminar on the Linguistic and Psychological Foundations of Language Teaching. With a constant inflow of teaching assistants alert to needs and problems it is hoped that the program will never become static, at no matter what stage of apparent effectiveness, but continue to adapt to the interests and objectives of each new wave of undergraduate students.

At its present stage of development, the French Department program may be described in terms of the schema presented in Figure 1.

FIGURE 1.

| Goals | Continuing<br>Terminal |
|---|---|
| Pace | Placement for appropriate level<br>General courses (101-104)*<br>Accelerated groups for future majors and minors (133, 134)<br>Intensive courses for faster progress (105, 106, 107)**<br>Independent study<br>Proficiency tests for faster advancement |
| Modality<br>(Approach) | Modified audiolingual<br>Active modified direct method (eclectic)<br>Reading approach (123, 124)<br>Conversational approach (113, 114)<br>Films as a regular supplement (documentaries and feature films)<br>Computer-assisted instruction (PLATO system) with aural-oral practice in the classroom |
| Content | Literature (including Black Literature of French, expression, and women's studies)<br>Civilization and culture (144)<br>Contrastive French and American culture (154)<br>Scientific and technical material (164)<br>Newspapers and magazines (174)<br>Individually selected content (199) |

*Elementary: First semester 101; Elementary: Second semester 102. Intermediate: First semester 103, 113, 123, or 133; Intermediate: Second semester 104, 114, 124, 134, 144, 154, 164, 174, 199.

**105 = 101 + 102; 106 = 102 + 103; 107 = 103 + 104.

Only about 36% of the students at the 200 (advanced) level in the French Department studied the language for a semester or more in our elementary and intermediate classes. A mere 4% began their study of the language with us. Two-thirds of the students in the elementary and intermediate courses do not continue the study of the language after the fourth semester. Our program is, therefore, designed to meet the needs of both of these groups: the continuing and the terminal students. After a core program of two semesters, students wishing to continue beyond the fourth semester are given accelerated instruction to prepare them to meet the challenges of the advanced level: courses are in French, accuracy and thoroughness in learning are stressed, and students are given some basic training in literary appreciation as well as in understanding the values, attitudes, and institutions of the French people. This frees us to design the rest of the courses for the needs and special interests of our terminal students.

To enable students to work at the level and pace which suit their needs, placement tests are administered to incoming freshmen with high school language experience; proficiency tests are organized at the beginning of the fall semester and at the beginning and end of the spring semester so that hard-working students can move ahead as they are able, and computer-assisted courses using the PLATO system,[8] supplemented by aural-oral practice in the classroom, are available throughout the sequence.

At the third semester level, after students have had a fair chance to decide their learning preferences, we begin to provide more specifically for different modalities of learning. We commence a sequence of two courses (123, 124) for students who do not particularly care about oral communication in French, but prefer to concentrate on developing their skill in reading. French literary works are read in the original language and discussed in English. For those desiring to develop their aural-oral skills more intensively, a supplementary course which meets for two hours per week (113) is available. In the fourth semester, students can choose from seven distinct courses: a course exclusively devoted to oral communication (114); three courses in which reading has the primacy: one with readings from French literature with discussions in English (124), the second devoted to the extracting of information from scientific and technical material (164), and the third to the reading of newspapers and magazines with most discussion in French but with opportunity to discuss really controversial issues in the native tongue (174); a course on French culture and civilization with readings and discussions in French (144); a course on contrastive French and American culture with materials drawn by instructor and students from many sources, both French and American, with discussions in English; and, finally, a general four-skills course with literary and cultural readings (104) for students who have no particular modality or content preferences. In the specialized courses grammar is treated as required for efficient comprehension or expression. The effectiveness of our attempt to provide special interest courses can be judged by the fact that the non-specialized 104 sections have been reduced over the past year from seven to three as students have begun actively to select among the alternatives.

Teaching assistants who have participated in our training and have sufficient experience and maturity to branch out on their own are encouraged to develop these diversified courses as they and their students would like. Consequently, the "Hawthorne effect" of an experimental atmosphere and enthusiasm suffuse many of these classes and should continue to do so as new groups of instructors and students find their own way. 114 has been described by one student as "a workshop that works," and 144 as "the most enjoyable class I've had in a few years." A student in 154 says "In five weeks in this course I have learned more about France and the French people than in three years of regular French. Granted I may be unable to speak or write French well at the end, but I really believe I will have a basic understanding of the way of life, social and political structure. I actually enjoy this class." These are from "requirement" students, and are but a few from many such comments. We do not have all the answers and many more things can be done,[9] but at least we are on our way.

## The Non-Major
## at the Advanced Level

Of our majors, 70% gave as one reason for selecting this particular language for study the fact that they had begun it at secondary level, whereas only 42% of the electives cited this as a deciding factor. It seems that only 15% of our foreign-language majors have studied another language for four years or more, whereas 33% of our electives have studied another language for this period of time. Of the majors, 38% have parents who speak a foreign language, while only 28% of the electives are in this situation. It seems, then, that our electives are an interesting group of people who have an intrinsic interest in foreign-language study.

The fields in which they hope to use the language are very diverse. Of the majors, 57% expect to teach the language (the 10% who have no plans will probably teach the language anyway), but the electives expect to use their knowledge in science, anthropology, philosophy, music, journalism, business, aviation, law, inner-city medicine, linguistics, engineering, social work at home, social and religious service abroad, in diplomacy, international law, interpreting, library science, advertising, speech therapy, archaeology, astrophysics, and, as one student put it, "active service in today's action army." All of these things and many more were cited by particular students.

What are we providing for this 62% at the 200 level? One student of Russian wrote that he would like:

> Reading and discussion courses in the language in areas of history (both social and cultural-intellectual), economics, government, contemporary affairs and life as exemplified by current newspapers and magazines, etc. I would certainly like to see something more than pure literature courses on the one hand and pure grammar on the other. Though these two are important aspects of the language, they are not the only important ones. How about some variety? A language student cannot live by literature courses alone.

The interests of the elective group are varied. Many want to read the foreign literature but an introduction to techniques of literary criticism, designed for majors, does not really meet their needs, interesting as it may be to others. They are interested in many things besides. In descending order of choice they mentioned: oral communication, reading in their own fields, translating and interpreting, and contemporary life styles and values. More sparsely checked were: contrastive study of societies and cultures, philosophy, art history, film, music, operas, songs, cultural and political history, and linguistic analysis. A few here and there would like practice in situational language use for social workers, and more history of the language. (Several students specially wrote in "poetry." Does this indicate that it is insufficiently treated in literature courses in some departments?) What a wide open field! Surely none of us can say: What else can we offer besides courses in literary criticism and literary history?

What can we conclude from these findings? It seems that interest in foreign-language study is far from dead among students other than our majors despite the prolonged neglect from which they have suffered. We have often bemoaned the fact that we spend much of our time producing more teachers of future foreign-language teachers in a seemingly unending cycle. Surely this is because we have not realized who many of our students really were. It seems our clientele is much more broadly based and shows much more potential good will than we have hitherto believed. It is for us to use our imagination in devising courses which will keep this interested group with us and attract more of their kind.

A foreign-language teachers' association in a big Canadian city recently asked me to address them on the subject: "Is it a matter of survival?" That is a question worthy of some meditation.

## FOOTNOTES

[1] R. J. Nelson, "Foreign Language Study: Bride or Bridesmaid?" *ADFL Bulletin*, Vol. 4, No. 3 (1973): 19.

[2] The College of Liberal Arts and Sciences of the University of Illinois at Urbana-Champaign requires two years of high school foreign language for

entrance and an additional two semesters of the same foreign language for graduation. A student may satisfy the requirement with three semesters each of two foreign languages. The L.A.S. College requirement was upheld by a two-thirds majority of the assembled L.A.S. faculty and student representatives in the spring of 1972, and again by a four-fifths majority in the spring of 1973. A number of departments in other colleges require varying lengths of study of humanities subjects chosen from a list which includes foreign languages. In many cases, the departments specify that this foreign-language study must be at the intermediate level and above. For this reason many departmental requirement students may be considered electives because they have chosen foreign languages from a list of up to fifteen other humanities subjects.

[3] By the time this article appears in print the conventional majors and minors at the University of Illinois at Urbana-Champaign will have been replaced by fields of concentration.

[4] P. Pelc and S. Sauder, "A Survey of Student Attitudes toward Elementary and Intermediate French Courses at the University of Illinois," in Wilga M. Rivers, Louise H. Allen, et al., eds., 1972, p. 199.

[5] L. A. Jakobovits, "Research Findings and FL Requirements in Colleges and Universities," *Foreign Language Annals* 2 (1969): 436-56, and Robert L. Politzer, "Student Motivation and Interest in Elementary Language Courses," *Language Learning* 5 (1953-54): 15-21.

[6] James McGlathery, "A New Program of Substitute and Supplementary German Language Courses," and Richard C. Figge, "The Beginning German Program: Rethinking the Problems," in Wilga M. Rivers, Louise H. Allen, et al., eds., *Changing Patterns in Foreign Language Programs* (Rowley, Mass.: Newbury House, 1972).

[7] Since the author left the French Department at the University of Illinois at Urbana-Champaign for Harvard in July, 1974, the development of the program has not necessarily followed the lines described.

[8] The PLATO system is described in detail in Richard T. Scanlan, "The Application of Technology to the Teaching of Foreign Languages," in Wilga M. Rivers, Louise H. Allen, et al., eds., 1972, pp. 84-87.

[9] I have discussed possible approaches to this stage of foreign-language study in "Conservation and Innovation," in Wilga M. Rivers, Louise H. Allen, et al., eds., 1972, and in "Foreign Languages in a Time of Change" and "From the Pyramid to the Commune: The Evolution of the Foreign-Language Department," Chapters 11 and 12 in this book.

## 14

# UNIVERSITY OF ILLINOIS QUESTIONNAIRE
# ON INTERESTS
# IN FOREIGN LANGUAGES

---
*See the Acknowledgment on page 169.*

---

A *75-item questionnaire,* divided into general sections, sections for requirement students, and for electives, majors, and minors, was administered at the University of Illinois at Urbana-Champaign in the *100 and 200 level courses* (elementary, intermediate, and advanced levels, but excluding courses which might also contain graduate majors), in all departments teaching foreign languages at the end of the fall semester of 1972-73. For the original questionnaire, see Section F.

### Analysis

After elimination of questionnaires with insufficient information for category identification, 1821 questionnaires were processed by computer by the Office of Instructional Resources.

Completed questionnaires fall into the following categories:

| | Levels | |
|---|---|---|
| 101: | 545 students |
| 102: | 265 |
| 103: | 441 |
| 104: | 223 |
| 200: | 347 |
| (Total 1821) | |

Note: 101 and 103 are always larger than 102 and 104 in the Fall semester at Urbana. The position is reversed in the

Spring semester. (101-102 are elementary level, 103-104 are intermediate level, and 200 is advanced level.)

### Languages

| | |
|---|---|
| Arabic: | 8 students |
| Chinese: | 7 |
| French: | 733 |
| German: | 518 |
| Greek (Classical): | 20 |
| Hebrew (Modern): | 10 |
| Hindi: | 8 |
| Latin: | 98 |
| Persian: | 10 |
| Russian: | 129 |
| Spanish: | 180 |
| (Total 1721) | |

The discrepancy between level and language totals is due to some incorrect coding of languages by students.

In the following information O = overall, while appropriate abbreviations are used for specific languages and levels are indicated where relevant. Note that percentages will not always add to 100% because of rounding by the computer and later rounding by the reporter + some omissions by students.

For comparisons in this report the following languages were selected (sample size indicated):

| | |
|---|---|
| French | 733 |
| German | 518 |
| Spanish | 180 |
| Russian | 129 |
| Latin | 98 |
| Modern Hebrew | 10 (ethnic identification Q. 54) |
| Persian | 10 (exotic or specialized) |

### Categories of students

| | |
|---|---|
| Majors | 172 |
| Minors | 146 |
| Electives | 416 |
| Requirement | 1298 |
| (Total 1932) | |

(LAS Requirement 993, Departmental Requirements from other colleges: approximately 305)

> Discrepancy explained by the fact that a number of electives had decided to complete minors in their electives and checked both categories. In later analysis, this discrepancy has been corrected by evidence from other sections of the questionnaire. Some students are required by their colleges to complete Humanities sequences from which they may select foreign languages: they may therefore check that they are completing a Departmental requirement and/or that this is an elective from possible humanities sequences. The number for Departmental requirement students has been calculated from evidence in various sections of the questionnaire.

## A.  Requirement Students

1.  Students who would *not have studied* a FL if it had not been required (Q. 27):    O = 66%

2.  Students who *enjoy learning* a foreign language even though it is a requirement (Q. 28):    O = 54%
    —at 101 level    O = 54%
    —at 102 level    O = 49%
    —at 103 level    O = 46%
    —at 104 level    O = 54%

3.  Students who *would have tried to include* a FL if there had been no requirement (Q. 47):    O = 33%
    (These students will be dubbed Voluntary Requirement VR for comparison with Non-Voluntary Requirement NVR)

4.  Omitting those who were neutral on 3, there were:    OVR  = 385 students
    ONVR = 770 students

5.  The *OVR students,* self-identified, who enjoy learning a FL despite requirement (Q. 28):    yes:  82%
    no:   17%

    (Some must have needed it for a special purpose)

6.  The *ONVR students* who enjoyed learning a FL despite requirement (this is the

percentage of those requirement students
left after OVR have been taken out):
—When asked elsewhere whether they
always disliked learning FL's, NVR 55%
agreed, as against 64% here. The discrepancy could be due to the reaction of some
to the word "requirement" in Q. 28).

yes: 35%
no:  64%

7. Students who *would have liked to continue* at 200 level (advanced), but
   cannot:

   | | OVR | ONVR |
   |---|---|---|
   | | 28% | 6% |

8. Students who *intend to continue* as
   electives, minors, or majors:

   | | OVR | ONVR |
   |---|---|---|
   | | 48% | 8% |
   | | 15% | 1% |
   | | 8% | 0% |

9. Students taking different levels on an *elective* basis (all O):

   Of students at this level

   | Level | % |
   |---|---|
   | 101: | 23% |
   | 102: | 24% |
   | 103: | 18% |
   | 104: | 16% |
   | 200: | 39% |

10. Students taking different levels as an *LAS requirement* (O):
    (Discrepancy between percentages in 9 and 10 is accounted for by
    Dept. requirements listed in 11.)

    Of students at this level

    | Level | % |
    |---|---|
    | 101: | 64% |
    | 102: | 68% |
    | 103: | 71% |
    | 104: | 71% |
    | 200: | 11% (presumably literature in translation or foreign culture) |

11. Percentage of "*free souls*" in elementary and intermediate courses,
    that is, electives, majors, minors, and VR:

    | | Elect. | MM | VR | Total % |
    |---|---|---|---|---|
    | 101: | 18 | 7 | 23 | 48 |
    | 102: | 15 | 8 | 20 | 43 |
    | 103: | 13 | 9 | 24 | 46 |
    | 104: | 12 | 10 | 21 | 43 |

12. To these percentages may be added *those who enjoy learning* a
    language even though it is a requirement, but who would not have
    studied one had there not been a requirement:

    Of students at this level

    | Level | % |
    |---|---|
    | 101: | 17% |
    | 102: | 13% |

|      |     |
|------|-----|
| 103: | 12% |
| 104: | 21% |

13. It seems then that the following percentages at each level *do not feel they are being forced to spend time on what does not interest them.*

|      | Of students at this level |
|------|---------------------------|
| 101: | 65% |
| 102: | 56% |
| 103: | 58% |
| 104: | 67% |

14. The figures in 13 (allowing errors for rounding and some omitted responses) complement almost exactly the answers to Q. 11: I can *see no use for foreign languages* in my life-style.

|      |     |              |
|------|-----|--------------|
| 101: | 31  | (+65 = 96)   |
| 102: | 37  | (+56 = 93)   |
| 103: | 34  | (+58 = 92)   |
| 104: | 29  | (+67 = 96)   |

15. *Other Colleges* (in student numbers)

|                        | Department Requirement | Elective and Minor |
|------------------------|:----------------------:|:------------------:|
| Agriculture            | 5   | 12 |
| Architecture           | 17  | 5  |
| Commerce               | 187 | 28 |
| Communications         | 1   | 22 |
| Engineering            | 5   | 11 |
| Library Science        | 2   | 0  |
| Fine and Applied Arts  | 41  | 24 |
| —of which Music        | 25  | 14 |
| Physical Education     | 1   | 0  |
| Other                  | 57  | 0  |

Note: Since some students did not indicate their college, these figures are gathered from various parts of the data and are therefore incomplete and indicative only.

16. Overall *sex ratio*:

|             |    |
|-------------|----|
| Female:     | 49 |
| Male:       | 42 |
| Not stated: | 9  |

(This was considered a sexist question by some who refused to answer it.)

Of declared males: 79% requirement; 21% elective, major, minor
Of declared females: 55% requirement; 45% elective, major, minor
Of undeclared: 75% requirement; 25% elective, major, minor

17. *Continued Study*
   Q. 43: *22%* of requirement students would have liked to continue at the 200 level but cannot.

QQ. 44-46: *28%* of all Requirement students intend to continue studying the language as majors, minors, or electives. Percentages of these requirement students in selected languages:

| | Fr. | Germ. | Span. | Russ. | Lat. | M. Heb. | Persian |
|---|---|---|---|---|---|---|---|
| approx. | 29% | 29% | 21% | 34% | 22% | 100% | 29% |

18. Examination of *Grade Point Average by language* reveals the following percentages (all levels):

| | Fr. | Germ. | Span. | Russ. | Latin | M. Heb. | Persian |
|---|---|---|---|---|---|---|---|
| sample size | (733) | (518) | (180) | (129) | (98) | (10) | (10) |
| 4.5-5.0 | 75 ⎡38 | 71 ⎡40 | 76 ⎡46 | 81 ⎡49 | 74 ⎡39 | 80 ⎡20 | 80 ⎡10 |
| 4.0-4.5 | ⎣37 | ⎣31 | ⎣30 | ⎣32 | ⎣35 | ⎣60 | ⎣70 |
| 3.5-4.0 | 16 | 12 | 17 | 10 | 15 | 10 | 10 |
| 3.0-3.5 | 4 | 5 | 4 | 2 | 4 | 10 | 10 |
| Omitted on Q: | 4 | 11 | 2 | 7 | 5 | 0 | 0 |

Comment: The data do not seem to support the widely held view that German and Latin generally attract a superior type of student. Russian only seems to have a slight edge (except for Modern Hebrew and Persian which have small samples, and are probably selected by students for personal reasons).

19. *Students' grades in FL*:

| | Fr. | Germ. | Span. | Russ. | Latin | M. Heb. | Persian |
|---|---|---|---|---|---|---|---|
| A | 39 | 42 | 48 | 46 | 67 | 70 | 30 |
| B | 40 | 39 | 39 | 39 | 21 | 30 | 60 |
| C | 15 | 12 | 13 | 9 | 5 | - - - | - - - |
| D | 3 | 2 | 2 | - - - | 2 | - - - | - - - |
| E | - - - | - - - | - - - | - - - | 2 | - - - | - - - |

From Q. 54: Percentages of students who feel a cultural or ethnic identification with this language:

| 11 | 28 | 12 | 19 | 7 | 90 | 10 |
|---|---|---|---|---|---|---|

20. *Background and opinions of LAS students:* QQ. 9-21 (sample size given)

| | LAS College (=1528) | LAS Req. (=1043) | NVR (=770) | VR (=385) | Dept. Req. Commerce (=187) | Elective* (=416) | Minors (=146) | Majors (=172) |
|---|---|---|---|---|---|---|---|---|
| Q. 9. Parents speak a FL | 25% | 22 | 20 | 29 | 24 | 28 | 32 | 38 |
| Q. 10. Friends speak a FL | 66 | 61 | 57 | 72 | 71 | 77 | 74 | 80 |
| Q. 11. See no use for FL's in their life-style | 29 | 42 | 51 | 14 | 20 | 7 | 7 | 3 |
| Q. 12. Have traveled in other countries | 43 | 39 | 35 | 53 | 53 | 53 | 49 | 57 |
| Q. 13. Would like to travel in other countries | 94 | 93 | 92 | 96 | 96 | 98 | 97 | 99 |
| Q. 14. English widely spoken so no need for FL | 21 | 30 | 36 | 11 | 16 | 7 | 3 | 4 |
| Q. 15. Interested in differences between languages | 51 | 35 | 25 | 63 | 66 | 76 | 77 | 87 |
| Q. 16. Interested in what goes on in other countries | 90 | 87 | 85 | 93 | 92 | 95 | 94 | 95 |
| Q. 17. Preparing for a field where FL will be useful | 45 | 30 | 22 | 60 | 57 | 61 | 79 | 91 |
| Q. 18. FL's require too much out-of-class study | 38 | 50 | 60 | 24 | 27 | 20 | 26 | 10 |
| Q. 19. Don't think any form of study should be required | 32 | 40 | 45 | 22 | 22 | 21 | 12 | 16 |
| Q. 20. Interested in how other countries look at things | 87 | 83 | 80 | 88 | 88 | 94 | 92 | 98 |
| Q. 21. Never liked learning FL's | 32 | 45 | 55 | 17 | 20 | 9 | 8 | 3 |

*Electives and Minors are spread through 100–200 levels. Majors are mainly, but not wholly, 200 level. See section 29 for distribution.

21. *Language experience by levels* (in percentages of students). Q. 5.

| This is | first | second | third | fourth | fifth | language studied |
|---------|-------|--------|-------|--------|-------|------------------|
| 200 | 53 | 31 | 12 | 3 | 1 | |
| 104 | 61 | 30 | 5 | 4 | 0 | |
| 103 | 46 | 41 | 9 | 2 | 1 | |
| 102 | 53 | 34 | 9 | 2 | 2 | |
| 101 | 32 | 53 | 10 | 3 | 1 | |

22. Studied *this* language *before coming to the University of Illinois* for x number of years. (Q. 6).

| for | 0 yr | 1 yr | 2 yr | 3 yr | 4 yr | 5 yr | 6 yr | 6+ yr |
|-----|------|------|------|------|------|------|------|-------|
| 200 | 12 | 7 | 16 | 12 | 33 | 8 | 5 | 6 |
| 104 | 13 | 5 | 34 | 24 | 15 | 4 | 2 | 3 |
| 103 | 29 | 10 | 31 | 17 | 6 | 2 | 2 | 2 |
| 102 | 25 | 9 | 41 | 18 | 4 | 0 | 1 | 1 |
| 101 | 57 | 6 | 28 | 6 | 1 | 1 | 1 | 1 |

23. *Studied this language before coming to U. of I.* (Q. 7).

| | HS | JHS | Elem. School | Jr. College | Univ. | Another Country | Native Speaker | Bil. USA |
|---|----|-----|-------------|-------------|-------|-----------------|----------------|----------|
| 200 | 56 | 12 | 8 | 2 | 4 | 3 | 1 | 4 |
| 104 | 65 | 12 | 6 | 1 | 2 | 0 | 0 | 1 |
| 103 | 52 | 7 | 7 | 3 | 3 | 1 | 1 | 2 |
| 102 | 61 | 9 | 5 | 1 | 2 | 0 | 0 | 2 |
| 101 | 33 | 6 | 4 | 1 | 1 | 1 | 0 | 2 |

24. Studied a *different* language before beginning this language (Q. 8).

| for | 1 yr | 2 yr | 3 yr | 4 yr | 5 yr | 6 yr | 7+ yr |
|-----|------|------|------|------|------|------|-------|
| 200 | 10 | 16 | 7 | 6 | 3 | 2 | 4 |
| 104 | 11 | 20 | 3 | 4 | 4 | 1 | 1 |
| 103 | 8 | 25 | 9 | 3 | 3 | 2 | 1 |
| 102 | 11 | 18 | 7 | 8 | 2 | 2 | 3 |
| 101 | 8 | 29 | 11 | 10 | 4 | 3 | 4 |

(Compare 21 above for percentages of students who have never studied another language.)

25. LAS requirement students who would enjoy learning a foreign language more if the *course content* were different (Q. 29): 41%.

26. *Differences in content preferred* (with some abstentions) QQ. 30-39:

| | Yes | No |
|---|-----|-----|
| Q. 30. More listening comprehension | 57% | 40% |
| Q. 31. More speaking FL themselves | 59 | 37 |
| Q. 32. More reading | 59 | 38 |
|     −literature (Q. 35) | 48 | 48 |
|     −of newspapers and magazines (Q. 40) | 61 | 35 |
|     −of scientific and technical material (Q. 41) | 19 | 77 |
| Q. 33. More writing in the language | 40 | 56 |
| Q. 34. More information about people who speak the language | 60 | 36 |
| Q. 36. More songs and music | 45 | 51 |
| Q. 37. More films | 67 | 28 |
| Q. 38. More information about current affairs | 58 | 38 |
| Q. 39. More analysis of language structure | 24 | 72 |

Course content preferences have not yet been analyzed by levels, by languages, by elective/non-elective, although data are available. A preliminary *analysis by college* has revealed distinct differences but because of small sample size in some cases it cannot be considered reliable. At a superficial level, *music* students (25) would be happiest with *aviation* students (34) (talking and listening to each other, singing and making music, and reading literature and magazines to learn about the people and events in other countries). Not even *engineers* (5) or *agriculturalists* (17) are interested particularly in scientific or technical reading (0-6%), and *commerce* students (187) are not particularly interested in learning to write the language, read its literature, or enjoy its music. *Architectural* students (17) are not very interested in learning to understand or speak the language; they want to be able to read (literature, newspapers, and magazines, but not technical material); they are interested in the people but not current events; they like films, but not songs or music.

27. The expressed *preferences for course content in specific languages* will be influenced to some extent by present content because of the wording of QQ. 30-42. For this reason the data will be most validly interpreted by the instructors in the respective departments.

*Percentage of 101-104 Requirement students of different languages* who would like the course to contain *more*:

|  | Fr. | Ger. | Span. | Rus. | Lat. | Heb. | Pers. |
|---|---|---|---|---|---|---|---|
| Listening Comprehension (Q. 30) | 66 | 59 | 51 | 68 | 28 | 100 | 71 |
| Speaking FL themselves (Q. 31) | 64 | 64 | 66 | 58 | 29 | 100 | 100 |
| Reading (Q. 32) | 63 | 59 | 57 | 79 | 52 | 40 | 57 |
| —of literature (Q. 35) | 56 | 47 | 42 | 50 | 46 | 40 | 43 |
| —of newspapers and magazines (Q. 40) | 67 | 66 | 61 | 71 | 26 | 60 | 43 |
| —of scientific and technical material (Q. 41) | 16 | 30 | 12 | 32 | 14 | 0 | 29 |
| Writing in the language (Q. 33) | 44 | 40 | 40 | 55 | 23 | 60 | 0 |
| Information about people who speak the language (Q. 34) | 67 | 54 | 58 | 76 | 62 | 60 | 100 |
| Songs and music (Q. 36) | 47 | 44 | 54 | 45 | 34 | 40 | 57 |
| Films (Q. 37) | 74 | 64 | 61 | 82 | 66 | 40 | 86 |
| Information about current affairs (Q. 38) | 64 | 56 | 61 | 68 | 32 | 60 | 29 |
| Analysis of language structure (Q. 39) | 23 | 27 | 21 | 50 | 23 | 30 | 29 |

# B. Electives, Minors, and Majors

(O) with special reference to the 200 level.

28.  *G.P.A.* (in percentages of each category).

| Sample Size O | | Electives (416) | | Minors (146) | | Majors (172) |
|---|---|---|---|---|---|---|
| *G.P.A.:*  5.0 | 46 | 15% | 59 | 21% | 50 | 16% |
| 4.5-5.0 | | 31 | | 38 | | 34 |
| 4.0-4.5 | | 31 | | 28 | | 35 |
| 3.5-4.0 | | 12 | | 8 | | 9 |
| 3.0-3.5 | | 3 | | 3 | | 3 |

Note: *These O figures for electives, minors, and majors cover 100 and 200 level classes.* At the elementary and intermediate (100) levels many students have not yet decided on a major or a minor, so a percentage of future majors and minors will be included in the Requirement category. More than half the majors at the University of Illinois (see section 32) enter with four or more years of high school language and move directly into the advanced level courses. Of the majors and minors in the sample a percentage will also be in the elementary and intermediate level courses, according to the data below (O) in which the division of minors and electives has been made from internal evidence within the questionnaire.

| | *101* | *102* | *103* | *104* | *In student numbers* |
|---|---|---|---|---|---|
| Electives | 18% | 15 | 13 | 12 | = 230 students |
| Minors | 5 | 7 | 5 | 5 | = 78 students |
| Majors | 2 | 1 | 4 | 5 | = 42 students |

*Of the samples in this section,* then, approximately 55% of the electives, 53% of the minors, and 24% of the majors are in the elementary and intermediate levels.

29.  At the 200 (advanced) level the breakdown of categories was (QQ. 22-26):

| | |
|---|---|
| Majors | 38% |
| Minors | 19 |
| LAS requirement | 11* |
| Commerce req. | 18** |
| Music req. | 6*** |
| Electives | 10**** (estimated) |

*LAS Requirement*: a six-hour sequence in a foreign literature can satisfy the Humanities requirement of the College.

**Commerce Requirement*: as an elective in List 1 of General Education sequences: eight-hour sequence in any language (intermediate or above).

***Music Requirement*: As an elective in the required Humanities Sequence: six or more hours involving literature or related humanistic studies using one foreign language at the 200-level or above ... or completion of intermediate-level of any foreign language (if not a curriculum requirement) plus one advanced course involving literature ....

****Electives = 39% in the data: would include many of the LAS, Commerce, and Music Requirement students (who elected to do FL rather than Art, Philosophy, History, etc.), and some minors. In this case the 10% estimated covers the remainder unaccounted for in the preceding categories.

30. *Students' grades in FL* in percentages of specific samples (Q. 2):

|   | Electives | Minors | Majors |
|---|-----------|--------|--------|
| A | 48% | 61% | 53% |
| B | 37 | 30 | 41 |
| C | 8 | 6 | 3 |
| D | 2 | 1 | --- |

31. *Language Experience,* in percentages (Q. 5):

| This is | first | second | third | fourth | fifth | language studied |
|---------|-------|--------|-------|--------|-------|------------------|
| Electives | 38% | 42 | 14 | 4 | 1 | |
| Minors | 29 | 51 | 14 | 5 | 1 | |
| Majors | 49 | 33 | 14 | 2 | 2 | |

32. Studied *this* language *before coming to the University of Illinois* for x *number of years* (Q. 6):

| | 0 yr | 1 yr | 2 yr | 3 yr | 4 yr | 5 yr | 6 yr | 6+ yr |
|---|------|------|------|------|------|------|------|-------|
| Electives | 43% | 6 | 13 | 8 | 22 | 2 | 2 | 3 |
| Minors | 36 | 13 | 14 | 8 | 21 | 4 | 1 | 3 |
| Majors | 10 | 3 | 19 | 12 | 32 | 9 | 5 | 8 |

54%

33. Studied *this* language *before coming to the U. of I.* (Q. 7):

| | HS | JHS | Elem. Sch. | Jr. Coll. | Another Univ. | Another Country | Native Speaker | Bilingual in USA |
|---|-----|-----|-----------|-----------|---------------|-----------------|----------------|------------------|
| Elect. | 41% | 7 | 5 | 1 | 2 | 1 | 1 | 3 |
| Minors | 45 | 4 | 7 | 3 | 5 | 2 | 1 | 4 |
| Majors | 58 | 12 | 10 | 1 | 3 | 2 | 1 | 5 |

34. Studied a *different* language *before beginning this language* (Q. 8):

| for | 1 yr | 2 yr | 3 yr | 4 yr | 5 yr | 6 yr | 7+ yr |
|-----|------|------|------|------|------|------|-------|
| Elect. | 7% | 15 | 8 | 17 | 6 | 3 | 7 |
| Minors | 10 | 18 | 13 | 9 | 7 | 5 | 10 |
| Majors | 12 | 17 | 6 | 8 | 4 | 1 | 2 |

35. *Some reasons for selection of this language* (QQ. 48-66):

| | Electives | Minors | Majors |
|---|---|---|---|
| Q. 48. Family interested in it | 18 | 18 | 19 |
| Q. 49. Friends studying it | 16 | 12 | 11 |
| Q. 50. Began studying it in H.S. or J.H.S. | 42 | 45 | 70 |
| Q. 51. Want to read literary works | 54 | 63 | 74 |
| Q. 52. Want to read sociolog/polit/econ/works | 31 | 31 | 37 |
| Q. 53. Want to read philos/psych works | 41 | 46 | 50 |
| Q. 54. Identify culturally or ethnically... | 28 | 28 | 37 |
| Q. 55. Important for international communication | 64 | 70 | 78 |
| Q. 56. Interested in langs. very different from Eng. | 37 | 39 | 41 |
| Q. 57. Had heard it was difficult | 24 | 30 | 20 |
| Q. 58. Had heard it was easy | 12 | 11 | 15 |
| Q. 59. Impressed by achievements of speakers of language | 31 | 38 | 37 |
| Q. 60. Close personal relations with a native speaker | 21 | 21 | 24 |
| Q. 61. Want to visit country. | 82 | 84 | 87 |
| Q. 62. Want to read research material | 29 | 28 | 28 |
| Q. 63. Want to understand films/radio | 61 | 65 | 77 |
| Q. 64. Want to correspond in language | 54 | 62 | 74 |
| Q. 65. Want to study in the country | 60 | 66 | 80 |
| Q. 66. Interested in the structure of the language | 51 | 66 | 76 |

36. Plan to use the language in *future work* (QQ. 68-69):

| | Electives | Minors | Majors |
|---|---|---|---|
| Q. 68. 1. *No plans* for use in future work | 38 | 18 | 10 |
| 2. Teaching major | 8 | 4 | 46 |
| 3. Teaching minor | 3 | 32 | 2 |
| 4. College teaching | 6 | 8 | 9 |
| 5. Science | 10 | 2 | 1 |
| 6. Anthropology | 1 | 1 | --- |
| 7. religious vocation, missions, etc. | 2 | --- | 2 |
| 8. social work | 2 | 1 | 1 |
| 9. overseas social service (Peace Corps, etc.) | 8 | 15 | 12 |
| Q. 69. 1. music | 5 | 5 | 2 |
| 2. journalism | 5 | 5 | 5 |
| 3. diplomatic or civil service | 8 | 20 | 16 |
| 4. business | 5 | 4 | 7 |
| 5. linguistics | 6 | 14 | 19 |
| 6. philosophy | 2 | 1 | 1 |
| 7. architecture | 1 | --- | --- |
| 8. engineering | 4 | 1 | --- |
| 9. other | 20 | 15 | 12 |

37. Needs *satisfied by types of courses provided* (Q. 70):

| | |
|---|---|
| Electives | 63% |
| Minors | 65% |
| Majors | 57% |

38. Would have liked to *combine* a foreign language *with the major in an interdepartmental structure* (Q. 73):

| | |
|---|---|
| Electives | 37% |
| Minors | 47% |
| Majors | 39% |

39.    If student could design *courses at 200-300 level to suit personal needs* they *would want* (QQ. 71-72):

|  |  | Electives | Minors | Majors |
|---|---|---|---|---|
| Q. 71. | 1. oral communication | 13* | 13 | 13 |
|  | 2. reading in own field | 7 | 10 | 3 |
|  | 3. writing/discussing business/advertising/ PR | 0 | 1 | 2 |
|  | 4. plays, operas, songs | 2 | 1 | 2 |
|  | 5. contrastive study of societies and cultures | 3 | 5 | 5 |
|  | 6. situational language use for social workers | 1 | 1 | 4 |
|  | 7. linguistic analysis | 2 | 2 | 2 |
|  | 8. translating and interpreting | 7 | 7 | 11 |
|  | 9. other (not yet analyzed) | 1 | 0 | 1 |

*Note: Q. 71 was answered by approximately 35% of electives and minors and 40% of majors. The figures given are percentages of the total sample. (The others were satisfied with courses offered, see 37 above.)

Q. 72. *Culturally enriching courses, unrelated to career needs,* in:

|  | Electives | Minors | Majors |
|---|---|---|---|
| 1. literature | 7** | 5 | 8 |
| 2. philosophy | 3 | 4 | 5 |
| 3. art history | 3 | 3 | 5 |
| 4. film | 3 | 3 | 5 |
| 5. music | 3 | 3 | 6 |
| 6. contemporary life-styles and values | 6 | 9 | 2 |
| 7. cultural and political history | 3 | 5 | 8 |
| 8. history of the language | 1 | 0 | 3 |
| 9. other (not yet analyzed) | 1 | 0 | 2 |

**Note: Q. 72 was answered by approximately 30% of electives and minors and 38% of majors. The figures given are percentages of the total sample.

# C. Specific Language Analysis (O): Across Levels

| | French (733SS) | German (518SS) | Spanish (180SS) | Russian (129SS) | Latin (98SS) | Modern Hebrew (10SS) | Persian (10SS) |
|---|---|---|---|---|---|---|---|
| 40. Fulfilling the *LAS language requirement* (Q. 22) | 63 | 58 | 62 | 29 | 59 | 40 | 60 |
| 41. *Majors* (Q. 26) | 11 | 6 | 11 | 16 | 7 | 0 | 0 |
| 42. Percentage majors at 200 level | 48 | 23 | 40 | 57 | 30 | 0 | 0 |
| 43. *Minors* (Q. 25) | 7 | 7 | 8 | 16 | 10 | 0 | 0 |
| 44. *Electives* (Q. 24) | 20 | 26 | 19 | 41 | 24 | 50 | 20 |
| 45. GPA (Q. 1): 5 (highest) | 10 | 10 | 7 | 16 | 16 | 10 | 0 |
|     4-4.99 | 63 | 61 | 69 | 65 | 58 | 70 | 80 |
|     3-3.99 | 20 | 17 | 20 | 12 | 19 | 20 | 20 |
| 46. *Average language grade* so far (Q. 2): | | | | | | | |
| A | 39 | 42 | 48 | 46 | 67 | 70 | 30 |
| B | 40 | 39 | 39 | 39 | 21 | 30 | 60 |
| C | 15 | 12 | 13 | 9 | 5 | 0 | 0 |
| D | 3 | 2 | 2 | 0 | 2 | 0 | 0 |
| 47. *Age* of student (Q. 3): under 21 | 82 | 81 | 78 | 69 | 85 | 80 | 80 |
| 48. Had a *break in education* (Q. 4) | 13 | 13 | 15 | 16 | 10 | 30 | 10 |
| 49. Have studied *two or more* foreign languages (Q. 5) | 60 | 64 | 53 | 85 | 53 | 100 | 40 |
| 50. Studied *this* language before coming to U. of I. (Q. 6): | | | | | | | |
| for  1 year | 7 | 7 | 10 | 5 | 5 | 40 | 30 |
|       2 years | 33 | 24 | 44 | 15 | 32 | 0 | 10 |
|       3 years | 17 | 14 | 11 | 8 | 10 | 10 | 30 |
|       4 years | 13 | 9 | 11 | 8 | 14 | 10 | 0 |
|       5+ years | 10 | 12 | 8 | 4 | 2 | 20 | 0 |
| 51. *Native speaker* or *U.S. bilingual* (Q. 7) | 1 | 4 | 2 | 6 | 0 | 0 | 10 |

## C. Specific Language Analysis (O): Across Levels (continued)

| | French (733SS) | German (518SS) | Spanish (180SS) | Russian (129SS) | Latin (98SS) | Modern Hebrew (10SS) | Persian (10SS) |
|---|---|---|---|---|---|---|---|
| **52. Studied *this* language *at* (Q. 7):** | | | | | | | |
| high school | 57 | 47 | 63 | 27 | 58 | 10 | 60 |
| Grades 7-8 | 12 | 5 | 8 | 4 | 6 | 10 | 0 |
| Grade 6 or earlier | 8 | 2 | 9 | 1 | 0 | 40 | 0 |
| Junior College | 1 | 3 | 2 | 0 | 1 | 0 | 0 |
| Another University | 2 | 2 | 1 | 6 | 0 | 0 | 0 |
| At school in another country | 1 | 1 | 1 | 2 | 0 | 20 | 0 |
| **53. Studied a *different* FL *before coming to* U. of I. (Q. 8):** | 40 | 63 | 51 | 86 | 58 | 100 | 30 |
| for  1 year | 9 | 9 | 12 | 6 | 6 | 10 | 10 |
| 2 years | 17 | 29 | 18 | 29 | 27 | 30 | 0 |
| 3 years | 6 | 10 | 5 | 15 | 10 | 30 | 0 |
| 4 years | 3 | 8 | 5 | 19 | 9 | 10 | 10 |
| 5+ years | 5 | 7 | 11 | 17 | 6 | 20 | 10 |
| **54. *Background and opinions of students by language* (QQ. 9-21):** | | | | | | | |
| Parents speak a FL (Q. 9) | 24 | 25 | 24 | 27 | 23 | 30 | 40 |
| Have friends who speak a FL (Q. 10) | 64 | 66 | 74 | 67 | 67 | 80 | 60 |
| See no use for FL (Q. 11) | 27 | 31 | 31 | 14 | 34 | 10 | 0 |
| Have traveled abroad (Q. 12) | 43 | 45 | 46 | 45 | 42 | 50 | 30 |
| Would like to travel abroad (Q. 13) | 95 | 95 | 94 | 93 | 97 | 90 | 90 |
| FL unnecessary because English widely spoken (Q. 14) | 20 | 22 | 26 | 5 | 28 | 30 | 0 |
| Interested in differences between languages (Q. 15) | 50 | 50 | 48 | 72 | 47 | 50 | 60 |
| Interested in what goes on in other countries (Q. 16) | 91 | 90 | 85 | 94 | 85 | 100 | 100 |
| Preparing for field where FL useful (Q. 17) | 40 | 48 | 48 | 67 | 47 | 10 | 60 |
| FL requires too much out-of-class study time (Q. 18) | 38 | 40 | 45 | 37 | 39 | 20 | 20 |

| | | | | | | | |
|---|---|---|---|---|---|---|---|
| No form of study should be required (Q. 19) | 33 | 29 | 37 | 18 | 39 | 20 | 40 |
| Interested in ways people in other countries look at things (Q. 20) | 88 | 84 | 84 | 95 | 83 | 90 | 90 |
| Never liked learning FLs (Q. 21) | 31 | 32 | 36 | 19 | 39 | 20 | 30 |
| *Requirement students only: 55-59.* | | | | | | | |
| *In percentages of requirement students (overall percentages in parentheses)* | | | | | | | |
| 55. Would *not* have studied FL if no requirement. In parentheses percentages of total SS (Q. 27) | 66 (47) | 62 (44) | 67 (45) | 55 (21) | 74 (48) | 50 (20) | 100 (60) |
| 56. *Enjoy* learning the FL even though it is a requirement (Q. 28) | 52 | 49 | 46 | 69 | 43 | 100 | 100 |
| 57. Would *enjoy FL more* if course content different (Q. 29). See 28 above for expressed preferences for course content (QQ. 30-42) | 49 | 41 | 30 | 48 | 20 | 25 | 17 |
| 58. *Would have liked to continue* but cannot (Q. 43) | 14 | 16 | 13 | 13 | 5 | 0 | 0 |
| Intend to continue: | | | | | | | |
| as major (Q. 44) | 3 | 3 | 3 | 0 | 2 | 25 | 0 |
| as minor (Q. 45) | 6 | 4 | 7 | 11 | 3 | 25 | 0 |
| as elective (Q. 46) | 21 | 23 | 10 | 24 | 17 | 50 | 33 |
| 59. *Would have tried to include FL* if no requirement (Q. 47) | 29 | 37 | 24 | 53 | 20 | 100 | 33 |
| *Present and future majors, minors, and electives only: 60-66. In percentages of this group* | | | | | | | |
| 60. *Selected this language because:* | | | | | | | |
| Family interested in it (Q. 48) | 11 | 30 | 12 | 11 | 7 | 60 | 33 |
| Friends studying it (Q. 49) | 13 | 20 | 14 | 11 | 4 | 30 | 33 |
| Began it in junior or senior high school (Q. 50) | 64 | 40 | 68 | 29 | 50 | 10 | 100 |
| Want to read the literature (Q. 51) | 51 | 45 | 47 | 52 | 53 | 20 | 33 |

## C. Specific Language Analysis (O): Across Levels (continued)

| | French (733SS) | German (518SS) | Spanish (180SS) | Russian (129SS) | Latin (98SS) | Hebrew (10SS) | Persian (10SS) |
|---|---|---|---|---|---|---|---|
| Want to read sociological/political/economic works (Q. 52) | 25 | 23 | 28 | 35 | 25 | 20 | 33 |
| Want to read philosophical/psychological works (Q. 53) | 34 | 35 | 40 | 34 | 39 | 20 | 66 |
| Feel cultural or ethnic identification with speakers of the language (Q. 54) | 16 | 47 | 24 | 23 | 13 | 90 | 33 |
| It is important for international communication (Q. 55) | 66 | 60 | 72 | 80 | 20 | 40 | 100 |
| it is very different from English (Q. 56) | 30 | 23 | 26 | 57 | 24 | 20 | 66 |
| Heard it was difficult (Q. 57) | 9 | 28 | 2 | 51 | 41 | 20 | 33 |
| Heard it was easy (Q. 58) | 15 | 12 | 46 | 0 | 15 | 0 | 33 |
| Impressed with achievements of speakers of the language (Q. 59) | 23 | 35 | 20 | 30 | 43 | 20 | 33 |
| Close relations with a speaker of the language (Q. 60) | 13 | 34 | 28 | 7 | 0 | 30 | 0 |
| Want to visit the country (Q. 61) | 89 | 87 | 86 | 82 | 22 | 100 | 100 |
| Want to read research material (Q. 62) | 21 | 34 | 18 | 43 | 31 | 10 | 66 |
| Want to understand films and broadcasts (Q. 63) | 68 | 62 | 68 | 55 | 0 | 30 | 100 |
| Want to correspond (Q. 64) | 58 | 54 | 60 | 48 | 0 | 80 | 66 |
| Want to study in the country (Q. 65) | 62 | 58 | 64 | 57 | 17 | 80 | 66 |
| Interested in the structure of the language (Q. 66) | 47 | 42 | 52 | 60 | 78 | 30 | 100 |
| 61. Want to use it for future work in (QQ. 68-69): | 66 | 68 | 76 | 71 | 63 | 30 | 100 |
| Teaching (below college) | 25 | 17 | 28 | 6 | 24 | 20 | 0 |
| Teaching (college level) | 2 | 5 | 2 | 6 | 9 | 0 | 0 |
| Science | 4 | 15 | 8 | 17 | 4 | 0 | 0 |
| Anthropology | 2 | 2 | 2 | 1 | 2 | 10 | 0 |
| Religious work | 0 | 2 | 0 | 1 | 0 | 0 | 0 |

| | | | | | | | |
|---|---|---|---|---|---|---|---|
| Social work | 2 | 2 | 12 | 0 | 0 | 0 | 0 |
| Overseas social service | 9 | 5 | 12 | 17 | 0 | 0 | 0 |
| Music | 6 | 8 | 4 | 4 | 4 | 0 | 33 |
| Journalism | 8 | 7 | 10 | 2 | 0 | 0 | 0 |
| Diplomatic or Civil Service | 9 | 7 | 18 | 17 | 0 | 0 | 33 |
| Business | 6 | 5 | 6 | 6 | 17 | 0 | 0 |
| Linguistics | 8 | 7 | 8 | 6 | 4 | 0 | 0 |
| Philosophy | 2 | 2 | 0 | 2 | 0 | 0 | 0 |
| Architecture | 0 | 2 | 0 | 2 | 0 | 0 | 0 |
| Engineering | 0 | 3 | 0 | 7 | 0 | 0 | 0 |
| Other | 11 | 15 | 24 | 17 | 30 | 10 | 33 |
| **62. Needs are satisfied by type of course provided (Q. 70)** | 58 | 60 | 60 | 58 | 76 | 70 | 100 |
| **63. Would like advanced courses in (Q. 71):** | | | | | | | |
| oral communication | 15 | 13 | 18 | 7 | 0 | 20 | 0 |
| Reading in my field | 8 | 10 | 2 | 8 | 7 | 0 | 33 |
| Business, advertising, and P.R. | 0 | 2 | 2 | 1 | 0 | 0 | 0 |
| Plays, operas, songs | 2 | 2 | 4 | 2 | 0 | 0 | 0 |
| Contrastive study of societies and cultures | 4 | 3 | 2 | 5 | 4 | 0 | 0 |
| Situational language use for social workers | 2 | 0 | 6 | 2 | 0 | 10 | 0 |
| Linguistic analysis | 2 | 2 | 2 | 1 | 4 | 0 | 0 |
| Translating/interpreting | 7 | 5 | 4 | 14 | 0 | 0 | 0 |
| **64. Would like culturally enriching advanced courses, unrelated to career needs in (Q. 72):** | | | | | | | |
| Literature | 9 | 7 | 4 | 2 | 4 | 0 | 0 |
| Philosophy | 4 | 3 | 4 | 5 | 2 | 0 | 0 |
| Art history | 4 | 3 | 2 | 1 | 0 | 0 | 0 |
| Film | 6 | 2 | 8 | 5 | 0 | 0 | 0 |
| Music | 2 | 2 | 6 | 6 | 2 | 20 | 0 |
| Contemporary life-styles and values | 4 | 5 | 12 | 8 | 6 | 0 | 0 |
| Cultural and political history | 2 | 3 | 0 | 6 | 0 | 0 | 0 |
| History of the language | 0 | 2 | 0 | 1 | 0 | 10 | 0 |

## C.  Specific Language Analysis (O): Across Levels (continued)

| | French (733SS) | German (518SS) | Spanish (180SS) | Russian (129SS) | Latin (98SS) | Modern Hebrew (10SS) | Persian (10SS) |
|---|---|---|---|---|---|---|---|
| 65. Would have liked to combine a FL with major in an interdepartmental structure (Q. 73) | 53 | 33 | 40 | 41 | 26 | 0 | 100 |
| 66. As well as this FL I have also studied (QQ. 74-75): | | | | | | | |
| French | -- | 30 | 32 | 37 | 30 | 60 | 0 |
| German | 11 | -- | 8 | 14 | 9 | 0 | 33 |
| Classical Greek | 0 | 0 | 0 | 1 | 9 | 0 | 0 |
| Modern Hebrew | 2 | 2 | 8 | 2 | 2 | -- | 0 |
| Japanese | 2 | 2 | 0 | 2 | 4 | 0 | 0 |
| Latin | 13 | 15 | 14 | 14 | -- | 0 | 33 |
| Russian | 4 | 3 | 2 | -- | 6 | 0 | 0 |
| Spanish | 21 | 18 | -- | 27 | 24 | 30 | 0 |
| Swahili | 0 | 0 | 2 | 0 | 0 | 0 | 0 |

### D. Foreign Language Needs and Interests (1973):
### By Language Groups and Levels
*(Prepared with the assistance of Paulette Pelc.)*

This part of the report focuses on information received from 1658 students of the major languages taught on campus: French, German, Spanish, Russian, and Latin. The number of questionnaires analyzed for the major languages is as follows: French (733 students); German (518 students); Spanish (180 students); Russian (129 students); and Latin (98 students). These figures do not represent enrollments in these languages. Of this sample, over one-half of the students studying each language were fulfilling the LAS graduation requirement, with French and Spanish having the highest percentages of requirement students, 63% and 62% respectively, with German next at 58%. The Russian group is distinctive in that only 29% of the students are fulfilling the LAS requirement. The Russian group is also unique in that among its total number of students it has the highest percentage of majors (16%), (followed by French and Spanish both with 11%), of combined elective and minor students (46%), and of elective students (32%).

Overall, 38% of the students at the 200 (advanced) level are majors, but there is considerable variability across languages; at the 200 level 57% of the Russian, 48% of the French, 40% of the Spanish, 30% of the Latin, and 23% of the German students are majors. Of the 62% who are non-majors at this level, 50% of the Spanish group and 43% of the German group are electives while 25% of both the German and the Latin groups are minors. Only 14% of the 200-level Spanish students are minors and 15% of the French.

Returning to the overall analysis by language, the Russian students have the highest university grade-point average with 81% maintaining an average of 4.0 or higher. 16% of both the Russian and the Latin students boast a 5.0 average while only 7% of the Spanish students and 10% of the French and German students have a 5.0 average. When asked for their average grade in foreign languages 67% in Latin claim an A, while only 39% of the French students have an A average.

The Latin group as a whole is the youngest (85% of the students are under 21) and only 10% have had a break in their education. On the other hand, 31% of the Russian students are 21 or over, and 16% have had a break in their education.

85% in Russian and 64% in German have studied two or more languages while 60% of French and 53% of Spanish students have studied another foreign language. (This discrepancy may be related to the higher percentages of students fulfilling the LAS requirement in French and Spanish.)

Even though students of Russian have studied more languages on the whole, 85% never studied Russian before coming to the University of Illinois. On the other hand, of students studying French 80% had studied the language before coming to the University of Illinois, 73% for two years or more, and 84% of the students of Spanish had studied the language earlier, 74% for two years or more. The figures for German were 66% and 59%. Not unexpectedly, it was found that the study of Spanish and French began early, in elementary or junior high school for a number of students (17% and 20%), and were the most frequently studied languages, along with Latin, in high school. Almost twice as much German as Russian is studied at that level.

Approximately 25% of the students in each language group have parents who speak a foreign language. 74% of the Spanish students have friends who speak a foreign language, perhaps because they, too, are fulfilling the LAS requirement.

Only 14% of the Russian students find no use for foreign language while 34% in Latin feel that it is not useful.

Nearly half of all the language groups have traveled, but almost 100% would like to do so.

28% of the Latin group and 26% in Spanish feel that English is so widely spoken as to make a foreign language unnecessary while only 5% of the Russian group feels this way. (The emphasis in Latin is, of course, not on speaking.)

Russian has a high 67% who plan to work in a field in which knowledge of a foreign language will be useful. Those who study Russian seem to feel that it is an integral part of their career orientation.

Latin (39%) and Spanish (37%) students feel most strongly that no form of study should be required, contrasting with 18% in the Russian group. Since 39% of the Latin students and 36% of the Spanish students never liked learning languages anyway while only 19% of the Russian students share this dislike, these may be the same students as those resenting any form of coercion in what they are learning. (Russian students, we may remember, have studied more foreign languages longer!)

From two-thirds to three-quarters of the requirement students state that they would not have studied a foreign language if there had been no requirement (with only 55% in Russian), yet 69% of requirement students in Russian and 52% in French are enjoying their foreign-language study despite the requirement, this percentage descending to 43% in Latin. Of those who responded, 49% in French and 48% in Russian felt they would enjoy their study more if the content were different, while only 20% of those who responded in Latin felt that a change in content would affect their enjoyment. The interpretation of the data at this point (QQ. 30-42) is difficult without more information on the type of course content the students of the different languages were experiencing.

30% of the French and German requirement groups, 22% of the Latin, 20% of the Spanish, and 35% of the Russian plan to continue the study of the language as an elective, a major, or a minor, and for all languages, except Latin, about one-seventh of them would have liked to continue had their program allowed it. 53% of the Russian, 37% of the German, and 29% of the French would have tried to include a foreign language in their program if there had been no requirement.

Within each language group, the reasons majors, minors, and electives give for selecting that language are as follows (in descending order of percentages).

*French*

| | |
|---|---|
| I want to visit a country where French is spoken | 89% |
| I want to understand films or radio broadcasts | 68 |
| I consider French important for international communication | 66 |
| I began studying French in junior or senior high school | 64 |

I want to study in a country in which French is spoken     62
I want to correspond     58
I want to read the literature     51

### German
I want to visit a country where German is spoken     87%
I want to understand films or radio broadcasts     62
I consider German important for international communication     60
I want to study in a country in which German is spoken     58
I want to correspond     54

### Spanish
I want to visit a country where Spanish is spoken     86%
I consider Spanish important for international communication     72
I began studying Spanish in junior or senior high school     68
I want to understand films or radio broadcasts     68
I want to study in a country in which Spanish is spoken     64
I want to correspond     60
I am interested in the structure of Spanish     52

### Russian
I want to visit a country where Russian is spoken     82%
I consider Russian important for international communication     80
I am interested in the structure of Russian     60
I am interested in languages which are very different from English     57
I want to study in a country in which Russian is spoken     57
I want to understand films or radio broadcasts     55
I want to read the literature     52
I heard it was difficult     51

### Latin
I am interested in the structure of Latin     78%
I want to read the literature     53
I began studying Latin in junior or senior high school     50
I am impressed with the achievements of the people     43
I heard it was difficult     41

It is interesting to note that, across languages, German students rate both family interest in the language and the fact that their friends study it as more important influences in selecting the language than do other students. Cultural and ethnic identification is highest among the German students (47%) and 34% of this group have personal relations with speakers of the language, the next highest in this category being Spanish with 28%. As might have been anticipated, for French, Spanish, and Latin early study rates more highly as a reason for selection. (Once these students have begun the study of the language, they simply continue it.) Higher percentages of students in Latin, Russian, and French are interested in reading the literature in their respective languages. German and Russian students also rate the reading of research material in the language of more importance in their selection of a language than do others.

Of all the groups, the students of Russian (80%) are most convinced of the importance of their language for international communication, followed by Spanish (72%) and French (66%). Russian students also like languages which are very different from English (57%) and are motivated to study Russian, at least partially, because they had heard it was a difficult language to learn (51%). On the other hand, 46% of the Spanish students had heard Spanish was an easy language to learn and marked this as one reason for selecting that language.

Spanish students (60%) are the most interested in corresponding in the language, closely followed by French (58%), and students of Latin (78%) and Russian (60%) are interested in the structure of those languages.

Of students who expect to use their language knowledge in future work, the majority are teaching majors in Spanish (28%) and French (25%). Spanish students also look toward work in diplomatic or civil service (18%) and home or overseas social service (12%). Use of the language for science (15%) vies with teaching (17%) for students of German, and students of Russian also see the language as useful for science (17%) and for overseas diplomatic and social service (17%). Latin students rate future use in linguistics higher (these students, too, were more interested in the structure of the language). More Russian and Latin students plan to enter college teaching (6% and 9%). More German and French students see some use for the language in music (8% and 6%) and Russian students in engineering (7%).

The Russian group has studied the most languages while for 47% of the Spanish students Spanish is their first foreign language.

Across languages French is the language most widely studied by all the other groups. Major, minor, and elective students of each of the major languages have studied the following (in descending order of percentages):

*French*:     Spanish (21%), Latin (13%), German (11%)
*German*:    French (30%), Spanish (18%), Latin (15%)
*Spanish*:    French (32%), Latin (14%)
*Russian*:    French (37%), Spanish (27%), German (14%), Latin (14%)
*Latin*:       French (30%), Spanish (24%), German (9%), Classical
              Greek (9%)

## E. Analysis by Levels
### (data follows questionnaire numbering)

101 = first semester; 102 = second semester; 103 = third semester; 104 = fourth semester; 200 = fifth and sixth semesters.

Figures in columns represent *percentages of the total number* of questionnaires received for that particular level (e.g., 101 = 545 SS or subjects). In some cases *yes* and *no* percentages are given (23/26); this is because these sections applied only to some of the respondents at that level (e.g., since not all 101 students were requirement students, only about 67% of them responded to Section C). In these cases, the proportions are important, e.g., for Q. 27 at 101 level 50/25 shows that 66% of requirement students would not have studied a foreign language if there had been no requirement (that is, 50% of the 101 class), whereas, in Q. 28, 40/34 indicates that 54% of these requirement students are enjoying studying the language even though it is a requirement. This does *not* indicate that only 40% of the class were enjoying the course, since a quarter of the class has not been included in this response (non-requirement students). In interpreting the data, this aspect must be continually borne in mind; the total of the yes/no responses for the question, in most cases, gives the percentage of the sample responding for that section, except for some choices, such as *Other,* to which not all students responded.

| Section A | | Overall (1,821 SS) | 101 (545 SS) | 102 (265 SS) | 103 (441 SS) | 104 (223 SS) | 200 (347 SS) |
|---|---|---|---|---|---|---|---|
| 1. | 1. | 11% | 10% | 10% | 12% | 9% | 14% |
|  | 2. | 30 | 26 | 28 | 31 | 28 | 39 |
|  | 3. | 34 | 34 | 36 | 33 | 39 | 32 |
|  | 4. | 14 | 15 | 15 | 15 | 16 | 8 |
|  | 5. | 4 | 6 | 4 | 4 | 3 | 2 |
|  | 6. | 1 | 1 | 1 | 1 | 0 | 1 |
|  | 7., 8., 9. | 0 | 0 | 0 | 0 | 0 | 0 |
| 2. | 1. | 44 | 45 | 44 | 37 | 39 | 54 |
|  | 2. | 38 | 36 | 35 | 42 | 31 | 37 |
|  | 3. | 12 | 12 | 17 | 16 | 13 | 6 |
|  | 4. | 3 | 3 | 3 | 3 | 4 | 1 |
|  | 5. | 0 | 0 | 0 | 0 | 0 | 0 |
| 3. | 1. | 80 | 85 | 82 | 82 | 78 | 71 |
|  | 2. | 16 | 10 | 14 | 15 | 20 | 24 |
|  | 3. | 3 | 5 | 2 | 2 | 1 | 5 |
|  | 4. | 1 | 1 | 2 | 1 | 1 | 0 |
| 4. | 1. (Yes) | 13 | 14 | 14 | 12 | 17 | 13 |
|  | 2. (No) | 86 | 85 | 86 | 87 | 83 | 86 |
| 5. | 1. | 46 | 32 | 53 | 46 | 16 | 53 |
|  | 2. | 40 | 53 | 34 | 41 | 30 | 31 |
|  | 3. | 9 | 10 | 9 | 9 | 5 | 12 |
|  | 4. | 3 | 3 | 2 | 2 | 4 | 3 |
|  | 5. | 1 | 1 | 1 | 1 | 0 | 1 |
|  | 6., 7., 8. | 0 | 0 | 0 | 0 | 0 | 0 |

*Section A*

| | | Overall (1,821 SS) | 101 (545 SS) | 102 (265 SS) | 103 (441 SS) | 104 (223 SS) | 200 (347 SS) |
|---|---|---|---|---|---|---|---|
| 6. | 1. | 7 | 6 | 9 | 10 | 5 | 7 |
| | 2. | 29 | 28 | 41 | 31 | 34 | 16 |
| | 3. | 14 | 6 | 18 | 17 | 24 | 12 |
| | 4. | 11 | 1 | 4 | 6 | 15 | 33 |
| | 5. | 3 | 1 | 0 | 2 | 4 | 8 |
| | 6. | 2 | 1 | 1 | 2 | 2 | 5 |
| | 7. | 2 | 1 | 1 | 2 | 3 | 6 |
| | 8. | 32 | 57 | 25 | 29 | 13 | 12 |
| 7. | 1. | 50 | 33 | 61 | 52 | 65 | 56 |
| | 2. | 8 | 6 | 9 | 7 | 12 | 12 |
| | 3. | 6 | 4 | 5 | 7 | 6 | 8 |
| | 4. | 1 | 1 | 1 | 3 | 1 | 2 |
| | 5. | 2 | 1 | 2 | 3 | 2 | 4 |
| | 6. | 1 | 1 | 0 | 1 | 0 | 3 |
| | 7. | 0 | 0 | 0 | 1 | 0 | 1 |
| | 8. | 2 | 2 | 2 | 2 | 1 | 4 |
| 8. | 1. | 9 | 18 | 11 | 8 | 11 | 10 |
| | 2. | 23 | 29 | 18 | 25 | 20 | 16 |
| | 3. | 8 | 11 | 7 | 9 | 3 | 7 |
| | 4. | 7 | 10 | 8 | 3 | 4 | 6 |
| | 5. | 3 | 4 | 2 | 3 | 4 | 3 |
| | 6. | 2 | 3 | 2 | 2 | 1 | 2 |
| | 7. | 3 | 4 | 3 | 1 | 1 | 4 |

| Section B | Overall | 101 | 102 | 103 | 104 | 200 |
|---|---|---|---|---|---|---|
| 9. | 25 | 22 | 25 | 22 | 28 | 31 |
| 10. | 67 | 66 | 62 | 64 | 65 | 79 |
| 11. | 27 | 31 | 37 | 34 | 29 | 5 |
| 12. | 44 | 43 | 42 | 39 | 41 | 56 |
| 13. | 95 | 94 | 96 | 92 | 96 | 99 |
| 14. | 20 | 22 | 32 | 23 | 19 | 4 |
| 15. | 52 | 48 | 38 | 43 | 48 | 84 |
| 16. | 90 | 89 | 85 | 89 | 92 | 95 |
| 17. | 47 | 45 | 35 | 39 | 35 | 75 |
| 18. | 38 | 40 | 40 | 51 | 43 | 15 |
| 19. | 31 | 31 | 41 | 38 | 29 | 18 |
| 20. | 87 | 84 | 82 | 85 | 90 | 95 |
| 21. | 30 | 37 | 38 | 37 | 29 | 7 |
| 22. | 57 | 64 | 68 | 71 | 71 | 11 |
| 23. 1. | 1 | 1 | 0 | 1 | 1 | 0 |
| 2. | 10 | 10 | 9 | 7 | 8 | 18 |
| 3. | 0 | 0 | 0 | 0 | 0 | 0 |
| 4. | 0 | 0 | 0 | 0 | 0 | 1 |
| 5. | 0 | 0 | 0 | 0 | 0 | 0 |
| 6. | 1 | 3 | 1 | 1 | 1 | 0 |
| 7. | 0 | 0 | 0 | 0 | 0 | 0 |
| 8. | 4 | 4 | 5 | 4 | 3 | 6 |
| 9. | 31 | 26 | 20 | 22 | 23 | 63 |
| 24. | 23 | 24 | 18 | 16 | 16 | 39 |
| 25. | 8 | 5 | 7 | 5 | 5 | 19 |
| 26. | 9 | 2 | 1 | 4 | 5 | 38 |

| Section B | Overall | 101 | 102 | 103 | 104 | 200 |
|---|---|---|---|---|---|---|
| 27. | 43/24 | 50/25 | 53/24 | 53/25 | 51/27 | 5/18 |
| 28. | 34/32 | 40/34 | 33/34 | 36/43 | 42/36 | 18/ 5 |
| 29. | 29/37 | 26/48 | 35/40 | 37/41 | 39/38 | 10/12 |
| 30. | 40/25 | 43/30 | 42/34 | 47/31 | 48/30 | 18/ 3 |
| 31. | 42/24 | 45/28 | 45/32 | 50/28 | 49/28 | 18/ 3 |
| 32. | 40/25 | 45/28 | 50/26 | 49/27 | 43/35 | 11/10 |
| 33. | 28/37 | 33/39 | 29/47 | 34/43 | 31/47 | 10/12 |
| 34. | 41/24 | 43/30 | 45/32 | 52/25 | 52/26 | 16/ 5 |
| 35. | 33/32 | 33/39 | 42/34 | 43/35 | 38/39 | 12/10 |
| 36. | 31/34 | 34/38 | 31/45 | 40/37 | 37/39 | 12/10 |
| 37. | 46/17 | 48/24 | 49/27 | 56/20 | 60/18 | 16/ 5 |
| 38. | 39/26 | 38/34 | 40/36 | 51/26 | 53/25 | 15/ 7 |
| 39. | 17/47 | 21/50 | 15/61 | 20/57 | 20/58 | 8/13 |
| 40. | 42/23 | 42/30 | 48/28 | 54/23 | 51/27 | 16/ 5 |
| 41. | 13/51 | 15/54 | 17/59 | 17/60 | 13/65 | 3/18 |
| 42. | 41/25 | 5/51 | 2/68 | 5/61 | 4/54 | 2/15 |
| 43. | 9/51 | 8/65 | 7/68 | 14/69 | 10/68 | 5/15 |
| 44. | 2/62 | 1/70 | 1/71 | 1/74 | 2/76 | 6/17 |
| 45. | 4/60 | 4/67 | 3/71 | 3/72 | 5/73 | 3/19 |
| 46. | 14/50 | 19/52 | 13/60 | 15/60 | 10/66 | 6/16 |
| 47. | 21/42 | 23/48 | 20/54 | 24/51 | 21/55 | 17/ 6 |

| Section D | Overall | 101 | 102 | 103 | 104 | 200 |
|---|---|---|---|---|---|---|
| 48. | 11/48 | 8/45 | 5/44 | 9/38 | 10/36 | 21/74 |
| 49. | 9/49 | 9/44 | 6/42 | 8/39 | 7/39 | 12/84 |
| 50. | 29/29 | 11/42 | 26/22 | 23/25 | 30/15 | 66/29 |
| 51. | 30/28 | 24/30 | 20/28 | 22/26 | 22/23 | 65/31 |
| 52. | 16/42 | 14/39 | 11/37 | 13/35 | 12/33 | 30/65 |
| 53. | 22/36 | 20/33 | 15/33 | 15/38 | 17/29 | 44/51 |
| 54. | 18/41 | 14/39 | 11/37 | 12/36 | 13/33 | 38/57 |
| 55. | 37/21 | 31/22 | 29/19 | 27/21 | 29/17 | 69/26 |
| 56. | 19/39 | 17/35 | 14/35 | 15/34 | 15/31 | 35/60 |
| 57. | 13/45 | 14/38 | 8/40 | 11/37 | 11/35 | 22/73 |
| 58. | 8/50 | 6/47 | 9/38 | 8/39 | 10/36 | 12/84 |
| 59. | 17/41 | 17/36 | 11/37 | 10/37 | 11/35 | 35/60 |
| 60. | 12/46 | 10/42 | 7/40 | 10/38 | 9/36 | 24/72 |
| 61. | 48/10 | 40/12 | 38/10 | 40/ 7 | 39/ 7 | 85/10 |
| 62. | 17/41 | 18/35 | 11/37 | 15/32 | 12/34 | 24/71 |
| 63. | 35/23 | 25/27 | 26/24 | 29/18 | 29/17 | 69/26 |
| 64. | 31/27 | 25/27 | 19/29 | 24/24 | 22/24 | 66/30 |
| 65. | 34/29 | 26/26 | 23/25 | 27/20 | 26/20 | 71/25 |
| 66. | 29/25 | 24/26 | 18/26 | 18/26 | 22/22 | 65/28 |
| 67. | 10/40 | 11/33 | 6/34 | 7/34 | 6/33 | 16/67 |
| 68. | | | | | | |
| 1. | 19 | 19 | 12 | 16 | 20 | 25 |
| 2. | 8 | 5 | 4 | 4 | 4 | 23 |
| 3. | 3 | 1 | 2 | 1 | 3 | 10 |
| 4. | 3 | 3 | 2 | 1 | 1 | 6 |
| 5. | 6 | 6 | 6 | 5 | 5 | 4 |

| Section D | Overall | 101 | 102 | 103 | 104 | 200 |
|---|---|---|---|---|---|---|
| 6. | 1 | 1 | 0 | 1 | 1 | 1 |
| 7. | 1 | 1 | 1 | 0 | 0 | 1 |
| 8. | 1 | 1 | 1 | 2 | 1 | 1 |
| 9. | 5 | 3 | 3 | 5 | 2 | 9 |
| 69. 1. | 3 | 3 | 2 | 2 | 4 | 5 |
| 2. | 4 | 3 | 3 | 5 | 4 | 5 |
| 3. | 6 | 5 | 4 | 5 | 4 | 12 |
| 4. | 3 | 2 | 3 | 2 | 1 | 6 |
| 5. | 5 | 3 | 3 | 3 | 2 | 12 |
| 6. | 1 | 1 | 1 | 1 | 0 | 1 |
| 7. | 0 | 1 | 0 | 0 | 0 | 1 |
| 8. | 1 | 1 | 2 | 1 | 0 | 1 |
| 9. | 9 | 9 | 8 | 7 | 5 | 15 |
| 70. | 36 | 35 | 32 | 26 | 26 | 58 |
| 71. 1. | 7 | 4 | 6 | 7 | 6 | 14 |
| 2. | 5 | 5 | 2 | 5 | 4 | 6 |
| 3. | 0 | 0 | 0 | 0 | 0 | 2 |
| 4. | 1 | 2 | 1 | 1 | 0 | 2 |
| 5. | 2 | 2 | 0 | 0 | 4 | 4 |
| 6. | 1 | 1 | 0 | 0 | 0 | 2 |
| 7. | 1 | 1 | 0 | 0 | 2 | 2 |
| 8. | 4 | 3 | 2 | 3 | 3 | 9 |
| 9. | 0 | 0 | 1 | 0 | 0 | 1 |

| No. | | | | | | |
|---|---|---|---|---|---|---|
| **72.** | | | | | | |
| 1. | 8 | 4 | 3 | 2 | 3 | 4 |
| 2. | 5 | 0 | 2 | 2 | 2 | 2 |
| 3. | 3 | 0 | 2 | 1 | 2 | 2 |
| 4. | 4 | 2 | 2 | 1 | 2 | 2 |
| 5. | 3 | 0 | 1 | 0 | 2 | 1 |
| 6. | 8 | 3 | 2 | 3 | 3 | 3 |
| 7. | 3 | 3 | 2 | 2 | 1 | 2 |
| 8. | 1 | 0 | 1 | 0 | 1 | 1 |
| 9. | 0 | 0 | 0 | 1 | 0 | 0 |
| **73.** | 41 | 17 | 14 | 13 | 16 | 20 |
| **74.** | 0 | 0 | 0 | 0 | 1 | 1 |
| **75.** | | | | | | |
| 1. | 1 | 1 | 1 | 3 | 1 | 2 |
| 2. | 22 | 9 | 8 | 7 | 14 | 12 |
| 3. | 9 | 2 | 3 | 5 | 4 | 5 |
| 4. | 1 | 0 | 0 | 0 | 0 | 0 |
| 5. | 0 | 0 | 0 | 0 | 0 | 0 |
| 6. | 3 | 1 | 0 | 0 | 2 | 1 |
| 7. | 0 | 0 | 0 | 0 | 0 | 0 |
| 8. | 2 | 0 | 1 | 1 | 1 | 1 |
| 9. | 1 | 0 | 0 | 2 | 0 | 1 |
| | 12 | 4 | 7 | 8 | 9 | 8 |
| | 1 | 0 | 0 | 0 | 0 | 0 |
| | 5 | 1 | 0 | 2 | 1 | 2 |
| | 1 | 1 | 0 | 0 | 0 | 0 |
| | 0 | 0 | 0 | 0 | 0 | 0 |
| | 16 | 4 | 9 | 8 | 14 | 11 |
| | 0 | 0 | 0 | 0 | 0 | 0 |
| | 2 | 0 | 2 | 0 | 1 | 1 |

## Q. 28:  *By Levels and Languages*

I enjoy learning a foreign language even though it is a requirement (Yes/No%). Sample size in parentheses. Since not all students in the sample were fulfilling a requirement and the figures are percentages of the total sample, the yes/no proportions in the responses are of interest, e.g., French 101: 46/38 indicates that more requirement students (55%) were enjoying the course than not enjoying it (45%).

|     | French | German | Spanish | Russian | Latin | Modern Hebrew | Persian |
|-----|--------|--------|---------|---------|-------|---------------|---------|
| 101 | 46/38  | 40/42  | 39/47   | 29/11   | 37/42 | 50/13         | 63/0    |
|     | (165)  | (169)  | (38)    | (55)    | (38)  | (8)           | (8)     |
| 102 | 37/37  | 34/50  | 23/59   | 29/36   | 32/55 |               |         |
|     | (126)  | (58)   | (22)    | (14)    | (22)  |               |         |
| 103 | 39/45  | 31/50  | 38/38   | 33/11   | (sample: |            |         |
|     | (221)  | (133)  | (40)    | (27)    | 1 omitted) |          |         |
| 104 | 38/37  | 49/25  | 45/45   | 30/20   | 24/59 |               |         |
|     | (94)   | (53)   | (38)    | (10)    | (17)  |               |         |
| 200 | 20/ 3  | 27/ 7  | 10/ 7   | 0/4     | 5/5   |               |         |
|     | (127)  | (105)  | (42)    | (23)    | (20)  |               |         |

## F.  Original Questionnaire

Since the questionnaire was designed for use with a particular kind of computer answer sheet, it is not reproduced here in its exact form. The following questions were asked and it is to these that the references in the above analysis refer (e.g., Q. 25, Q. 27). The computer sheet contained spaces for coded information on course number and level, college, sex, and specific language and was designed for nine choices. Persons wishing to replicate the study can obtain further information from Professor W. M. Rivers, Department of Romance Languages and Literatures, Harvard University, Cambridge, Mass. 02138. They are requested to communicate their results to her for comparison.

**Questionnaire on Student Interests in Foreign Languages**, UIUC, 1973.

(1 = yes; 2 = no, unless another code is indicated)

*Section A:*

1. *All-university grade-point average* to the nearest half-point according to the following code: 1 = 5; 2 = 4.5; 3 = 4; 4 = 3.5; 5 = 3; 6 = 2.5; 7 = 2; 8 = 1.5; 9 = 1.
2. *Average grade in foreign languages* so far: 1 = A; 2 = B; 3 = C; 4 = D; 5 = E.

3. *Age* using the following code: 1 = under 21; 2 = 21-24; 3 = 24-30; 4 = over 30.
4. I had a *break* in my education. (1 = yes; 2 = no)
5. This is the 1 = first; 2 = second; 3 = third; 4 = fourth; 5 = fifth *foreign language I have studied.*
6. I studied *this* foreign language before coming to the U. of I. for 1 = 1 year; 2 = 2 years; 3 = 3 years; 4 = 4 years; 5 = 5 years; 6 = 6 years; 7 = more than 6 years; 8 = 0 years.
7. I studied *this* foreign language: 1 = at high school; 2 = beginning at grade 7 or 8; 3 = beginning at grade 6 or earlier; 4 = at junior college; 5 = at another university; 6 = at school in another country; 7 = as a native speaker abroad; 8 = as a bilingual speaker in the U.S.A.
8. I studied a *different* foreign language before beginning this foreign language for: 1 = 1 year; 2 = 2 years; 3 = 3 years; 4 = 4 years; 5 = 5 years; 6 = 6 years; 7 = more than 6 years.

*Section B: For the following statements check 1 = yes; 2 = no.*
9. My parents speak a foreign language.
10. I have friends who speak a foreign language.
11. I can see no use for foreign languages in my life-style.
12. I have traveled in other countries.
13. I would like to travel in other countries.
14. English is spoken in most countries, so learning another language is unnecessary.
15. I am interested in differences between languages.
16. I am interested in what goes on in other countries.
17. I am preparing to work in a field where knowledge of a language will be useful.
18. Foreign languages require too much study time out of class.
19. I don't think any form of study should be required.
20. I am interested in how people in other countries look at things.
21. I never liked learning foreign languages.
22. I am taking this course as an *LAS* requirement. (If the answer to Q. 22 is *yes,* please move on to *Section C.*)
23. I am taking this course as a *departmental requirement* in: 1 = Architecture; 2 = Commerce; 3 = Communications; 4 = Engineering; 5 = Library Science; 6 = Music; 7 = Physical Education; 8 = Other (please specify); 9 = No. (If you answered Q. 23 affirmatively, please move to *Section C.*)
24. I am taking this course purely as an *elective* (not as part of a departmental requirement or as a minor). (If you answered yes to Q. 24, please move to *Section D.*)
25. I am taking this course as part of a *minor.* (If you answered yes to Q. 25, please move to *Section D.*)
26. I am *majoring* in this language. (If you answered yes to Q. 26, please move to *Section D.*)

*Section C: For LAS and Departmental requirement students only.*

(For each question in this section 1 = yes; 2 = no; always mark *No*—do not leave blanks.)

27. I would not have studied a foreign language if there had not been a requirement.

28. I enjoy learning a foreign language even though it is a requirement.

29. I would enjoy learning a foreign language more if the course content were different.

30-42.
    At the elementary and intermediate level I would prefer *more*:
    30. listening to the language being spoken.
    31. speaking the language myself.
    32. reading.
    33. writing in the language.
    34. information about the people who speak the language.
    35. literature.
    36. songs and music.
    37. films.
    38. information about current affairs.
    39. analysis of the language structure.
    40. reading of newspapers and magazines.
    41. scientific and technical reading.
    42. Other: (please specify, writing number 42 and your comment on the back of the answer sheet).

43. If my commitments for my major had permitted it I would have liked to have continued studying this language at the 200 level, but unfortunately I cannot.

44-46.
    I intend to continue studying this language as:
    44. a major.
    45. a minor.
    46. an elective (not part of a minor).

47. I would have tried to include a foreign language in my program even if there had been no requirement.

    (Students who answered *No* to *all* of questions 43-47 may pass in their questionnaires at this point.)

*Section D: To be completed* only *by students who answered* Yes to any of questions 24-26 or 43-47.

(In this section 1 = yes; 2 = no, unless otherwise indicated. Always mark No—do not leave blanks.)

48-66.

> I selected *this* language because
>
> 48.   My family is interested in it.
> 49.   My friends are studying it.
> 50.   I began studying it in junior or senior high school.
> 51.   I want to read literary works.
> 52.   I want to read sociological/political/economic works.
> 53.   I want to read philosophical/psychological works.
> 54.   I identify culturally or ethnically with speakers of this language.
> 55.   I consider it important for international communication.
> 56.   I am interested in languages which are *very* different from English.
> 57.   I had heard it was a difficult language to learn.
> 58.   I had heard it was an easy language to learn.
> 59.   I was impressed by the achievements of the speakers of this language.
> 60.   I have close personal relations with a speaker of this language.
> 61.   I want to visit a country where this language is spoken.
> 62.   I want to read research material.
> 63.   I want to understand films or radio broadcasts.
> 64.   I wish to correspond in this language.
> 65.   I wish to spend some time studying in a country where this language is spoken.
> 66.   I am interested in the structure of this language.
> 67.   I have another reason for studying this language. (Write on back of sheet under Number 67.)

68-69.

> (Answer these questions according to the code below. If not applicable, do not answer.)
>
> 68.   I want to use it for my future work: 1 = No; 2 = teaching major; 3 = teaching minor; 4 = college teaching; 5 = science; 6 = anthropology; 7 = religious vocation, missions, etc.; 8 = social work; 9 = overseas social service in Peace Corps, or other agency;
> 69.   for *future work* in: 1 = music; 2 = journalism; 3 = diplomatic or civil service; 4 = business; 5 = linguistics; 6 = philosophy; 7 = architecture; 8 = engineering; 9 = other (please specify on back of sheet under number 69).

70.   My needs are satisfied by the types of courses provided in this language. (If your answer is yes, move to Q. 73.)

71-72.

If I could design courses at the 200 and 300 level to suit my personal needs, I would want courses of the following types (mark as many as you wish according to the code):

71. 1 = oral communication; 2 = reading in my field; 3 = writing business letters and discussing business affairs, advertising, and public relations; 4 = plays, operas, and songs; 5 = contrastive study of societies and cultures; 6 = situational language use for social workers; 7 = linguistic analysis; 8 = translating and interpreting; 9 = other (please specify on back of sheet under number 71).

72. I would want culturally enriching courses, unrelated to my career needs, in: 1 = literature; 2 = philosophy; 3 = art history; 4 = film; 5 = music; 6 = contemporary life-styles and values; 7 = cultural and political history; 8 = history of the language; 9 = other (please specify on back of sheet under number 72).

73. I would have liked to have had the opportunity of combining a foreign language with my major in an interdepartmental structure.

74-75.

As well as this language I have also studied:

74. 1 = Arabic; 2 = Chinese; 3 = French; 4 = German; 5 = Classical Greek; 6 = Modern Greek; 7 = Modern Hebrew; 8 = Hindi; 9 = Italian.

75. 1 = Japanese; 2 = Latin; 3 = Portuguese; 4 = Russian; 5 = Scandinavian; 6 = Serbo-Croatian; 7 = Spanish; 8 = Swahili; 9 = other (please specify on back of sheet under number 75).

## G. For comparison: Harvard Questionnaire, January 1976
### Department of Romance Languages and Literatures
Wilga M. Rivers, Coordinator of Language Instruction

All totals for questions are given in percentages of the total number of responses to the questionnaire, except where explanatory footnote ** indicates otherwise.

### 1. First semester courses (labeled A): Elementary level

| Questions | French 114 SS (31%) | Italian 55 SS (15%) | Portuguese 14 SS (4%) | Spanish 184 SS (50%) | All languages 367 SS (100%) |
|---|---|---|---|---|---|
| Total responding | | | | | |
| 1. Fulfilling language requirement | 56% | 40% | 0% | 68% | 57% |
| 2. Would have studied it even if no language requirement | 66 | 81 | 100 | 58 | 63 |
| 3. Enjoying course as it is taught at Harvard | 89 | 82 | 93 | 82 | 82 |
| 4. Intend to continue studying this language | 45 | 40 | 71 | 25 | 35 |
| 5. Would like to continue (some have scheduling impediments) | 67 | 73 | 100 | 47 | 59 |
| 6. Years of high school study of this language before coming to Harvard | | | | | |
| 0 years | 46 | 87 | 100 | 39 | 51 |
| 1 year | 13 | 11 | 0 | 9 | 10 |
| 2 years | 25 | 2 | 0 | 23 | 19 |
| 3 years | 13 | 0 | 0 | 22 | 15 |
| 4 years | 3 | 0 | 0 | 8 | 4 |
| 5+ years | 0 | 0 | 0 | 2 | 1 |

| Questions | French 114 SS (31%) | Italian 55 SS (15%) | Portuguese 14 SS (4%) | Spanish 184 SS (50%) | All languages 367 SS (100%) |
|---|---|---|---|---|---|
| 7. This is the first foreign language studied | 26 | 4 | 7 | 32 | 24 |
| 8. Would enjoy the language more if it were taught differently | 10 | 31 | 0 | 27 | 21 |
| 9. Feel confident could use language to some extent independently | 63 | 74 | 93 | 83 | 75 |
| 10. Confidence for reading | 49 | 67 | 79 | 72 | 63 |
| 11. Confidence for conversation | 45 | 57 | 79 | 72 | 61 |

## 2. Third semester courses (labeled Ca):  Intermediate level

| Questions | French 133 SS (71%) | Italian 7 SS (4%) | Spanish 47 SS (25%) | All languages 187 SS (100%) |
|---|---|---|---|---|
| Total Responding | 74% | 17% | 30% | 60% |
| 1. Fulfilling language requirement | | | | |
| 2. Would have studied it even if no language requirement | 54 | 100 | 68 | 56 |
| 3. Enjoying course as it is taught at Harvard | 78 | 80 | 83 | 80 |
| 4. Intend to continue studying this language (into next semester at least)* | 44 | 71 | 70 | 50 |
| 5. Would like to continue (into next semester at least: some have scheduling impediments) | 55 | 71 | 83 | 61 |

| | | | | |
|---|---|---|---|---|
| 6. Years of high school study of this language before coming to Harvard** | | | | |
|    0 years | 0 | 0 | 8 | 2 |
|    1 year | 4 | 0 | 16 | 6 |
|    2 years | 18 | 0 | 18 | 18 |
|    3 years | 48 | 0 | 32 | 42 |
|    4 years | 20 | 0 | 18 | 19 |
|    5+ years | 10 | 0 | 8 | 10 |
| 7. This is first foreign language studied | 49 | 0 | 53 | 43 |
| 8. Would enjoy the language more if it were taught differently | 24 | 86 | 28 | 25 |
| 9. Feel confident could use language to some extent independently | 71 | 71 | 100 | 78 |
| 10. Confidence for reading | 67 | 71 | 98 | 75 |
| 11. Confidence for conversation | 53 | 43 | 79 | 59 |
| 12. Studied this language at a lower level at Harvard | 12 | 71 | 45 | 23 |

*Question 4. Most Harvard Ca students reach the *required* level of proficiency on the Harvard Placement Test by the end of the third semester course.

**Question 6. Some students did not complete this question. Percentages were worked out on French 115 SS, Spanish 38 SS, Italian 7 SS. Those not responding are accounted for by the number responding to Question 12, viz., they had begun their study of the language at Harvard, and in the case of Italian and Spanish by some students from a bilingual family environment who had not had previous formal instruction in the language.

# 15

## TEACHER - STUDENT RELATIONS: COERCION OR COOPERATION?*

In *Teachers and the Children of Poverty*, Robert Coles quotes a child from an urban slum who speaks of his school experience in the following terms: "Are you trying to figure out if school makes any difference to us, because if that's it, I can tell you, man, here in my heart, it don't, much. You learn a few tricks with the numbers, and how to speak like someone different, but you forget it pretty fast when you leave the building, and I figure everyone has to put in his time one place or the other until he gets free . . . ."[1] This child is not speaking of the foreign-language class specifically, but what he says may well express the attitudes of many of our early foreign-language dropouts and even of those who stay two or three years in the high school course. Harry Reinert, in an investigation of the attitudes of students toward foreign languages, found that "well over half of them indicated that college requirements—either for admission or graduation—influenced their original enrollment in foreign language classes" and that "both by word and deed these students showed that once they had completed these

---

*Reprinted from *New Teachers for New Students*, published by the Washington Foreign Language Program, Seattle, Washington, and the American Council on the Teaching of Foreign Languages, New York City, New York, at Seattle, Washington, 1970.

requirements, they intended to have nothing more to do with foreign language."[2] "Traditional requirements with their standards of credit hours and grades have unfortunately developed into a system of timeserving"[3]—these words written in 1944 might well have been written in 1970. It may be that the present tendency for some foreign-language requirements to be eliminated will serve foreign-language teachers well by forcing them to examine the relevance in this late twentieth-century period of their objectives as reflected in what actually goes on in their classrooms (as opposed to the aims set out in syllabuses and in the literature), as well as their views on whom they do, and do not, welcome in their classes and the types of learning experiences they provide for their students.

The tyranny of requirements has made it possible for many a teacher to present a sterotyped, unimaginative course to his conscripted clientele. Not many students, we would hope, have had to suffer under such procedures as were employed in one advanced class in a New York high school in 1970. Most of the year was spent "reading" one French novel; for this, the class was divided into two groups, each of which prepared alternate sections. The sections were then subjected to grammatical and lexical dissection. By this method, no student officially read the whole novel or even a consecutive half of it. Such nonsensical teaching would never be endured by successive groups of students—unless they were coerced into the class by some obligation extrinsic to foreign-language study.

If foreign language is to maintain its position in the school curriculum unprotected by external requirements, we will need to convince students as well as administrators that it has a fundamental and unique contribution to make to the educational experience, a contribution which the students can perceive as relevant to their real concerns. For years, protagonists of foreign languages have made extravagant claims about the remarkable vocational value of their subject. A foreign-language major, we have said, can become a diplomat, a foreign correspondent, an executive in an international business complex, or a private secretary to a man who travels from world capital to world capital. What we have not been willing to admit is that ours is, vocationally speaking, an auxiliary study. A diplomat needs a solid background of history and political science, and, in his adolescence, the future diplomat does not know which language he will need in later life. A foreign correspondent needs to be a first-rate journalist. A company with international branches needs first of all a man with engineering training, business experience, or advertising or public relations expertise. The businessman who travels the world wants first and foremost a person who can handle competently his correspondence and reports, and keep unwelcome intruders away from his door. The student has a right to expect more from a study which is going to take a great deal of his time and energy for a number of years than a half-developed skill which he may or may not find useful at some hypothetical moment in his future career. And the administrator needs more convincing reasons than the vocational ones for continuing the foreign-language program in his school.

The unique contribution of foreign-language study that is truly educational, in the sense that it expands the student's personal experience of his environment, and truly humanistic in that it adds a new dimension to his thinking, is the opportunity it provides for breaking through monolingual and monocultural bonds. Such an experience reveals to the student that there are other ways of saying things, other values and attitudes than those to which his native language and culture have habituated him. Through this process, he may develop new attitudes to ideas and peoples that will reduce his bondage to the familiar and the local, while increasing his sympathy for persons of other cultures and languages. The new-generation student in our schools is internationalist and interculturalist in his aspirations; he is also brutally direct in demanding the rationale of what we are doing and what we are asking him to do. This basic contribution which foreign language can make to his development is one which he would welcome, but he must see that what we do in our classrooms really achieves such a purpose or he will drop out as soon as he conveniently may. If, as Harold Taylor has said: "The first task of education . . . is to raise the level of awareness and response to *all* ideas, events, people and objects,"[4] then foreign language, taught with this end firmly in view, can still claim that it has a rightful place in the overall educational program of the school.

Can our teachers meet the challenge of providing the genuinely mind-stretching experience of exploring other ways of thinking? Certainly teachers trained only in habit-formation techniques of skill training will find it difficult to deal with sensitive areas of attitudes and values; and teachers for whom cultural understanding means the description of picturesque costumes worn for religious festivals or the measurements of the Eiffel Tower will find it difficult to explain why students are disturbed in Berlin, in Paris, and in Tokyo. The teacher of the future will need to be well read, alert to current trends, receptive himself to ideas other than those of his own culture, and flexible enough to reexamine his own ideas at regular intervals in order to keep in touch with a new generation and a rapidly changing world. Such a teacher is not produced by a rigid teacher training program where the "right" answers and the "right" techniques are forced upon him as he is shaped and molded. Coercive training can only produce either a coercive teacher or a rebel against all that this training held to be of value. The teacher of the future needs to be given a deep understanding of the bases of what he is trying to do so that he will be able to adapt familiar techniques intelligently and develop new ones as circumstances change and new demands are made upon him. His association with those who train him must bring him to the realization that only a person of open mind, willing to consider and weigh many points of view, can develop such qualities in those who study with him.

We have paid lip service to this cultural objective for a number of years, but students and faculty do not see that any such enrichment is evident in those who have spent a year or two in our classes. They sometimes accuse us of rationalizing the irrelevance of our subject. The approach of most teachers is built on the belief that students must attain a high degree of language skill before they can really perceive and appreciate cultural differences reflected through language. Such training is, of course, important; it is our primary task and must not be neglected. We must ask ourselves, however, how we can give some part of this mind-broadening experience to every student no matter what his level of attainment in the language. It seems evident that any degree of cultural understanding will require a depth of discussion and thought which our high school students cannot cope with in the foreign language. Insistence on the exclusive use of the foreign language in the classroom and the more recent emphasis in some circles on the discouraging of questions from students in order to maintain this artificial atmosphere have meant the reduction of classroom "discussion" to trite questions and answers on the content of what is seen, heard, or read. The questions which are of real interest to the students are thus suppressed, and their misconceptions remain unidentified. Acting out roles is one way for the language student to get the feel of cultural differences, but, without some frank discussion, the learning of cultural differences must remain at the stage of such overt manifestations as greetings, festivals, or eating habits, viewed out of context and interpreted by the student according to his own culturally determined values and attitudes. The interest of the students in the foreign culture must be fostered from the beginning with research projects using any and all materials available, whether in the foreign language or not, with the encouragement of vigorous discussion at the points of contrast. Such projects need not take valuable time away from the language learning activities that should rightfully occupy the time the teacher has with his students; the projects should be given as out-of-class assignments, and class time should be taken only for discussion of the findings.

A study of two widely used Level 4 texts shows that even at this stage the questions on reading passages are still at the level of content (mere recall or identification of specific details), and are so structured that the one right answer must emerge. With this type of question, it is easy for the teacher to imagine that the whole class is alert and participating intelligently, whereas they are merely giving the teacher "the right answer and the right chatter,"[5] a thing they learn to do with equal ease in the foreign or the native language. Such practices are stultifying to intelligent students who revel in bull sessions and the discussion of controversial issues with their fellows. At the advanced stage, some discussion must be permitted in the native language if the student does not yet have the fluency to handle complex ideas. Such discussions are motivational and encourage the student to pursue more diligently the difficult goal of full control of the foreign language. In this period of open and uninhibited discussion, our students will no longer suffer one-way "communication" in which the teacher has all the advantages. The day of "the silent generation" to which many of our teachers themselves belonged has passed. Our new generation of teachers must be trained to handle discussion, to welcome expression of student opinion, to be willing to admit when they do not know the answer, and to cooperate with students in finding out the things they most want to know about the foreign people and the ways they think and react.

Having established a truly educative purpose in foreign-language study other than mere skill training, the foreign-language teacher of the seventies will have to answer the question: "Is this experience of value to all students?" It is the task of the educator to consider the needs of all youth: the gifted, the average, the less able, and, of particular emphasis at this time, the disadvantaged. For too long the foreign-language teacher has sought a privileged role in the school: only an elite of bright, alert, well-motivated students was acceptable in his class—all others were, in his view, "incapable of learning a foreign language." Sometimes the mathematics teacher, the science teacher, the history teacher, and the art teacher have felt the same way about their students, and would have preferred a select group—yet students of all levels of ability and all backgrounds still come to be taught.

The foreign-language teacher of the past found himself unable to teach any but the more intelligent and more highly motivated students because he had turned foreign language into an abstract study of grammatical forms and relationships, followed by the close analysis of modes of expression divorced from the stream of common life—classical tragedy, nineteenth-century prose—which, with his academic approach, he was unable to relate, as they may well be related, to the preoccupations and concerns of the present day. In a reversal of trends, he may have moved away more recently from a traditional presentation to one involving drills and repetitive practice of inert phrases, material which students have felt to be of little concern to them at a stage when the body of educative experience presented to them in other subjects emphasizes productive and creative thinking. Despite his initial advantage, then, the foreign-language teacher has also frequently lost the gifted students, who see foreign-language study as sterile and unrewarding.

We may ask with these students why, in most schools, they must be forced to accept a uniform foreign-language diet established by tradition or by the uncontested prestige of college professors unacquainted with, and often uninterested in, the interests and capacities of high school students. After the elementary general-purpose textbooks have been completed, who has decided that all foreign-language students, no matter what their abilities or interests, must study a series of literary "masterpieces," often of a bygone era? How frequently are such senior students allowed to participate in the selection of what they will do with their time and energies? Some may be interested in contemporary social problems, some in history, some in scientific developments, some in the arts or the everyday experiences of a foreign people, and some in the modern novel or contemporary theatre. The interests of boys may well be different from the interests of girls. Some high schools do make provision at this stage for personal choice and decision, providing resource materials for individual and group research projects in which students read, listen to, and discuss all kinds of material in the foreign language, but such progressive programs are all too few. If the final high school years provide only "more of the same," it should not surprise the foreign-language teacher when even the better students are reluctant to continue beyond the minimum requirement.

Even at earlier levels it is possible to allow students some autonomy in the selection of activities according to their personal predilections if at least some part of the program is individualized. Should we expect all students, even the inarticulate, to want to develop their speaking skills primarily? Some in this television generation, if allowed to choose, might prefer to look and listen. (Teachers should be aware of research that shows a different rate of native-language development for boys and girls, in the girls' favor; this has a cumulative effect,[6] and may affect personal preferences at a certain age). Some students may prefer to range beyond the rest of the class in reading (graded readers which cover a wide variety of topics are available in the more commonly taught languages). Such individualization of choices requires imaginative planning by a classroom teacher who is willing to go beyond a steady, uniform, universal diet for at least part of the time. An experimental study of Robert Politzer and Louis Weiss has shown that "better results were obtained by the pupils of those teachers who went beyond the procedures strictly prescribed by the curriculum, teachers who were concerned with supplementing the curriculum rather than merely implementing it." It seems that "the efficiency of the individual teacher increase(d) with the amount of his *personal* stake and *personal* contribution to the instructional processes."[7] To complete the picture, involvement in personally selected tasks is intrinsically motivating to normal students whose natural enjoyment of cognitive exploration has not been completely stifled by the formalism of an educational system which overemphasizes such extrinsic rewards as grades and promotions.[8]

Some schools have already experimented with student involvement in decision-making; at the McCluer High School, for example, teachers and students work cooperatively in "a non-graded curriculum stressing individualized learning through small group activities and team teaching."[9] More teachers will need to launch out into new instructional approaches, and teachers coming into the profession will need to be made aware of new possibilities in providing the proper environment for learning if foreign languages are to keep the interest and allegiance of a voluntary clientele.

To move down the scale of ability, not infrequently a student of very average ability becomes fascinated with foreign-language study. For him, it has provided a new beginning at a stage when an accumulation of undigested facts or principles from earlier years has given him a feeling of hopelessness in certain other subject areas. Everyone begins the foreign language at the same time, and he feels he has as much chance as his neighbor to assimilate it. Such students are often more successful with some aspects of foreign-language study than others. Sometimes a very average or less gifted student will find that he can understand anything he hears in the foreign language, but is unable to use the language actively with any fluency. The tests most teachers devise penalize this type of student severely, and, despite his high degree of motivation and undoubted skill in one area, he may find himself advised not to continue with the language. His teacher does not realize that many people are very popular because they listen appreciatively, mur- muring from time to time only "Yes," "of course not," or "you're absolutely right." An individualized program will enable a student of this type, or a student who can read with ease but has inhibitions in speaking, or a student who can converse fluently but is a poor reader, to continue his study with a special emphasis in the area in which he feels most at home.

Finally, what has the foreign-language teacher to offer to the disadvantaged student? He may say: "I cannot teach the disadvantaged. They cannot learn a foreign language. Why—some of them cannot even read or write their own language with any degree of success!" Again, if foreign language does have some genuine educational value, it must surely have something to offer to those whose backgrounds have limited their horizons. It will not, however, be success- ful in the hands of a teacher who doubts the success of his enterprise even before it begins. Studies of students of a low socio-economic status have shown that they already suffer from a feeling of insufficiency, and readily accept the implications of defeat that the unconvinced teacher finds hard to conceal in his relations with them. The teacher expects them to fail, and they fail. If success is to be achieved in teaching foreign languages to disadvantaged students, teachers-in-training and experienced teachers alike will need to study the preoccupations, value systems, and characteristic approaches of these young people.[10] With an understanding of their preferred modes of learning, the teacher can choose materials and design lessons which will utilize these to the full.

Students of disadvantaged groups prefer the concrete to the abstract, and respond to concrete material for which they see an immediate application. They therefore enjoy learning foreign words and phrases which they can employ immediately in the context of their class or with minority group children in their neighborhood who speak the language. Since they are not motivated by deferred rewards but seek immediate gratification, the promise that they will eventually be able to use the language fluently means little, whereas actual use of the language immediately, even in simple forms, in face-to-face interaction, is motivating. They learn through activity, through seeing, hearing, touching, manipulating, and role-playing. The teacher should use: visual presentations (flash cards, drawings, films); things the students can hold, open, shut, or pass to each other; music, songs with tapes, guitars, drums, action songs, and action poems. The vocabulary used should be practical, and should deal with the objects and actions commonly used by the students. The characters and incidents presented to them in the foreign language should never appear to be "prissy" or effeminate. These students appreciate firm leadership from the teacher, and are not anxious to work in small groups in which they will need to make group decisions. Since, in their neighborhood environment, they are accustomed to learn orally rather than through the written word (which may even present them with some difficulty in their native language) reading the foreign language will not appear to be of vital importance to them.

Since disadvantaged students are motivated by concrete, clearly visible rewards, it seems appropriate that the foreign language they are to be taught should be selected with an eye to languages spoken in their home neighborhood; in this way, the practical tangible value of the foreign language becomes obvious. Alternatively, black students today have a yearning for a clear and unambiguous identity, and are seeking this identity more and more through the exploration of their lost African heritage. There is, therefore, clearly a case for the teaching of Swahili, or some other African language, in high schools, as many black groups have been demanding. Teachers of Spanish, French, and German should be foreign-language teachers first, rather than desperate defenders of hard-won fiefdoms; they should be advocates of more foreign-language learning, not of more learning only of Spanish or French or German. If we genuinely believe in the fundamental value of some foreign-language study for all students, then surely we should exploit this desire to learn a specific language among one large group of disadvantaged people. Swahili, or Arabic, or Yoruba will give students insights into how language operates just as surely as the more commonly taught languages, and will give them equal insights into other ways of thinking and other sets of cultural values.

The immediate response of many teachers will be: "But we don't have teachers of Swahili readily available." The answer is that we must acquire them. Swahili is considered one of the less difficult languages to learn in the Defense Language Institutes, and it does not have a strange script. The logical approach would appear to be to provide intensive training courses in Swahili for practicing foreign-language teachers, who could then introduce the language as a further offering of their language departments. Would not this also help some middle-class Americans to understand a completely different culture and the aspirations of a group of young nations striving to advance into modern statehood? Young teachers-in-training are sometimes invited to undertake the learning of a completely different language as one of their education courses in order to experience afresh the problems of language learning. Courses of this type could be used for giving them some basic knowledge of Swahili. It seems better for trained language teachers to take up this cause rather than leave it in the hands of linguistically unsophisticated amateurs.

This same line of reasoning should apply in areas where there is a strong concentration of immigrant groups speaking a particular language, since students learning a language for educational, rather than vocational, reasons will be more motivated if the language they are learning can be used and heard in everyday life.

Finally, the success of foreign languages in the years to come must lie with those teachers whom we are training at the present time. They will need to innovate, to experiment, to initiate new programs. We must train them to expect and to respect a new clientele. With the experience they themselves have of participation in decision-making and of planning for change, they will be much more fitted than any preceding generation to work with their students in developing new approaches, new techniques, and a new place for foreign languages in the educative process.

## FOOTNOTES

[1] R. Coles, *Teachers and the Children of Poverty* (Washington, D. C.: The Potomac Institute, 1970).

[2] Harry Reinert, "Student Attitudes Toward Foreign Language–No Sale!" *Modern Language Journal,* 54(1970): 107.

[3] Otto K. Liedke, "A Historical Review of the Controversy between the Ancient and the Modern Languages in American Higher Education," *German Quarterly,* 17(1944): 1-13, reprinted in M. Newmark, *Twentieth Century Modern Language Teaching* (New York: Philosophical Library, 1948), pp. 11-21.

[4] Quoted by A. E. Lean in *And Merely Teach* (Carbondale: Southern Illinois University Press, 1968), p. 58.

[5] John Holt, *How Children Fail* (New York: Dell, 1970), p. 42. Originally published by Pitman, 1964.

[6] Dorothea A. McCarthy, "Sex Differences in Language Development" in R. G. Kuhlen and G. G. Thompson, eds., *Psychological Studies of Human Development* (New York: Appleton-Century-Crofts, 1970), pp. 349-353.

[7] R. L. Politzer and L. Weiss, "Characteristics and Behaviors of the Successful Foreign Language Teacher," Stanford Center for Research and Development in Teaching, Technical Report No. 5 (Palo Alto, April 1969), pp. 69-70.

[8] E. J. Murray, *Motivation and Emotion* (Englewood Cliffs, N.J.: Prentice-Hall, 1964), pp. 74-82.

[9] F. H. Wood, "The McCluer Plan: An Innovative Non-Graded Foreign Language Program," *Modern Language Journal,* 54(1970): 184-87.

[10] Two useful references are H. Sebald, *Adolescence: A Sociological Analysis* (New York: Appleton-Century-Crofts, 1968) and A. Shumsky, *In Search of Teaching Style* (New York: Appleton-Century-Crofts, 1968).

# 16

# INDIVIDUALIZED INSTRUCTION
# AND COOPERATIVE LEARNING:
# SOME THEORETICAL CONSIDERATIONS*

Individualization of instruction or of the learning environ-ment is neither a new concept nor an American one. It seems to skip gaily across the Atlantic at one period or another. Rousseau and Pestalozzi in Europe influence Horace Mann and Dewey in the United States.[1] The same beliefs that Dewey held are reflected in the British informal elementary school of the nineteen-sixties[2] which applies ideas drawn from the research of Piaget in Geneva.[3] This British movement in turn inspires Weber's Open Corridor in a school in Harlem.[4] Nor should we forget the enduring and pervasive influence on early childhood education everywhere of Froe-bel, Montessori, and Susan Isaacs.

These influences cannot even be clearly delimited within precise episodes in educational experience, although the names of certain schools and school systems do spring to mind. The beliefs they embody have persisted, as a constant-ly surfacing underground, wherever teachers have cared more deeply about their students than about their subject matter. Lest anyone think individualization of instruction, under its present name, emerged full-grown on the educational scene with the *Britannica Review of Foreign Language Education,* Vol. 2, in 1970,[5] allow me to quote from a history of American education published in the early fifties:

> In city school systems around the country it was found
> in 1948 that 40 percent of the cities had adopted some

---

*Paper given at the session on Individualized Instruction at the Fourth International Congress of Applied Linguistics (A.I.L.A.), Stuttgart, Germany, August 26, 1975.

form of individualized instruction. More than half of the cities over 30,000 population had adopted such programs, and the trend toward still more individualized instruction for those cities that used it was strong.[6]

Individualized approaches such as the Dalton or Contract Plan, the Winnetka Plan, and the "unit method," which achieved world-wide recognition, were on their way in the twenties.[7] Technical implementation has evolved and concepts have been enriched, with more emphasis on individual development rather than the older emphasis on individual differences, but the "unipacs" and the LAPs (learning activity packets) of today and the "assignments" of yesterday are in the same family line.[8] Why then, we may ask, is there such a resurgence of interest and energy in this area at this particular period in history?

We will gain some insight into this question if we first identify the essential philosophy that is basic to what we may regard as intermittent waves of an ebbing and flowing tide. This essence is, to my mind, captured in the following quotation. Each person

> . . . is born a unique individual, and development is *in* this individual. His world of inner needs and meanings is personal, lived out in the human relationships into which he is born and with people whose world has been equally individually determined. He has particular, specific bits of experience and particular, specific expectations, and it is these that he brings to his relationships—meeting people with differing experiences and expectations. His development is individual and uneven in pattern and pace and made even more individual by the personal route of his interests.[9]

In this quotation, we have all the emphases of the individualization movement of today and from it we can also see what individualization is not. Our students have their own inner needs. They come with an individual perception of what is meaningful and valuable which they have acquired within a cultural milieu (in which ethnic, socio-economic, and sub-cultural influences have played a role). They are maturing (developing) at an individual rate, so that they have their own preferred pace, mode, and style of learning which may vary at any particular stage. They have individual goals and expectations and, therefore, their motivation is intensely personal but purposeful. It is the "personal route" of their interests which dictates the content which will absorb them. They learn through active experience, particularly as they interact with others. This experience is genuinely shared, because each individual in the group contributes his or her personal experiences to the communal enterprise; the individual's inner world is thus "lived out" in human relationships. Individualization cannot, then, be "isolated learning"[10] as independent study would make it, although some individuals may prefer to work on their own on certain occasions (or even a great deal, depending on their preferred style of learning). We may note that no mention is made here of "abilities" or "aptitude" which, in this context, are comparative expressions. The proponent of individualization does not compare students but allows each to learn as his or her individual nature permits. There are no non-learners in the human family.

A fine philosophy and one with a distinguished and respectable ancestry, I hear you say, but is it relevant to our day and age (if I may use an overworked expression of the late sixties)? What, then, distinguishes the world in which our young people are growing up? And here, I speak of world-wide trends.

It is an era of mechanization, standardization, and homogenization. It is the throw-away age. It is an age of anonymity and depersonalization. In the United States, we are our Social Security numbers which computers devour or reject. It is interesting that the U.S. Internal Revenue Service and the Blue Cross/Blue Shield Health Plans, among others, depend on the computer to spit out those returns and claims which do not conform to certain patterns. You give too much to charitable causes for a person of your income bracket: this is suspect. You have had too many illnesses this year for a person of your age, occupation, or social milieu: this must be investigated. You must not stand out from the crowd. Of course, investigation may show that you are just a harmless oddity, in which case you can be reinserted in the computer and ignored. For many of our generation, their skills also have become rapidly dispensable as automation demands only a few who can be trained rapidly for a specific task and replaced as rapidly if they fall out. No wonder it is an age of the alienation of the young who have never experienced a period when they really counted, when their contribution to society was considered essential. The brief euphoria of 1968 when they were heeded, because they were a substantial statistic, has faded and society has again turned its attention away from those for whom there is not as yet a place, and perhaps never will be. This is the kind of world which we have created or allowed to creep up on us.

This is not, however, a world to which our young people yearn to belong. They see it as a world careering ahead without direction—careering perhaps toward disaster. Our young people know more about what is going on in the world—what is being done with their world—than any previous generation and they don't like it. They demand a role. They see the need for responsible individuals independent of the system, willing to stand out and live by other values than those of the corporate yes-man on the make—self-directed individuals who can work and think with others. They see the need to reassert the values of cooperation over those of individualism in the service of one's own interests. They wish to be able to choose. They need an education which will help them to develop their ability to think, to weigh alternatives, to work without compulsion, and to accept responsibility for their choices.

This is a world which has dedicated its efforts to universal education, frequently referred to as "mass education"—a formula which clearly indicates that we are talking here of instruction, not education. There cannot be education of a mass. There can be manipulation of a mass or exploitation of a mass. There can be education only of persons, of individuals. Even the concept of universal instruction can be a cruel delusion and a frustrating deception when it means trying to pour new wine into old bottles. Instruction for failure in the system of another age is not good enough. Parents and students have seen this trap and are unwilling to play society's little game. Even where the school system is willing to face reforms so that the uneducated become educated and the "disadvantaged" become advantaged, can society open up opportunities for them all to play a self-fulfilling and satisfying role? Education must provide individuals with the kinds of opportunities for development which will enable them to create worthwhile lives for themselves, not merely prepare them to fit into a pattern or a temporary slot.

This is a world in which knowledge, or at least factual knowledge, is accumulating at an exponential rate and becoming obsolete almost as fast as it is accumulating. This is not the time for merely acquiring a body of knowledge. It has become imperative for our young people to learn how to learn, how to assess facts, how to evaluate new knowledge, and how to put knowledge to use. Education, then, must encourage creative, heuristic thinking, boldness in application, and ability to function autonomously.

So more than ever we need to educate, rather than instruct. Much of what we taught in an earlier period, our students already know from informal sources: television, magazines, personal experience of travel, and extended contacts.

These, then, are forceful reasons for a reconsideration of our educational approach. Where education and societal needs do not keep pace, something must crack and the present breakdown in many educational systems throughout the world is noteworthy. Our education must, in some way, face up to the world as it is today and prepare our young people to do something in it and about it. From these preoccupations springs the present resurgence of emphasis on the individual, on the person, and on developing educational procedures which maximize opportunities for participation in cooperative planning and implementation of purposeful activity, for responsible decision-making and self-direction, for the building of a strong foundation of self-confidence and appreciation of one's uniqueness and for raising levels of aspiration, for encouraging originality, creative endeavor, and flexibility of mind which will enable each person to adapt to new circumstances and recognize new opportunities. This is not an easy task, but it is most certainly an urgent one.

What can this possibly have to do with foreign-language teachers who surely know that their task is implanting another language? No new knowledge there. For too long, foreign-language teachers have claimed a place apart, rarely recognizing that theirs is an educational task like that of any other teacher. It is not for foreign-language teachers to train for rigid performance and unthinking reproduction while their fellow educators are seeking to develop flexibility and willingness to experiment.

Here a word from Georgia Green, one of the younger generation of generative semanticists, seems appropriate. In an interesting linguistic analysis of the verb *teach,* Ms. Green shows that in English we are really dealing with two homophonous verbs, as indicated by their semantic and syntactic properties.[11] In other words, the verb *teach* does not behave in all respects like the verb *give.* The two sentences

1a. Mary gave John an apple,
1b. Mary gave an apple to John,

are synonymous, whereas the two sentences

2a. Mary taught John linguistics,
2b. Mary taught linguistics to John,

are not.

3a. "The teacher taught Jane the meaning of responsibility"

implies that Jane learned it, whether the teaching was explicit and voluntary or implicit and involuntary, whereas:

3b. "The teacher taught the meaning of responsibility to Jane"

implies an explicit act on the teacher's part, but does not presume learning by Jane. This distinction is particularly appropriate in the present discussion. What we think we teach is not necessarily what our students learn. Much of what they learn comes from their associations with teachers, peers, and other significant contacts in and out of school and from all kinds of activities. What is learned in the long run is determined by the personal perception of the situation by each student: what is important to them individually and how the situation affects their sense of well-being (of security, belonging, and self-esteem, to use Maslow's terminology[12]). We should, therefore, be much more sensitive to the learning environment we create and the qualities of the relationships within it, rather than attributing to our organization of explicit teaching the major role in student learning.

Let us look now at foreign-language teaching and see what kinds of demands this change of attitude lays on our profession, because it does require a change of attitude on our part. How, then, can foreign-language teaching fit into the picture I have just drawn and still be true to its own nature as a discipline?

Recent research in second-language acquisition in natural environments makes it abundantly clear that different people at different ages acquire a second language in different ways and at different rates. Hatch, after an in-depth analysis of fifteen observational studies of forty children learning a second language without formal teaching, concludes that there is little basis at present for talking about universals in second-language acquisition. She observes that "the differences seem very great indeed."[13] One child with two and a half hours' exposure to English a day was able to speak the language like a native after five months, another with greater exposure to English each day had said only a few words of English in two years.

Hatch distinguishes in these studies[14] "rule-formers," who sorted and organized the input from the beginning, from "data-gatherers," who seemed merely to accumulate segments of language without any identifiable systematizing, yet the members of each of these three groups seemed to acquire the language in their own good time and in their own way. Some learners experienced interference from their first language in expressing themselves; others did not but explained items to themselves in their first language. Some switched and mixed languages; others did not. Some merely inserted second-language vocabulary items, as they acquired them, into a first-language matrix; others occasionally used direct translations from the first to the second language, and so on. In a study of an adolescent Spanish speaker learning English, again without formal training,[15] we find the subject trying to express adult ideas on a wide variety of topics, employing strategies of simplification and reduction, circumlocution for words he could not remember, gestures and repetition of words for increased intensity, and borrowing features of his native-language structure when it could help him.

Such is the diversity of natural language-learning. Hatch concludes that in natural environments learners will do whatever is within their power to communicate, making the most of what they have in the second language and supplementing this, where necessary, with what they can transpose from their other means of communication: their first language. How familiar such a variety of communication strategies sounds to the foreign-language teacher who has tried to encourage students, at whatever stage, to express themselves freely with what they have learned.[16] Yet many teachers still try to push students through the same series of hoops, expecting the "right" answer as output. Where ability to communicate is our aim, as in so many programs, we must relax and allow place for the varied developmental and idiosyncratic processes of the individual to operate, while ensuring that the student has frequent contact with a wide variety of language structures and expressive vocabulary. We must encourage our students to struggle to express what is within them, to fight their way out from the restricting strait-jacket of their minimal knowledge. This is by no means an easy thing for them to do. In this way, with our help, they can develop confidence in themselves and learn that what one wants to do one can do with perseverance and imagination. While increasing their satisfaction in personal achievement, we will be contributing something beyond mere language knowledge to their development as individuals.

The little research we have from natural second-language-learning thus supports the observations of every experienced teacher of foreign languages in a formal setting: that there is in any class, no matter how large or small, a wide range of *individual differences in styles, strategies, and pace of learning.* We must do something about this. Students who cannot learn a language at the pace we set and in the way we present it must no longer be sloughed off like so much dead tissue.[17] By not allowing them to learn at their own pace and in their own way, we attack them at the level of security, a very basic level in Maslow's hierarchy of needs. The rickety foundation to which the student is required to add level after level of unconsolidated information cannot but give way and the student, it seems, is a "failure." We find it so easy to blame the student, rather than ourselves, or the system. If we, as foreign-language teachers, are to have a role in the "education of the masses," which is the education of a mass of individuals, then something must be done to face up to this "problem." Let us say rather "situation" and acknowledge openly that "problem" is another word by which we shift the responsibility from ourselves to others. The mechanics of providing for different paces and styles will have to be worked out in relation to any particular situation.[18] This is not my province in this chapter. It is discussed by other speakers and by the writers cited in my footnotes. The Gerry Logans, Steve Levys, and Fred LaLeikes[19] have made it work in areas as widely separated physically and situationally as California, New York City, and Wisconsin. We can learn from their experience.

*Ah! programming!* the initiated murmur, as soon as the question of individual pace of learning is raised. It always seems so much easier to find an answer for this aspect of personal style than for the others. We just lift time restrictions and let our students learn as quickly or as slowly as they comfortably can, allowing for learning and relearning, testing and retesting, until they have mastered the material. The answer seems purely organizational—complicated perhaps, but feasible.

There are several other questions to be considered, however, at this point: About what kind of programming are we talking? Do we mean one program for all students? Can programming, as we know it, really teach language use as we now understand it?

About the kind of programming, except for very sophisticated computer programs not readily available to most foreign-language teachers,[20] we are, for the most part, talking about refinements of the two classical types of programming: linear programming with minimal-step progression, originally developed by Skinner, and Crowder's intrinsic programming with built-in trial-and-error factor and opportunities for branching to accommodate faster and slower learners.[21] In both cases the program is basically the same for all students, although intrinsic programming allows for more variation in assimilation of the material, since it provides extra practice for the student who does not select the right answer according to the program. This summary statement is not intended to ignore the diligent work of foreign-language programming researchers who have tried to develop more sophisticated versions of these basic types, by taking into consideration Carroll's proposals for "designed learning,"[22] and by incorporating the auditory and oral aspects of language and the inferencing aspects of reading. However, step-increment and feedback (reinforcement through immediate knowledge of success or failure) remain the basic principles of their programs.[23]

The programming system shows a clear relationship with some types of individualized instruction. Programming requires precise specification of the terminal behaviors which the student should be able to demonstrate after completion of the program, just as some forms of individualized instruction require the writing of performance or behavioral objectives. The latter do not seem to differ in any significant way from the specifications of terminal behavior of the programmers.

*A performance objective* explains the purpose for requiring a particular form of behavior, the conditions under which this behavior will occur, and how it will be evaluated (the criterion by which the student will demonstrate that they have achieved the required behavior). Valette and Disick[24] give the following example of a performance objective:

1. *Purpose*: To demonstrate knowledge of twenty vocabulary words.

2. *Student Behavior*: Write out and spell correctly the word that corresponds to each of the twenty definitions given.

3. *Conditions*: On a twenty-minute classroom test.

4. *Criterion*: At least thirteen of the twenty items must be entirely correct in order to pass.

The constant use of the word "behavior" and the precision of the specifications in statements of objectives show clearly the line of descent from behavioristic programming. It seems clear also that only the most trivial or mechanical aspects of language use can be so specified for all students. It is disheartening to see a fine ideal like individualization of instruction being equated with such precise dissection of living wholes of language and language use into atomistic morsels. These segments have an undeniable place, since there is much detail to be mastered in any language (what I have called *micro-language learning*[25]). When, however, attempts are made to deal with macro aspects of language use, or skill-using,[26] in the same way, we realize the simplistic view of language learning on which the approach is based and the elaborate paraphernalia involved in carrying it through to its logical conclusion.

The following examples will demonstrate what I mean:

( i ) *Objective for oral production*:

After completing all the written assignments and the laboratory practice drill accompanying Unit 8, the student will go to the laboratory and record his oral responses to eight aural stimuli of the following form:
Stimulus: I like ice-cream. Does Martha?
Student: Yes, Martha likes ice cream too.
A response is acceptable if, and only if:
1) the appropriate subject is used.
2) the correct verb is used.
3) the response is complete.
4) the pronunciation is good enough to be easily understood by the teacher.
At least five of the eight responses will be correct.[27]

( ii ) *Objective for Level 1 interaction*:

The student will make a comment about the weather and will follow the comment with a question which he will ask a classmate. When the classmate answers his question the first student will follow the answer with another question. The classmate will answer this question; then the first student may pose a second question to his classmate.[28]

(iii) *Objective for a literature assignment*:

Each student will write a description of the protagonist describing at least four physical characteristics and three personality traits.[29]

(iv) *Objective for class discussion*:

The student *will volitionally participate* in each class discussion by contributing a total of *at least three* questions and/or complete-sentence comments per discussion.[30]

Naturally one would expect teachers to have clear ideas on the direction in which they wish the class to progress and students will need precise instructions on what is expected of them in an assignment or task. In Carroll's model of school learning,[31] one important element determining the amount of time a student *needs* to spend in learning is the quality of instruction, defined by Jakobovits in his application of Carroll's model as "the extent to which it is made clear to the learner what it is that he is supposed to be learning."[32] Whether what he is to do is clear to the student is dependent to some degree on his ability to understand instructions. That these instructions should, however, take the form of elaborate "behavioral objectives" has yet to be demonstrated to the satisfaction of this author who continues to feel that behavioral objectives and individualization of instruction are incompatible terms. Behavioral objectives imply that someone, the teacher or the materials writer, will decide precisely what someone else will do and how. The fact that the writer of Objective (iv) above could use the expression *"volitionally participate"* in an objective which stated the exact number of interventions required of each student in a class discussion illustrates a certain blindness to the authoritarian nature of behavioral objectives. Even when students are working with individual packets, their learning may be even more teacher-directed than in many classrooms. (No one has as yet suggested that all behavioral objectives should be tailored to the needs of each individual student, thus making the task of writing them infinite!) As usually presented, they leave very little room for flexibility or for adaptation by students who may not feel inclined to do just what has been stated, but who may very well be learning a great deal in their own way.

Individualization must imply choice and some latitude in modality and style of learning; otherwise, the only individual thing about it is the pacing: students are allowed to complete the predetermined, detailed assignments with which the teacher confronts them at their own speed of learning. This is precisely what programming was supposed to do, and for this we do not need another name. Let us use programming where it is appropriate (for learning basic features of phonology and language structure, for instance) and let us keep the name "individualization of instruction" for the richer, more humanistic approach outlined in the earlier part of this chapter.

Since teachers are individuals too, let us say that performance objectives are an integral part of some programs that are individualized, but that they are neither a sufficient nor a necessary feature of individualization. For those teachers or students who feel comfortable with them they may be a helpful prop, but those who enjoy the challenge of adapting to an evolving situation may ignore them.[33] Either way, let us raise our sights and those of our students to a fuller and more normal use of language than can ever be confined within the limits of a circumscribed "objective."

Which brings us to the *"personal route" of our student's interests.* In a preoccupation with pace of learning, we may well change the outward form of the learning situation in highly visible ways while retaining the same old content. To do this, after all, may require only technical manipulation: adapting the textbook, writing assignments, and putting our usual handouts, exercises, and tests into folders with answer keys. Attention to the students' interests requires much more of us: it requires a fundamental rethinking of what we are about.

In recent years, as a profession, we have felt the pressures of a narrowing world. When one group changes its major objectives, we all seem to change. So we have moved to a worldwide emphasis on oral communication skills, often to the almost total exclusion of reading and writing, from an overemphasis on literature and literary style to a wide-scale rejection of anything that might be branded "literature," from a translation-burdened course to the vilification of translation. Now we seem to be drifting imperceptibly back to a re-emphasis on reading. In many cases, the swing has occurred without personal conviction on our part that the change had anything to do with our own students in their unique situation. Now is the time for assertion of individual priorities, thoughtfully established in consultation with our students and their community.

As teachers of languages we have great freedom. A language may be learned for a number of different purposes, each with a variety of possible contents. Anything in the language, anything that can be expressed in the language, facts about the language itself, facts about language: all or any of these are our province. It is we, and we alone, who have restricted ourselves to a certain approach, to certain procedures, to a certain type of content. Our students abandon language study because they do not know the choices available to them or because we do not allow them to choose. If we are convinced of the need to tailor opportunities for learning to the individual, we must take seriously the individual's personal interests in learning a language.[34] Individualization of instruction implies *diversification* of objectives and content. Some students may want only to read and to read in a narrowly defined area: this is their prerogative. Some may want to communicate spontaneously; others may wish merely to be able to pronounce the language acceptably (as for opera and newscasting); others may wish to be able to communicate freely in the aural-oral mode, but not to write; still others may want to read poetry, or to find out about the customs and daily lives of the speakers of the language, or to translate instructions for making prestressed concrete. Individualization, sympathetically conceived, makes such diversity possible, as no previous system has done. Again, it is a matter of attitude on our part: we must work with our students in establishing what they are really seeking in learning the language, rather than imposing on them our view of their needs. This may add further organizational complications, but we cannot speak sincerely of "individualization" without it.

In our enthusiasm for techniques adopted by colleagues in mathematics, science, or the arts, we may forget that we are seeking an approach which is true to the nature of our discipline. Unless we are careful, packets, carrels, and individual tests may conspire to isolate students from their fellows. The term "individualization of instruction" itself may be leading us astray with its connotations of separateness and segmentation and its seeming focus on receptive learning. For both language-related and educational reasons I propose we use the term *cooperative learning.*

Language is essentially a vehicle for the communicating of ideas, emotions, and experiences, whether in the oral or graphic medium. We call languages "dead" when they no longer function in this way, and we rediscover them in tombs and caves or in the sepulchral depths of silent libraries. If our students' new language is not to be stillborn, it needs at all stages to be used for some form of real communication.

The essence of language is *macro-language use*: listening to something someone wants to share (ideas, songs, plays, news, plans, and projects), telling something we want others to hear, writing something we intend to be read (by ourselves at a later date or, more frequently, by others), reading what others want to communicate (to inform ourselves or enjoy) and then sharing what we have read with others through action or discourse. Students do not move easily from isolated micro-language learning (learning about facts of language and how smaller elements combine into larger segments) to normal uses of language. Whitehead has said that in training a student "to activity of thought, above all things, we must beware of . . . 'inert ideas'—that is to say, ideas that are merely received into the mind without being utilised, or tested, or thrown into fresh combinations."[35] How peculiarly appropriate this is to language learning! Facts we learn about language are "inert ideas" until they are tossed about, recombined in original ways, and tested for their communicative potential in the natural give-and-take of interaction between individuals or in the dynamic interchange within groups. "The acquisition of skills," said Dewey, "is not an end in itself. They are things to be put to use, and that use is their contribution to a common and shared life."[36]

One of the demands on modern education, as outlined in the earlier part of this chapter, is to reestablish the values of cooperation in an increasingly depersonalized world. It has been suggested that we need an interdependent learning model "in which cooperation is structured to be as productive of results as competition."[37] Since language use, if it is to be developed with confidence, needs just such an accepting, cooperative atmosphere, free of cross-comparisons, here is an area in which we can take the lead. In cooperative learning, all can succeed because each has something unique to contribute to the enterprise, and because success is not an external standard constructed to exclude, but the individual perception of the attainment of a self-selected goal. With acceptance of diverse goals, and individual emphasis on how the language will be used, this is not a vain dream. Ongoing individualized programs have shown us how it may be implemented.

Cooperative learning implies full participation of both teacher and student, and the interaction of student with student. It implies participation in planning and the opportunity to make effective choices. It implies student helping student, student helping teacher; it implies small group activity, large group instruction, interacting in pairs, or leaving another individual alone if that is what he or she prefers. It implies sharing what one has discovered with others. This is surely what education, as opposed to instruction, is about: "a deliberate and conscious sharing of responsibility for learning."[38] As students are given responsibility, they develop responsible attitudes, even if for a while there are "shavings on the floor."

Cooperative learning means a new role for the teacher, as well as for the student. Instead of dispenser of knowledge from a podium to which all eyes are raised in expectant vacuity, the teacher becomes an adviser, guide, helper, supporter, partner in a cooperative venture. Since so many of the problems the student has in developing confident language use are emotional ones, this new relationship cannot but promote better language learning through the reduction of tensions. In education, "it is the *process* and not merely the result that is important."[39] Through cooperative learning, sound language learning becomes sound education as well.

## FOOTNOTES

[1] R. F. Butts and L. A. Cremin, *A History of Education in American Culture* (New York: Henry Holt and Co., 1953), pp. 218-21, 329-31.

[2] A. Clegg, "Why Did We Change?" Selections from *Revolution in the British Primary Schools* (Washington, D.C.: N.A.E.S.P., N.E.A., 1971), in C. E. Silberman, ed., *The Open Classroom Reader* (New York: Random House, 1973), p. 82.

[3] R. S. Barth, *Open Education and the American School* (New York: Agathon Press, 1972), pp. 34-36, and L. Weber, in Silberman, ed. (1973), pp. 150-54, extracted from *The English Infant School and Informal Education* (Englewood Cliffs, N.J.: Prentice-Hall, 1971).

[4] Silberman, ed. (1973), supra, n.2, pp. 36-37.

[5] Chicago: Encyclopedia Britannica. The series has now become the *ACTFL Review of Foreign Language Education* (Skokie, Ill.: National Textbook Co.). Vol. 2 took as its main theme "Individualization of Instruction" and contains a very comprehensive "Rationale for the Individualization and Personalization of Foreign-Language Instruction" by Lorraine A. Strasheim.

[6] Butts and Cremin (1953), supra, n.1, p. 590.

[7] Butts and Cremin (1953), supra, n.1, p. 589. In the Dalton Schools in New York while Helen Parkhurst was headmistress (1916-1942) pupils studied in "laboratory brigades," without tests or examinations, with the aim of having the more capable students raise the standards of the backward ones. The students were also self-disciplined. As a further demonstration of the cross-Atlantic influence, Parkhurst drew her inspiration from Maria Montessori. Crossing the Pacific, we find a similar implementation of individualizing principles described in K. S. Cunningham and D. J. Ross, *An Australian School at Work* (Hawthorn, Australia: Australian Council for Educational Research, 1967), an account of the educational program at the Melbourne Church of England Girls' Grammar School from 1939 to 1955 in which this author participated.

[8]F. M. Grittner and F. H. LaLeike, in *Individualized Foreign Language Instruction* (Skokie, Ill.: National Textbook Co., 1973), use the term "unipac"; LAPs are discussed by J. K. Phillips in "Individualization and Personalization," Chap. 8 of G. A. Jarvis, ed., *Responding to New Realities, ACTFL Review of Foreign Language Education,* Vol. 5 (Skokie, Ill.: National Textbook Co., 1974), pp. 233-34, along with FLAPs (Foreign Language Activity Packets) and DISKs (Dewey Independent Study Kits). The latter, appropriately enough in the light of our discussion in the introductory paragraph, are used at the John Dewey High School in Brooklyn which has conducted an individualized foreign language program since 1969: see S. L. Levy, "Foreign Languages in John Dewey High School, New York City: An Individualized Approach," in R. L. Gougher, ed., *Individualization of Instruction in Foreign Languages: A Practical Guide* (Philadelphia: Center for Curriculum Development, 1972). G. E. Logan, whose pioneering work at Live Oak High School in California dates from 1967, still uses the term "assignment": see G. E. Logan, *Individualized Foreign Language Learning: An Organic Process* (Rowley, Mass.: Newbury House, 1973).

[9]L. Weber in Silberman, ed. (1973), supra, n. 2, pp. 152-53. She is summarizing Nathan Isaacs's explication of Piaget's views.

[10]Grittner and LaLeike (1973), supra, n.8, p. 92, discuss the dangers of this approach.

[11] G. M. Green, *Semantics and Syntactic Regularity* (Bloomington and London: Indiana University Press, 1974), pp. 156-67: "The *Teach* Conspiracy." Green points out that this distinction is basically that between *apprendre* and *enseigner* in French. It is interesting that *apprendre* can be used for both the teacher's and Jane's part in the interaction.

[12]These terms are used by A. H. Maslow in his hierarchy of basic needs, set out in *Motivation and Personality,* 2nd ed. (New York: Harper and Row, 1970), Chap. 4. For a more detailed application of this theory in second-language teaching situations, see W. M. Rivers, "Motivation in Bilingual Programs," Chapter 8 of this book. E. W. Stevick also applies it to foreign-language instruction in "Before Linguistics and Beneath Method" in K. Jankowsky, ed., *Language and International Studies* (Washington, D.C.: Georgetown University Press, 1973), pp. 99-106. See also the discussion of "defensive" and "receptive" learning in E. W. Stevick, "Language Instruction Must Do an About-Face," *Modern Language Journal* 58 (1974): 379-84

[13]See the case studies assembled by E. Hatch in *The Second Language: Case Studies in Second Language Acquisition* (in preparation). Further information from E. Hatch, Dept. of English, University of California at Los Angeles.

[14]The observations in this paragraph are from E. Hatch, "Second Language-Learning–Universals?" *Working Papers on Bilingualism* 3 (1974), 1-17. Toronto, Canada: Ontario Institute for Studies in Education.

[15]G. Butterworth, "A Spanish-speaking adolescent's acquisition of English syntax," unpublished M.A. thesis, UCLA, 1972.

[16]For a lengthy discussion of autonomous interaction, with many suggestions for its implementation, see W. M. Rivers, *A Practical Guide to the Teaching of French* (New York, London and Toronto: Oxford University Press, 1975), Chap. 3, or

the companion volumes, W. M. Rivers, K. M. and V. Dell'Orto, *A Practical Guide to the Teaching of German* (1975), and W. M. Rivers, M. M. Azevedo, W. H. Heflin, Jr., and R. Hyman-Opler, *A Practical Guide to the Teaching of Spanish* (1976).

[17]The author remembers vividly an Australian "slow learner" of French who found it difficult to put two sentences together to express meaning but who, having married a Frenchman, is now happily bringing up a family in Paris and "talking a stream" with practically native precision.

[18]For a useful discussion of three modes of individualized instruction, see V. M. Howes, "Individualized Instruction: Form and Structure," in V. M. Howes, ed., *Individualization of Instruction. A Teaching Strategy* (New York: Macmillan, 1970), pp. 69-81.

[19]See references in note 8.

[20]For a flexible system of computer-assisted instruction, see the description of PLATO (Programmed Logic for Automated Teaching Operations) at the University of Illinois, in R. T. Scanlan, "The Application of Technology to the Teaching of Foreign Languages," in W. M. Rivers et al., *Changing Patterns in Foreign Language Programs* (Rowley, Mass.: Newbury House, 1972). Despite the sophisticated potential of modern computer languages, computer programs for foreign-language learning are still dependent on the programmer. Until some foreign-language materials writers begin to utilize fully the innovative possibilities of the technological developments, even computer-assisted instruction will remain basically similar to classical programming.

[21]Programming in theory and practice is discussed at length in W. M. Rivers, *Teaching Foreign-Language Skills* (Chicago: The University of Chicago Press, 1968), pp. 88-97.

[22]J. B. Carroll, "Psychological Aspects of Programmed Learning in Foreign Languages," in T. Mueller, ed., *Proceedings of the Seminar on Programmed Learning* (New York: Appleton-Century-Crofts, 1968), p. 63.

[23]See T. Mueller, "The Development of Curricular Materials (Including Programmed Materials) for Individualized Foreign Language Instruction," in H. B. Altman and R. L. Politzer, eds., *Individualizing Foreign Language Instruction* (Rowley, Mass.: Newbury House, 1971), pp. 148-55, and J. Ornstein, R. W. Ewton, Jr., and T. H. Mueller, *Programmed Instruction and Educational Technology in the Language Teaching Field* (Philadelphia: Center for Curriculum Development, 1971). For a rounded statement of Skinner's views, see B. F. Skinner, *The Technology of Teaching* (New York: Appleton-Century-Crofts, 1968). Skinner does not pass all teaching over to the program. On p. 254, he says, "The contact between teacher and student characteristic of classroom teaching is particularly important when the contingencies are social. In exposition, discussion, and argumentation (written or spoken), in productive interchange in the exploration of new areas, in ethical behavior, in the common enjoyment of literature, music, and art—here the teacher is important, and he is important as a human being."

[24]This definition of a performance objective and the description of an objective which follows are taken from R. M. Valette and R. S. Disick, *Modern Perform-*

*ance Objectives and Individualization: A Handbook* (New York: Harcourt Brace Jovanovich, 1972), pp. 17-18.

[25] "Micro-language learning" and "macro-language use" (used later in this paper) are concepts which are explained and applied in Rivers (1975), supra, n. 16, pp. 87-88, and in Rivers et al. (1975 and 1976), supra, n.16, Chap. 3.

[26] For the distinction between skill-getting and skill-using, see Chapters 2 and 3 of this book.

[27] From E. B. and P. J. Hartley, "Teach Yourself to Write Behavioral Objectives— An Exercise for Foreign Language Teachers," in *American Foreign Language Teacher* 3, No. 2 (1972), p. 17. The behaviorist ancestry of the objectives is clearly demonstrated in this article by the sentence: "Remember that a *behavioral* objective is some activity that is *observable* and *measurable*" (p. 18, italics in the original).

[28] From F. Steiner, *Performing with Objectives* (Rowley, Mass.: Newbury House, 1975), p. 78.

[29] Hartley (1972), supra, n.27, p. 17.

[30] Ibid., p. 18. Italics in the original.

[31] J. B. Carroll, "A Model of School Learning," *Teachers College Record* 64 (1963), 723-33.

[32] L. A. Jakobovits, *Foreign Language Learning: A Psycholinguistic Analysis of the Issues* (Rowley, Mass.: Newbury House, 1970), p. 95.

[33] For two sides of the debate on behavioral or performance objectives, see F. M. Grittner, "Behavioral Objectives, Skinnerian Rats, and Trojan Horses," *Foreign Language Annals* 6 (1972), 52-60, and Steiner (1975), supra, n.28.

[34] This subject is discussed at length in Chapter 13 of this book, "The Non-Major: Tailoring the Course to Fit the Person—Not the Image."

[35] A. N. Whitehead, *The Aims of Education* (New York: New American Library, 1949), p. 13. Original copyright: Macmillan, 1929.

[36] J. Dewey, "The Need for a Philosophy of Education," in R. D. Archambault, *John Dewey on Education* (New York: Random House, 1964), p. 11. Original publication date 1934.

[37] I. H. Buchen, "Humanism and Futurism: Enemies or Allies?" in A. Toffler, ed., *Learning for Tomorrow: The Role of the Future in Education* (New York: Random House, 1974), p. 139.

[38] R. S. Barth (1972), supra, n.3, p. 28.

[39] J. Dewey in Archambault (1964), supra, n.36, p. 4.

# 17

# STUDENTS, TEACHERS, AND THE FUTURE*

In the everyday hurly-burly of the school, it is easy to become time-bound. Yet the future is pressing in on us at a faster and faster pace according to the futurologists—those late twentieth-century prophets who are endeavoring to cushion the shock of societal change. If the future is purchased by the present, as Samuel Johnson maintained,[1] our best preparation for it is to recognize the directions of change in our present situation, so that adjustment and adaptation become natural, non-threatening processes. Knowing that change, sometimes continuous and imperceptible, at other times sudden and jolting, will be a way of life for us all in any educational enterprise, we must ensure that those joining us in the profession are prepared mentally and temperamentally to comprehend and accept new purposes while retaining the essence of our discipline.

## Changing Relations

*Teacher-student relations* are changing from the traditional teacher-directed situation to one of teacher-student interaction with shared decision-making. Foreign language teachers, along with colleagues in other fields, must identify what each student needs and wants; as educators they must then provide for a balance of these two if the student is to be

*Revised version of a Working Paper for the Steering Committee of the MLA Foreign Language Program for the Seventies, 1973. Originally published in *Foreign Language Annals* 8 (1975), 22-32.

motivated to learn. Whether individualization of instruction in its present form is a lasting wave is immaterial. The emphasis it places on attention to individuals, sensitivity to their needs and interests, and closer rapport between teacher and students in a student-centered program will continue to influence the planning of cooperative teacher-student learning experiences.

*School and community* are no longer separate entities, with the student moving out of one and into the other. The school must go out into the community, as part of the community, to learn from the community and serve community needs; conversely, the community impinges on the curriculum and activities of the school. Foreign language teachers must know their community, use the community, and design foreign language programs which reflect the preoccupations and interests of the community.

*Foreign language programs and other subject areas* can no longer operate in the same institution in hermetic juxtaposition. For a meaningful educational experience all aspects of the curriculum must interrelate. Foreign language teachers must consider what they can gain from and bring to an integrated curriculum. Sometimes their contribution may be in developing an auxiliary skill to widen the student's perspective in other areas. Certainly it will mean looking beyond their traditional preoccupation with belles-lettres to involvement with the ways of thinking and acting of people who speak the language, their history, their environment, their community structures, their influence beyond their own shores, and their ways of interacting politically, commercially, economically, and artistically with other peoples. Only a few foreign language teachers are prepared professionally or emotionally to move in this direction at present. Very few are being prepared to do so in our colleges and universities.

## Changing Directions

The educational emphasis is moving *from the mechanistic to the humanistic.* Foreign language teaching is no longer seen as the inculcating of certain skills, but as part of the formative education of a human being: an experience which broadens the way the individual views life, the world, and the people he encounters. To survive in this changing atmosphere, foreign language teaching must show that it has something to contribute to the quality of life. At present, foreign language teachers talk about this need, but only a few have been able to develop programs which achieve this effect. More experimentation is needed with the kinds of learning materials and the types of learning environments which will make such an outcome possible and probable.

Foreign language teaching is moving *from an elitist to a comprehensive view* of its task. As a profession we must consider much more seriously what the study of a foreign language can contribute to the education of all students, with their widely diverse abilities, interests, and modes of learning. We must give serious consideration to ways of presenting languages so that all kinds of students can learn them efficiently and pleasurably.

Interest in languages is now turning increasingly *from the languages of far-away places to languages at home*—the languages of local areas, neighboring states, or nearby countries. This trend is demonstrated not only in bilingual programs but in moves to preserve the ethnic heritage of America's immigrant groups and in the emphasis, for instance, on the Spanish of the Western Hemisphere and the French of Louisiana, Canada, and Africa (as the ancestral home with which a considerable segment of the population identifies). Teachers must be prepared to readjust the perspective of their teaching accordingly, taking their students into local and neighboring communities, where this is feasible, and bringing representatives of these groups into the schools.

The profession is moving rapidly *from orthodoxy to heterodoxy*. With this in mind, leaders and teachers alike must be on their guard against any tendency to impose a monolithic approach, no matter how estimable. In methodology this means a clear preference for eclecticism: selecting the approach, the content and materials, the organizational pattern, the techniques, and the pacing to meet the needs of particular individuals in a specific situation. Teachers and students should be encouraged to think through the implications of each situation as it arises and develop their programs to meet the perceived purposes of their encounter. In this way the Hawthorne effect of the "do your own thing" project will be more widely generalized and more students and teachers will profit from at least some exciting classes.

Innovation in language teaching is becoming a movement *from the base to the apex.* Teachers are less anxious to listen to "experts" and are becoming more willing to learn from other teachers. As a profession we should encourage classroom teachers to try out their own ideas and provide them with frequent opportunities to share their successful experiences with others.

## The Present State of the Field
## from the Point of View of the Classroom Teacher

To the ordinary classroom teacher the field appears confusing, demanding, and threatening.

*Confusing.* The classroom teacher often feels like a pawn in a game played for professional advancement through leadership in "innovation" by "experts" with little or no experience of the realities of today's classrooms. Teachers feel pressured into new approaches (which for the experienced teacher are often cyclical), only to be left stranded, and vilified for their insufficiencies, as the tide turns. Teachers who were coaxed or coerced into audiolingual teaching are now being told it is a failure despite clear evidence of successful learning in many of their classes. Many of these teachers also saw such evidence of successful learning in their pre-audiolingual classes and are likely to experience it again in a post-audiolingual period. Understandably, they are in no mood to suffer the same experience twice in a decade. The shocks of accelerating changes in society, in the curriculum, and in student-teacher relations are exacerbated by constant demands for innovation before the last, or next-to-last, recommendation has been consolidated or seriously evaluated in longitudinal fashion. For long-term improvement we need to encourage absorption of the best of what has been tried into the fabric of ongoing practice, rather than expecting continual replacement. For any realistic evolution, the *teachers themselves must be involved in determining new directions for the profession.* Instead of rapidly conceived and prematurely acclaimed "innovations," we need carefully planned pilot experimentation in which local teachers and students are active participants at all stages, widespread inservice discussion and training, appropriate restructuring based on the experience of many, and considered longitudinal evaluation of effectiveness in specifically stated situational contexts before recommending the adoption or discarding of any new approach.

At the moment there appear to be in the profession a number of thrusts which are not necessarily convergent. As primary objectives we find emphasis on communicative competence, cultural understanding, development of reading skill, integration of foreign languages in humanities programs, career utility, and the fostering of listening comprehension through films, radio, TV, and plays. We hear strong advocacy of behavioral objectives, individualization of instruction, peer teaching, cognitive-code learning, mini-courses, total immersion programs, the long sequence, the terminal course, programmed and machine-aided instruction and learning through community involvement—all laudable in themselves but as varied as a smorgasbord. Which path is the ordinary classroom teacher to follow?

*Demanding.* As well as being expected to rethink their philosophies and reorient their techniques at intervals of five years or less, teachers are the recipients of a plethora of recommendations which require the development of new materials and the adaptation of old ones. To perform these tasks effectively, the teacher must have near-native fluency and accuracy, the technical training of a textbook writer or materials developer, excellent organizing ability, a superlative memory, and the temperament and capacity to provide answers and design activities for all kinds of levels and types of work at the same time. Nor do our teachers have any assurance that extra time to do all that is now expected of them professionally will be forthcoming, or that they will be given the opportunity to acquire the specialized training they will need to do it efficiently.

*Threatening.* The superior teacher can meet these demands, given sufficient physical stamina and resourcefulness, teaching aides, and some money for acquiring supplementary materials. The average or less-skilled teacher cannot. The latter may try, with ineffectual results and much discouragement, or may prefer to take refuge in a closed-door, traditionally textbook-dominated classroom.

For many teachers, then, there is a *continuing need for inservice workshops, institutes, and training sessions* for the maintenance and development of language skills, and for practical training in materials development and in pedagogical techniques to enable them to implement a variety of approaches and courses for the types of students in their groups. Such training sessions should be planned and taught by experienced and successful teachers who can demonstrate what they are discussing, and guide in the practice of techniques and the production of materials which teachers can use in their own classes. In other words, we need much more teacher-to-teacher exchange of ideas and experience.

Primacy in any planning should be given to the continuing development and consequent emotional serenity of the classroom teacher—who will remain the key figure in any projected advance for the profession.

## Future Demands on the Classroom Teacher in View of Changing Relations and Directions

An unpredictable future will require of our teachers first and foremost *flexibility*—the ability to work out many things for which they were never trained.

*Flexibility in their attitude to the students and the curriculum.* The teacher can no longer be the master passing down to the disciple what he or she has learned. New knowledge is accumulating and multiplying too fast for this approach to continue. The teacher must cooperate with all types of students in optimalizing their opportunities for learning, in developing new content and appropriate activities for teaching the real uses of language as determined by the language user, and in meeting community needs and interdisciplinary demands.

*Flexibility in working patterns.* Teachers will be expected to break up the more easily controlled lecture-practice class hour to allow for a variety of groupings, scheduling patterns, and differentiated teaching approaches.

*Flexibility in approach and methodology.* Teachers will need to be able to select methods and techniques which suit the particular needs of certain students in a given situation, and to be able to switch from techniques of one type to techniques of another as the situation changes.

*Flexibility in approach to student achievement.* A plurality of student needs and objectives and the diversification of content and activity will require a variety of ways of evaluating the appropriate level of achievement in specific cases and situations. Many teachers, traditionally trained and oriented, find a flexible viewpoint toward evaluation very difficult to achieve.

## What Steps Can Be Taken
## to Ensure Development of a
## Flexible, Future-Oriented Profession?

### A. *The New Teacher; Pre-Service Training*

1. Development of an approach to teaching begins with the way we have been taught. Most future teachers spend a large part of their four years of undergraduate (and perhaps one year of graduate) study in rigid, conventional, lecture/discussion type classes for which typically they are examined in a two- or three-hour regurgitation session at the end of the semester. At present, many instructors in elementary schools, high schools, and junior colleges are open to experimentation with content and presentation, but such innovation is still rare at the undergraduate level of foreign language departments in senior institutions. It is here that the problem must be attacked—unpopular as such an approach may be.

Flexibility in undergraduate programs means not only willingness to broaden the curriculum to meet the needs of today and tomorrow, but a new approach to presentation, participation, and evaluation. The value of the undiluted lecture must be reassessed and opportunities provided for students to select topics, find out for themselves, take the lead, work in groups, and share in the development of their learning experience, bearing personal responsibility for their level of achievement. If such a radical change at the undergraduate and graduate level is to be achieved, a vigorous profession-wide discussion of the matter must be precipitated.[2] The profession must be convinced of the need for *thorough training of future college teachers,* not only in the advanced study and research of their chosen specialty, but in broader areas of general pedagogy (the not-so-simple practice of teaching) and language learning, ways of developing appreciation of and insight into another literature and culture, materials development, and the principles and techniques of evaluation.

Once the college classroom is open to innovation, diversification, variations of approach, new alliances, and the recognition of the validity of a variety of objectives we may expect teacher trainees with a quite different outlook to begin appearing in teacher-training programs.

2. We may then begin to apply *criteria of selection* to our teacher-training applicants which will screen out the rigid, authoritarian personality from the adaptable, outgoing, and community-oriented. Not everyone who knows a foreign language well, or who has studied it conscientiously, is a suitable candidate for our foreign language teaching corps. We need guidelines that will help us to select the type of person our unpredictable and unconventional future demands.

3. We must then *reassess the adequacy of our present teacher-training programs.* Some are excellent, and it is these exceptions which are reported in the journals and at professional meetings.

It may be well at this stage to face frankly some of the long-standing reasons why much foreign language teacher training provides insufficient preparation for the real life of the schools.

Teacher training typically takes place in either the foreign language department or in the college of education (more rarely in both, in which case it is often repetitious because of lack of coordination among the various courses). In neither case has the typical instructor any specialized training for this task.

Teacher training has a low priority in faculty assignments in foreign language departments and increasingly in colleges of education. Those who do train teachers are often trying to get out of it as soon as they can or are caught in it for want of an acceptable "field of research."

In the foreign language department, the teacher-training instructor is often a person who has not experienced high school (or elementary school) since leaving it as a student. Sometimes the instructor was educated in another country and has never lived through the experience of the American high school. Such instructors may or may not keep abreast of educational developments and needs in the schools; in any case, they may have more absorbing "intellectual" preoccupations (theoretical linguistics, the study of poetry, comparative literature) which provide the few vivid presentations of the semester. The rarer individual who has actually taught in the schools may be fighting to "rise above it" in the eyes of colleagues.

In colleges of education esteem for foreign language teaching is often low. A part-time instructor is considered sufficient, or students are trained in classroom practice with students of other subjects for want of an expert in the area. Where qualified foreign language instructors are available, they may or may not be keeping in touch with current trends in the schools, and they may or may not know the various languages their students are to teach and the problems peculiar to those languages.

As a profession we must publicize the qualities and qualifications we expect of those who prepare teachers for the schools of today and tomorrow. We must seek to recruit open-minded, perceptive persons who will grow as they teach, and we must take steps to see that the qualifications we expect are readily obtainable in responsible institutions and are respected by accrediting bodies. It is only in this way that we can build up the prestige of what is presently regarded, in the main, as a low-grade activity, and thus attract to it first-class, professionally-trained personnel who will be willing to devote their undivided efforts to their field.

Keeping up with the field is difficult in a period of rapid change. For this reason trainers of teachers should have some close association with an ongoing teaching program, whether in a laboratory school, within a foreign language department, or in association with a local school district. Their teacher training work should not be a second string to a "more scholarly" pursuit. Until such an ideal situation obtains, there is need for some source of information, such as a newsletter, which will draw the attention of teacher trainers, as well as administrative personnel in school districts who are responsible for inservice training, to important trends, useful recent publications, reports of experimentation, and sources of assistance to teachers.

As an interim measure, serious attention should be paid to providing further training for those teacher trainers who have been shanghaied into the task with insufficient background, as well as others who have gradually slipped behind or come back into the work after years of absence from the field.

*The nature of the training offered needs to be reexamined at regular intervals.* In this regard the National Council of State Supervisors of Foreign Languages has performed a service for the profession in issuing a carefully prepared and succinct position paper.[3] One cannot emphasize too much the necessity for a thorough command of the language the trainee is to teach and the culture of its people (in both senses of this word). Linguistic and psycholinguistic insights tied closely to the needs of the classroom teacher are also valuable and important. For the rest of the teacher's professional preparation, from a theoretical or a practical point of view, there is frankly too much that is essential for it to be covered in one short, rushed course. The all-too-brief methods course is often packed into the same semester as the student-teaching experience, so that the student's ideas and perspective have no time to mature before he is hustled into the always nerve-racking first attempt at controlling a class and stimulating worthwhile activities at the same time. No wonder that to many young trainees actual problems of classroom management appear to be much more important than developing communication situations, so that much of what they learned in their methods course is perceived as irrelevant to the "real" task.

Hitherto we have been too modest in our requirements. We should advocate, and seek to see implemented, a dual system of a general methods course, to establish interest and perspective in the semester preceding the student-teaching experience, and a specific-language methods course, which would be essentially practical and tied to the needs of the teacher in the classroom. The latter should be given during the practice-teaching semester. Why two such courses? It is obvious that our flexible teachers of the future need a thorough theoretical background if they are to adjust and adapt their teaching to varying needs and a changing clientele, but also a thorough practical training in the designing and development of teaching and testing materials for courses they have not yet encountered or foreseen.

The general methods course which may be given with future teachers of various languages in the same class would normally be taught in the college of education where the instructor is in close touch with colleagues in educational theory, curriculum, and the teaching of germane subjects. The specific-language methods course, on the other hand, would normally be taught by a suitably trained instructor from the foreign language department who is in a position to keep up with new developments in the study of the language itself, the contemporary culture, the literature, and the artistic manifestations of its people.

The general methods course prepares future professionals, giving them a wide overview of the ramifications and complications of the field: the various theories of language, of learning, and of the learning of language which must be taken into consideration in designing activities for students of various ages, aptitudes, motivations, and needs, present and future; the long-accepted procedures and the experimental; the recurrent, often cyclical attempts at solving apparently intractable problems; the areas of controversy and their relationship to theoretical considerations and objectives.

The general methods course is the course for wide reading: for familiarizing oneself with the classics of the field and for following personal predilections as one discovers the many sources of information and stimulation available to the practicing teacher. It is this course which reveals to our future teachers the potential of their chosen field. It gives them the background of knowledge which frees them at a later stage to innovate and develop their courses to meet the needs of changing and evolving situations beyond what they could have anticipated in their early training.

For content in the general methods course, we can list at least the following: the place of foreign languages in the curriculum and in the general education of the student; their interaction with other areas of study; the intricate relationships between objectives and approaches or methods; the theoretical background to language acquisition and the development of skill in the various areas of language use; interpersonal relations in foreign language study; interaction and transactional analysis, the psychology of groups, the sociolinguistic and emotional problems of communication; the rationale and organization of individualized programs, community-oriented programs, and programs for special-interest and career objectives; the theoretical assumptions and the operation of various types of bilingual programs; when and how to design intensive courses and mini-courses; patterns of scheduling and staffing, the open classroom, the school without walls, and their implications for effective foreign language teaching; principles of evaluation; aptitude and motivation; the supportive role of media in foreign language learning; where to find information to keep abreast of educational trends; the problems and changing objectives of the different levels of institutional instruction; research and recent experimentation in foreign language learning and teaching. A general methods course can combine future

FLES, junior high school, and high school teachers, even junior college instructors, thus ensuring that future foreign language teachers in the various types of institutions will have some understanding of each other's aims, problems, and working conditions and be thus prepared to contribute to regional and local cooperative endeavors.

What of the specific-language methods course? It is in this course that the student practices techniques and day-to-day operations, designs activities and situations, refines evaluative procedures and instruments, and learns how to interest and motivate the various types of students. Since this course is taught while the student is actually participating in some form in the life of a school community, students will now understand the importance of the meticulous work of materials evaluation, adaptation, and use, and the necessity for imagination and resourcefulness in creating learning situations and in stimulating genuine interaction.

The teacher trainer now has time to involve the students in actual construction of materials and the design of exercises and activities which they will use. Since the class is language-specific, students learn to cope with the major problems of the language they will teach. This course is the place for discussing and working with the appropriate components of various levels of instruction; for microteaching; for the planning and preparation of elementary, intermediate, and advanced level courses, units, lessons, kits, individualized learning packets, culture capsules, games, and situational encounters; for practicing the organization and conduct of small-group learning; for detailed evaluation of textbooks, recorded materials, visuals, and tests; for learning to operate equipment and integrate it into the lesson; for seeking suitable original materials to supplement the standard fare; for discovering and recording sources of realia and contemporary information about the language and the countries where it is spoken; for establishing the relative usefulness of professional journals. Students will try out what they have designed on each other, meanwhile profiting from the instructor's expertise in the language to correct faults in pronunciation and language use. In this course the needs of teachers at various institutional levels will be different, and this fact can be exploited by providing students with the opportunity to experience individualization and personal planning in action, recombining the group for sharing where needs coincide.

It must be emphasized that neither of these courses should be designed merely to support future teachers through their first week or month of classroom teaching, although some of this preparation is needed. Rather, they should lay the foundations for a lifetime of professional growth and involvement by providing students with both the theoretical understanding and the practical experience they need if they are to be able to adjust and readjust whenever new emphases and objectives require unanticipated responses of them. The inevitable trauma of the first day or the first week can be faced only in an actual encounter with students.

4. The reality of interaction with students in a school (*internship experience*) will give the future teacher the experience which creates confidence, rather than a simulation of this experience through peer teaching in a methods class or in a videotaping session where the students are obliging, well-motivated, and already know what is expected of them. Microteaching of this type is useful for the study of techniques, but its artificiality should be recognized and its place delineated. A period of practice under guidance is essential if what is being learned is to have reality for the trainee.

Regrettably, some institutions do not provide for an internship at all. Much has and could be written about the inadequacies of what actually takes place in those that do. Many students have to work with teachers who are out of touch with present needs. Some teachers require students to do exactly as they do; others leave their student teachers to do as they please without any help or guidance, and sometimes without even a supportive presence in the classroom. Many student teachers never see an exciting lesson during their whole internship. The length of time in the schools is frequently inadequate and often in one block, so that students have no opportunity to reflect on their experiences and then try again in another setting. For many students the experience is a bitter one, coming too late for them to change their career plans, whereas others, more fortunate, have had a carefully organized para-teaching experience,[4] which gave them an early opportunity to decide whether or not their career choice was congenial to them.

It is time for the profession as a whole to realize that, with all the demands which will be made on the teacher of the future, a pre-service training period, no matter how well organized, will not be sufficient. Schools must be encouraged to provide a mentor for each new teacher during his or her first semester of autonomous teaching—an experienced teacher with whom the new professional may discuss the design of courses, activities, and tests, as well as the inevitable day-to-day problems which result from lack of experience with student relations and classroom management. *Such supervised initiation into the profession must be recognized as an essential element in a teacher's training* and not a haphazard increment for those who are lucky. It is this first semester with full responsibility for the learning of one's students which is the crucial period for the development of professional skills and attitude, rather than the short interlude of pre-service experimentation.

5. *How can the profession help the teacher trainer to improve the training program?* There is a need for easily available films and videotapes of successful teaching of all types for all kinds of objectives to strengthen the practical side of pre-service and inservice training. Professional organizations should establish libraries of these materials for specific languages and make them readily available for rental or purchase.

Professional organizations should seek out and identify teacher-training programs which the users (students, classroom teachers, and department heads) recognize as successful, their characteristics should be described, and accounts of their operation circulated to stimulate the improvement of other programs.

## B. *Inservice Training*

1. More teacher-to-teacher workshops should be organized at the local and regional levels to *reach teachers from the base.* National organizations can help by providing packaged workshops which teachers can utilize as they please in their own districts. These could contain tapes of significant lectures, discussion materials based on simulated situations, films or videotapes of pilot programs of an innovative nature or of extra-curricular activities such as language camps and fairs, and projects for community involvement programs. Teachers should be encouraged to give their own demonstrations at local and regional workshops and initiate discussion of problems which are real to them.

2. *Dissemination of teacher-prepared materials and ideas* for teachers to use should be encouraged at the regional and district level, rather than the national level, so that teachers can interact in workshops and inservice conferences with the originators of the materials.

3. Opportunities for *interaction among instructors of different institutional levels* should be organized locally—not so that one group may "talk at" the other groups, but for exchange of information and combined action for the improvement of programs and the publicizing of what is really being accomplished. FLES and junior college instructors particularly need this support.

4. We must *break down the parochialism of the French/German/Spanish teacher* without arousing feelings of insecurity about future jobs. Teachers of the well-established languages must be kept informed of national and local needs for a variety of languages, and be encouraged to involve themselves in efforts to broaden the range of language-learning opportunities by arousing local interest, training persons fluent in these languages in teaching techniques, and helping develop programs for teaching them. Where a need is clear but trained teachers are not available to meet it, practicing foreign language teachers should be encouraged and enabled to take crash courses in the less-taught language with a view to establishing a program, rather than leaving the

field to enthusiastic amateurs with no notion of how to teach a foreign language.

5. Local foreign language teachers should be encouraged to *interest themselves actively in current movements and language-related activities* which go beyond their usual sphere: the bilingual and ethnic heritage movements, the opening of lines of communication through language and the study of culture with Third World countries, the open university and the development of continuing education, the possibilities opened in many communities by cable television, such activities as the Bicentennial which provide opportunities for celebrating the contributions to national development of the speakers of many languages. National organizations should help teachers plan not only for active participation in these activities but also for the opportunity they provide for many students to use the languages they are learning in making visitors to their area welcome, by acting both as guides and hosts.

### Influencing the Decision Makers

What goes on in the classroom will continue to be dependent to a large degree on the types of materials readily available. Since these are, for the most part, produced commercially, the profession must *invite the editors of publishing houses to share in their discussions* and try to influence the orientation of new materials, rather than leaving such important considerations to the ad hoc decisions of editors and individual materials writers.

Teachers should be given more training in evaluating materials for specific purposes and the needs of specific groups of students. In journals directed to the needs of the classroom teacher, the traditional book review should be largely replaced by users' reports. Several such reports grouped together can help teachers to gauge the usefulness of the materials under discussion for their own situation.

In view of the tendency toward diversification of courses for a plurality of student needs and interests, the trend in published materials should be toward flexible groupings of interrelated (and sometimes alternative) materials from which teachers may select those which develop the particular skills or content they wish to emphasize.

The *public* and *administrators* interact, since administrators are sensitive to the priorities set by the community.

To improve the image of the profession we should, first of all, do less public breast-beating. We can educate the public on the values of foreign language study by *keeping the press, national and local, well supplied with succinct, well-reported accounts* (accompanied by photographs) of successful and innovative language teaching, that is, of interesting things actually taking place, not vague statements on what the profession ought or hopes to do. Accounts of worthwhile programs in language learning, community involvement, or bilingualism, such as those featured in certain centerspreads in *Accent on ACTFL* (e.g., the Skyline Center of the Dallas Independent School District,[5] the individualized program in Dale City, Virginia,[6] a Day in Arcachon[7]) should be made available inexpensively for distribution to newspapers, school boards, P.T.A.'s, administrators, or radio and TV stations in local districts. Teachers can be encouraged to talk to local groups or write short items for local news media if national associations make easily available informational kits, regularly updated, from which they can draw factual material. Some of this factual material should be in pamphlets for school administrators and counselors. Students should also be able to take home interesting facts and figures to their parents.

To improve attitudes toward foreign language learning in the wider community, we should *encourage and promote more learning of languages by adults* through programs planned to meet their needs in junior and community colleges, continuing education, and elementary and intermediate courses at senior institutions. This strategy will succeed only if adults have interesting and successful learning experiences related to real uses of language in their personal or professional lives. From this point of view, improving the teaching of foreign languages for specific purposes in junior colleges is of immense importance to the profession. Junior college instructors should work with companies who can use

personnel fluent in certain foreign languages. National associations can help by locating such companies and alerting
junior colleges and other adult education groups to their
needs. University departments should help colleagues in other
fields who need to acquire a foreign language for advancing
their research or for initiating or maintaining overseas
contacts.

Research is urgently needed into the type of language and
content appropriate for foreign language courses for students
interested in business, advertising, public relations, tourism,
fashion, the sciences, architecture, the arts, engineering, and
so on.

The best long-term policy for changing community attitudes is undoubtedly to increase the number of interesting
and effective school programs, thus reaching the decision-
makers of the future. The future of foreign language teaching
is in the hands of our present teachers and those they train.
Let us not wait for others to promote us or find answers to
our problems. In us lie the seeds of our future.

## FOOTNOTES

[1] *The Rambler,* No. 178.

[2] See, for example, Warren C. Born, ed., *Toward Student-Centered Foreign-Language Programs. Reports of the 1974 Working Committees of the Northeast Conference on the Teaching of Foreign Languages* (New York: The Conference, 1974).

[3] Keith Crosbie *et al., Foreign Language Teacher Education in 1971: A Position Paper.*

[4] One such program is described in full in S. and A. Shinall. "To Teach or Not to Teach: Is Para-Teaching the Answer?," *French Review,* 46 (1973), 766-72.

[5] September 1972.

[6] April 1973.

[7] November 1972.